The Home Energy Decision Book

Sierra Club Books
TOOLS FOR TODAY

Sierra Club *Tools for Today* books chart a bright new path through the 80s. They're practical, easy to read, full of information, thoroughly illustrated—the perfect tools for decision making in changing times. Whether you're refitting your home with new solar equipment, refurbishing your kitchen, redesigning your lawn to include edibles—any of the thousand ways to make an adventure of prudent, ecologically sound living—turn to the perfect guide, *Tools for Today* books.

Books in This Series

The Living Kitchen by Sharon Cadwallader
Your Affordable Solar Home by Dan Hibshman

Sierra Club Books
TOOLS FOR TODAY

The Home Energy Decision Book

by Gigi Coe, Michael R. Eaton, and Michael Garland

illustrated by Bill Wells

SIERRA CLUB BOOKS
San Francisco

FIRST EDITION

Printed in the United States of America.

A Yolla Bolly Press Book

The Home Energy Decision Book was produced in association with the publisher at The Yolla Bolly Press, Covelo, California. Editorial and design staff: James and Carolyn Robertson, Dan Hibshman, Don Yoder, Diana Fairbanks, Juliana Yoder, and Barbara Youngblood.

The Sierra Club, founded in 1892 by John Muir, has devoted itself to the study and protection of the earth's scenic and ecological resources—mountains, wetlands, woodlands, wild shores and rivers, deserts and plains. Its publications are part of the nonprofit effort the club carries on as a public trust. There are more than 50 chapters coast to coast, in Canada, Hawaii, and Alaska. For information about how you may participate in the club's programs to enjoy and preserve wilderness and the quality of life, please address inquiries to Sierra Club, 530 Bush Street, San Francisco, California 94108.

Library of Congress Cataloging in Publication Data

Coe, Gigi.
The home energy decision book.

(Tools for today)
"A Yolla Bolly Press book."
Bibliography: p.
Includes index.
1. Dwellings—Energy conservation. I. Eaton, Michael R. II. Garland, Michael. III. Title. IV. Series.
TJ163.5.D86C63 1984 644 83-19574
ISBN 0-87156-811-X

The authors gratefully acknowledge permission to publish the thermogram on the cover: VANSCAN™ Thermogram, by Daedalus Enterprises, Inc.

Contents

Acknowledgments

We wish to express special appreciation to the people who helped us find information: Deborah Blevis, Peter Cleary, Bonnie Cornwall, Gautum Dutt, Steve Gates, David Goldstein, Jeff Harris, Mark Levine, Cynthia Praul, Art Rosenfeld, Judy Tretheway, Bruce Wilcox, and the staff of the Office of Alternative Technology library.

Robert Weisenmiller, Richard Sextro, Michael Manetas, and Elena Jones reviewed and critiqued the manuscript and provided valuable advice.

Others who have given valuable encouragement and support and who deserve our special thanks are Jim, Carolyn, Barbara, Diana, Dan, and Don of The Yolla Bolly Press and Mikos Fabersunne and Gayle Cribb.

Chapter One
The Range of Choices

The Range of Choices

Higher energy prices have spurred a search for ways to make homes and apartments use energy more efficiently—for better ways to run appliances, heat water, cool in summer, and warm in winter. Consumers have been helped by government, utilities, and a growing number of businesses selling energy conservation materials and services. One result of this assistance is that people interested in home energy efficiency now face a bewildering array of choices, products, and claims.

This book is a road map, not a "how-to" book. A how-to book assumes you already know what is best for your home, budget, and lifestyle. This book helps you to survey the range of options, determine your own priorities, understand the basic steps of energy conservation and solar energy measures, and project the rough costs and benefits that will result.

An energy efficiency project can be thought of as an investment: an investment of money, time, and personal energy. This investment returns benefits that range from the pragmatic—lower utility bills, a more comfortable home, or a house with a higher resale value—to the far reaching—a cleaner environment, self-reliance, or greater national security. On a strictly financial basis, investments in energy conservation compare favorably to many other types of investments.

To help you sort through choices and make decisions based on your own goals, ability, and budget, we have created three categories, or levels, of residential energy investments according to the time, money, and complexity involved and the energy and cost savings that result.

Level I energy investments are basic energy conservation techniques that are relatively inexpensive, don't require structural alterations, and yield a high return for every dollar invested. Whatever your goals, the basic conservation measures of Level I are an essential step to improving the comfort of your home and saving energy. In most houses, these actions are easy to accomplish and cut utility bills significantly—often by more than a third—with a modest capital investment.

Level II measures require greater dollar expenditures than Level I measures and may involve structural modifications to your house; a remodeling project presents excellent opportunities for carrying out these energy improvements. Level II measures help you to the next stage of home energy efficiency by making use of more efficient equipment—furnaces, heat pumps, and the like—and by using energy supplied from a renewable resource: the sun. If these measures are well planned, they can be good investments that also improve the quality of your home, increase comfort, and add to the resale value of the house.

Level III incorporates energy improvements that are best carried out in the course of a home expansion or major renovation or when building a new home. These improvements include both energy efficiency measures and solar energy strategies. Not only can Level III projects provide an attractive return on your investment when completed as part of a home addition, but they can also bring you a step closer to energy independence.

The solar energy measures in Levels II and III include active solar water heating, passive solar space heating, and the use of the sun for indoor lighting. Neither Level II nor Level III includes energy options that are very expensive now but may become economic for household use in the near future: active solar space heating or cooling, photovoltaic cells, and wind energy.

About Our Approach

This book is for people who want to save energy in their homes but aren't sure where to start or how to approach the decisions they face. It is also for people who want to understand all the consequences and trade-offs of their energy investment decisions. Owners of single-family homes will find the book most useful, but there is valuable information here for renters and people who live in multifamily buildings. This book is for people whose interest in home improvement does not at present go beyond the need to save energy; it is also for those who want to reduce their utility bills in the course of a remodeling project, major renovation, or building addition.

This is not a technical book. It does not show you how to weatherize or remodel a house, but it does provide a comprehensive survey of the possibilities and the tools you'll need to calculate the costs and benefits of different options. It is above all a practical guide to the range of home energy projects.

If you are new to the subject, you'll find it easiest to read the book from the beginning. When you encounter an unfamiliar term, consult the glossary at the end of the book.

If you are already familiar with the subject, this approach may not be the most efficient. The chapter titles and the index will steer you quickly toward the information you need. As you use this book, there will be times when further research will be necessary. This will be true if you decide, for example, to invest in a solar addition. The reference section at the end of the book lists the best how-to books and design manuals currently available, as well as general books on subjects related to home energy conservation.

How to Use This Book

Successful home energy projects follow a logical progression—from an evaluation of your goals, resources, and opportunities, then to an estimation of costs and benefits, and then to financing and initiating construction. The chapters in this book follow the same progression.

Chapter 2 looks at the reasons to invest in home energy efficiency. Use the information here to sort out your motives and goals. Understanding goals is most important during the planning and construction phase as you face trade-offs among cost, energy savings, comfort, and other factors.

Once you have established your goals, the next step is to find out how you use energy and where the opportunities for savings lie. Chapter 3 helps you survey your house, looks at energy audits, and explains how to get the most out of one. Use this chapter to get a better understanding of your house, apartment, or condominium and to identify areas for savings. The chapter includes a checklist to fill out as you survey your home. You will be using this information in later chapters to decide which actions are appropriate to your house and what kind of savings you can expect.

Chapter 4 introduces the range of Level I conservation measures. You will gain a better understanding of what is involved in all the basic energy conservation measures from this chapter, as well as general rules about costs, savings, and applications.

Chapter 5 is a companion to Chapter 4. It contains a series of case studies that show how energy efficiency measures perform in different areas of the United States. The case studies look at a typical house in seven different climate zones and show which conservation measures are a priority, what the average contractor-installed costs are, and what kind of annual energy savings you can expect. No case study will duplicate your situation exactly, but you can use the notes included with each case study to help you compare your house with the one under discussion. You can then use the cost and savings estimates for the house and climate closest to yours as guides in planning your own strategy. Also use them to compare benefits of different energy conservation choices—for example, the relative costs and savings of double glazing and triple glazing.

Chapter 6 describes Level II investments, and Chapter 7 presents case studies to help you evaluate energy and dollar benefits for these measures in your climate. Use Chapter 6 to gain an understanding of the general opportunities, problems, and benefits involved. The case studies in Chapter 7 will guide your decision making by providing the rough costs and annual percentage savings of passive solar heating, solar and heat pump water heating, and new furnaces for your location.

Chapter 8 introduces Level III investments—those that are appropriate to a home addition. It is not a substitute, though, for the technical discussions of solar energy that appear in the books in the reference section. Use the information in Chapter 8 to survey your opportunities and narrow down to an approach appropriate to your home and needs.

Chapter 9 gives you the tools to determine the economics of your project and looks at different ways to finance it. Use these tools to estimate financial benefits and financing options. In this chapter, you can use information you've developed throughout the book to compare the benefits of home energy investments with other financial investments, as well as to estimate your rate of return, tax benefits, and payback.

The Range of Choices

The measures in Level I are easy to accomplish and require little skill or training if you plan to do them yourself. Moreover, if you decide to move to the next level you will be building on improvements you have already made. This basic conservation package includes insulation, weatherstripping, window treatments, efficient appliances, and landscaping to save energy. Together these measures can lower your monthly utility bill by 10 to 50 percent.

Decisions about these basic energy conservation measures are simpler and the payoff is more easily predicted than the more ambitious measures of Levels II and III. Level I tactics cost less, and their installation, whether you use a contractor or do it yourself, rarely disrupts your home. The benefits are straightforward: a more comfortable home, dollar savings, and a lower energy bill. Your decisions depend on a few simple factors: how much time and money you have, what technical and financial assistance is available, and the physical characteristics of your home.

Level II measures build on the investments of Level I by using the sun, new heating and cooling equipment, and natural ventilation to increase savings.

Should you embark on these extensive home energy improvements, saving money will probably not be your sole motivation. Other factors come into play, such as aesthetics, improving the quality of your home, greater comfort, and increasing the resale value of your house. While you can realize greater energy and dollar savings with these meas-

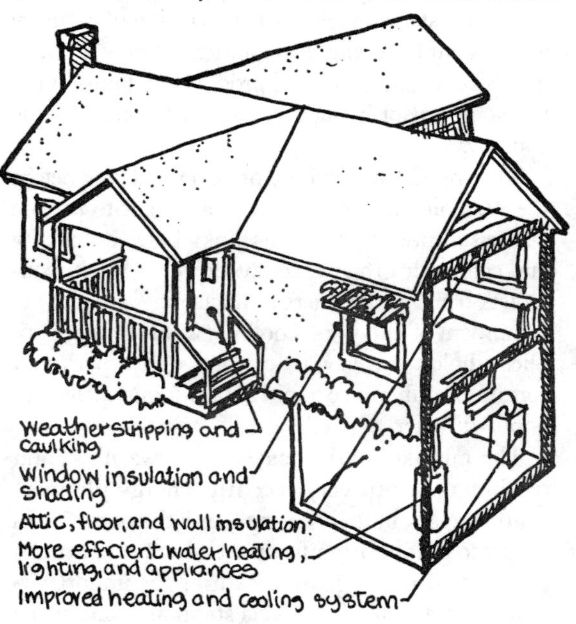

LEVEL I MEASURES

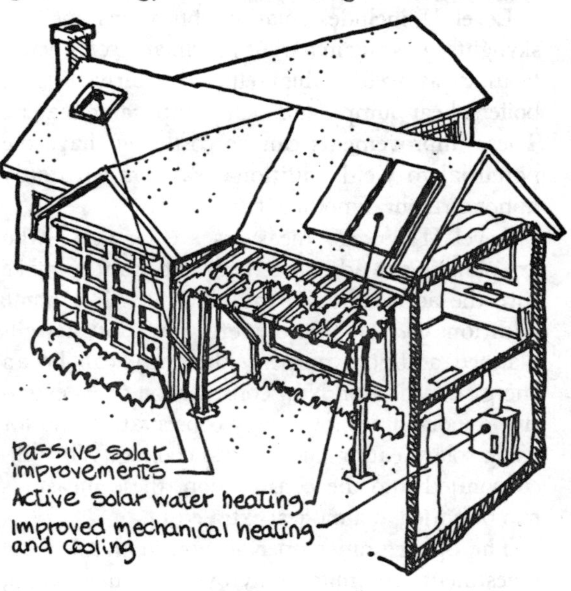

LEVEL II MEASURES

LEVEL III MEASURES

ures than if you had stopped at Level I, financial analysis will not support your decision in every case. Because a Level II investment is larger, and because your energy use is lower after completing Level I measures, Level II measures will take longer to pay back in savings.

Level II includes solar modifications such as skylights, glassing in a front porch, and solar water heating, as well as high-efficiency furnaces and boilers, heat pumps, and heat pump water heaters. These improvements can be costly but have the potential to yield additional savings with only minor structural modifications.

Level III energy measures are for those who are planning to add on a room and want to make sure the addition is energy efficient. Most home additions *increase* home energy use, but a well-planned addition, properly designed, can be an energy contributor. New construction offers extensive opportunities for energy conservation and for using solar heating and natural cooling. When incorporated into the construction, these measures can be added at a modest extra cost.

The opportunities open to you at this level of investment are limited only by your imagination, your budget, and the lifestyle you want to lead. If you do not want the maintenance and operation responsibilities of a solar system, many of the energy efficiency measures of Levels I and II can be incorporated in an addition—preventing it from becoming a drain on your pocketbook.

Why Save Energy? The Larger Context

For many people, energy is first a matter of dollars and cents. Throughout this book you will find information to help you determine the rough costs and returns from a range of efficiency measures. In most houses, these investments compare favorably with traditional financial investments, and they lead to increased comfort.

But energy savings mean more than just improved cash flow and personal comfort. Energy efficiency benefits the national economy: Individual actions to save energy lead to lower energy prices, reduced interest rates, and a lower rate of inflation. Energy efficiency also contributes to local jobs and community development, to national security, and to the quality of life for our children and grandchildren.

CONSERVATION AND THE ECONOMY

For decades, economists and policymakers linked economic growth with the increasing consumption of energy. Energy supplies grew and production costs fell, fueling the expansion of industry and encouraging the development of new, energy-intensive technologies and products and improving the standard of living for families throughout the country.

The era of falling energy prices ended long before the 1973 oil embargo, but it took longer to update our assumptions about the links between energy and economic growth. Today, however, most economists believe that energy efficiency—and the development of inflation-proof renewable energy supplies—holds the key to continued prosperity. A continued adherence to old assumptions spells economic disaster.

The mistakes of the past serve as warnings and reminders. Until very recently, energy planners continued about their business as if the past was an accurate guide to the future. Unbuilt or partially constructed power plants, natural gas import terminals, and synfuels projects stand as monuments to these errors. Utilities trying to complete large power plants now stagger under the weight of massive cost overruns. And consumers have no alternative but to pay the bills. When national leadership has attempted to point the way, it has as often as not been the wrong way.

The most spectacular example of the failure to understand the changing relationship between energy and the economy is in the Pacific Northwest. An ambitious plan to build five large nuclear power plants, conceived in the 1970s by the Washington Public Power Supply System (WPPSS), fell apart in the early 1980s. With one plant near completion and three others halted in various stages of construction, WPPSS decided that it could no longer afford to continue construction on plants whose costs had escalated dramatically and whose electricity was not needed. In 1983, WPPSS defaulted on bonds worth $2.5 billion, the largest such default in U.S. history.

One unfortunate result of this adherence to outdated assumptions is the draining away of capital from new industries that could provide the foundation for an energy-efficient economy. Forty percent of U.S. capital is invested in energy industries and energy-related activities. Businesses, including those developing the technologies and making the equipment to eliminate energy waste, face a higher cost of capital because of these mistakes.

Energy efficiency should be a top national policy, not an afterthought or a consequence of our mistakes. Reducing energy demand by increasing energy efficiency results in lower long-term energy prices and helps to stabilize the costs of other goods and services as well. And it helps keep dollars in this country, strengthening consumer buying power and stimulating growth throughout the economy.

CONSERVATION AND THE COMMUNITY

The average family pays 6 percent of its total income to heat and cool its home and run lights and appliances. These dollars flow outward: to the oil company, to the electric or natural gas utility, to the heating oil suppliers. From there the money moves even further away: to oil and natural gas wholesalers, to import firms, to foreign companies or governments.

Dollars invested in conservation travel in significantly different circles. The insulation you purchase is likely to be made in another region, but the wholesaler and retailer who sell it and the company that installs it employ people from your community. When they get your dollar, they are likely to spend it locally, perhaps on goods or services you yourself provide. Economists call this the multiplier effect. For every new dollar spent locally, two or three dollars are spent on local goods and services. This "recycling" of dollars has a subtle but profound effect. It contributes to local jobs, to increased incomes, and to the economic stability and growth of your community.

CONSERVATION AND SECURITY

Energy efficiency and renewable energy sources make our energy system stronger and more reliable, because each of our conventional fuel sources is in many ways quite vulnerable to disruption. The "pipeline" that brings us oil from Saudi Arabia—our largest foreign supplier—is long and fragile. The oil fields themselves are vulnerable to enemy attack or sabotage; the pipelines that transport oil from the fields are long and easily severed; and tankers are easy targets.

This dependence on foreign supplies of oil has shaped many of our defense and diplomatic policies—from the recent increases in defense spending to the development of a warmaking capability, the Rapid Deployment Force, designed specifically as a means to secure Middle Eastern oil fields and pipelines if necessary. But true security will come only from energy independence. Already, declining U.S. oil imports have undercut the political and economic power of the OPEC countries. These trends increase world stability and can reduce the likelihood of an escalation of tensions leading to war.

Domestic energy sources are more reliable, but because of our highly centralized production and delivery system they too are vulnerable to disruption. The Alaskan pipeline and the tankers that carry oil to the West Coast and through the Panama Canal are susceptible to accident, earthquake, or sabotage. Underwater pipelines and oil drilling platforms on the outer continental shelf have similar vulnerabilities.

Natural gas supplies are only somewhat more secure. Natural gas deliveries depend on a network of pipelines, pumps, and electronic controls that span the continent. Much of our supply comes from other countries, and the new natural gas pipeline from Alaska will be subject to many of the vulnerabilities that characterize the existing oil pipeline.

The sensitivity of our electric grid has received much attention in recent years. The two New York City blackouts and other, less publicized occurrences highlight the weakness of the system to outages caused by lightning, accident, or the failure of a transmission line or power plant.

Conservation of conventional energy sources and reliance on decentralized renewable energy sources benefit both the individual and the nation. Energy-efficient homes can better weather the effects of shortages or blackouts. A nation that depends on an extensive network of decentralized, domestic energy supplies is better able to stand on its own during times of international instability.

CONSERVATION AND THE FUTURE

The energy policies we adopt and the energy investments we make today will help shape the next century. Homes already built will make up over 80 percent of U.S. residences in the year 2000. With the cost-effective Level I conservation measures described in this book, the energy use of all houses at that time could be 30 percent below the 1980 level. What does this mean? A report prepared by the Solar Energy Research Institute titled *A New Prosperity* concludes that basic conservation measures in residential and commercial buildings can "produce" the equivalent of 8.1 million barrels of oil per day—an amount about as large as U.S. imports from OPEC at their peak in the late 1970s—at about half the cost of providing electricity, oil, and gas to these buildings from new conventional sources. Reducing energy use in this way would lift an enormous burden off the U.S. economy.

Energy conservation on this scale has substantial environmental benefits. Many of the environmental consequences of energy production and consumption are known. Burning coal to produce electricity creates air pollution and acid rain, for example, reducing crop and forest productivity across this country and Canada. Other serious environmental effects are suspected but not confirmed. One of these is the possibility of climatic changes from the release of carbon dioxide as fossil fuels are burned. This possibility, if confirmed, will require concerted worldwide action. Energy efficiency measures, by reducing the amount of fuel burned, limit the scope of the problem and the dislocations that will result should we have to curtail our use of fossil fuel.

More efficient fuel use in the industrial nations will also help alleviate world tensions arising from inequities of wealth and resource consumption. The United States, with less than 10 percent of the world's population, uses over 30 percent of the energy consumed worldwide. Compared to its industrial trading partners, the United States is an inefficient user of energy, requiring 50 to 100 percent more energy than Western Europe or Japan to produce equivalent goods and services. As resources grow increasingly scarce—particularly energy—international competition for them is becoming a major source of global tension. And this situation is bound to continue until people and nations choose strategies that emphasize efficiency, conservation, and the use of indigenous renewable resources.

Thus the most important consequences of our shift toward energy efficiency may occur in the future. Using resources wisely ensures that they will be more plentiful and less costly in the years to come. By conserving now, we leave fewer long-term environmental problems for our children and grandchildren, and they will inherit a safer world.

Chapter Two
Making Decisions

Making Decisions

Most successful home energy projects proceed from a clear sense of purpose and a commonsense assessment of goals, skills, time, project costs, and overall benefits. The best measure of eventual success is satisfaction: Is what you got what you really wanted? Does it match your targets for time and money invested as well as for performance? As with any major changes involving lifestyle and home, personal values and individual judgments weigh heavily as you make choices.

Setting Goals

The goals you set for your project reflect your personal wishes, your commitments, and the qualities you value in a home. You may be seeking more affordable comfort or you may be reaching for energy independence. You may bring a hard-headed, dollars and cents approach and see your energy-saving project foremost as a way to save money. Perhaps you're just partly interested in saving energy, but you recognize that, when remodeling or adding onto a house, it makes sense to increase the insulation and provide for some solar heating to make winter days more comfortable.

To help you define your goals we have established some rough categories that we refer to throughout the book: saving money, increasing your home's resale value, greater comfort, adding a room, and environment and security. These categories will help remind you of your original priorities when you are making choices during the planning and construction stages. The better you understand what you want out of your project, the more successful the outcome will be.

SAVING MONEY

Economics may not be your only consideration, but few people can afford to ignore the investment opportunity and cash flow implications of a home energy improvement project. If you view your energy project mainly as an investment, then both a careful cost estimate and a realistic evaluation of energy benefits are essential.

To help you balance economic factors, references to costs and savings are made in Chapters 4 to 8 and further details are presented in the case studies of Chapter 5 and 7. Chapter 9 gives you a way of performing your own economic analysis and provides information on financing a home energy project. Chapter 9 also discusses the tax benefits of your investment.

When weighing economic factors alongside your other objectives, keep in mind the limitations of all attempts to predict dollar savings. Estimates of savings are hypothetical and often based on shaky assumptions. Your future savings will be influenced by how fast energy costs rise, for example—but forecasts of future energy prices are speculative, and, over the past decade, experts have generally guessed low. Moreover, if energy costs rise steeply, they may overtake your savings, leaving you with fuel bills as high as they were before you made the investment. Your savings are no less real, but they are in the form of *avoided* costs, not reduced expenditures (see "Estimating Energy Savings" in Chapter 9).

Other factors that affect savings defy quantification: lifestyle, home management, personal thresholds of comfort. Suppose, for example, you

Minimum comfort, rising utility bills

Increased comfort, more stable utility bills

economize on the use of your heater or air conditioner by keeping your thermostat at 65° F or lower in the winter and at 80° F or higher for the summer. To keep your utility bills in check, you have learned to live less comfortably. The addition of insulation may not reduce your bills by much because you are simply not using enough heating or cooling energy to allow significant savings. After you complete your project, however, you may discover that you can raise your thermostat in the winter and lower it in the summer without facing increased utility bills. You might want—and can now afford—greater comfort in a more efficient home.

Climate, the size of your family, the type of fuels you use, and their cost also influence how much money you save. And how much money are you willing to invest? As a general rule, unless you have already invested in conservation measures, you can spend twice your annual expenditure for heating and cooling and see financial benefits that pay back your investment in three to four years.

In this book we approach the problem of estimating savings through the use of case studies, introduced in Chapter 5 and extended in Chapter 7. If your primary interest is saving money, the case studies will help you estimate annual savings and set your investment priorities.

INCREASING YOUR HOME'S RESALE VALUE

Energy-conserving homes sell more easily than their uninsulated counterparts in most areas. As the cost of fuel continues to rise, they become even more attractive to homebuyers. Even so, the question of energy efficiency standards for new housing has been a subject of intense political controversy for the last decade. Public agencies have sought to impose stricter energy efficiency standards on new home builders; builders have answered that these additional measures have boosted house prices and even further excluded hard-pressed families from the housing market.

If the claims that energy efficiency measures hurt the sale of housing were ever true, they are certainly not true today. Over the last few years, progressive builders and many lenders have come to recognize that—because an energy-efficient house costs less to live in—energy efficiency measures expand the pool of those whose income makes them eligible to purchase a new or older home. Similarly, energy efficiency measures may be part of the solution—not part of the problem—to selling your home, now and in the future. What is important is the bottom line of monthly payments.

Traditionally lenders have considered four factors: loan principal payments, interest, taxes, and insurance. Today energy costs are an important fifth factor. Some lenders have redesigned their eligibility formulas to reflect the significance of energy costs, but the practice, although it would expand the pool of homebuyers, is not yet widespread.

Because income has not kept pace with inflation in the cost of either energy or housing, people are more concerned than ever about paying an increasingly higher share of their income for energy. And this concern is beginning to affect their attitudes about home and condominium purchases. In *Decision for the 80's*, a study of consumer preferences, the National Association of Home Builders found that nearly 80 percent of the homebuyers surveyed in all regions of the country consider energy to be an important factor when buying a home. Homebuyers are also willing to pay extra for energy improvements. Nearly all those surveyed consider the energy situation serious or extremely serious.

Real estate brokers and appraisers surveyed in twenty-two cities throughout the United States estimate that a well-weatherized house is worth from 5 to 9 percent more than one that is not. A third of those surveyed said an energy-efficient home is easier to finance. Most say that being able to tell a customer a house is well insulated helps make a sale, and that having to admit that a house is poorly insulated diminishes it appeal. Nearly all of the appraisers and real estate brokers expected energy-saving features to increase in importance in determining the value of a home. Table 2-1 shows that energy-efficient homes increase in value well beyond the cost of the efficiency measures.

TABLE 2-1
THE AVERAGE WELL-INSULATED HOUSE: COSTS AND RETURNS

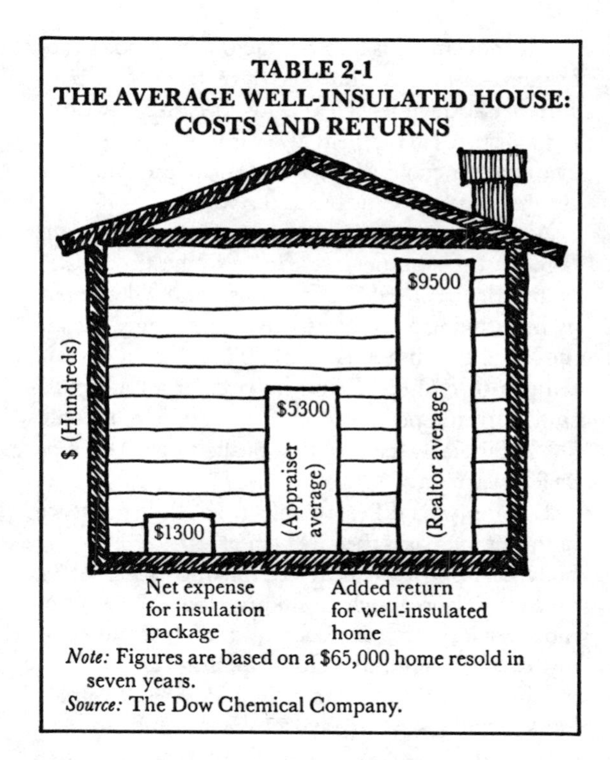

Note: Figures are based on a $65,000 home resold in seven years.
Source: The Dow Chemical Company.

GREATER COMFORT

The purpose of a house is to provide shelter and comfort. Historically, most of the technical advances that provided the comfort we enjoy have involved costly oil, gas, or electricity. Energy efficiency measures make comfort more affordable without cutting into other household necessities.

Until recently, many people falsely equated saving energy with sacrifice, hardship, and discomfort. The opposite is true. An energy-efficient home is less drafty, less noisy, and stays warmer in winter and cooler in summer with less energy, allowing use of rooms that would otherwise remain closed off. Increasing comfort is a legitimate and achievable goal, even though most utility and government conservation programs do not stress this consideration.

The "physics" of comfort is complex but important. Body comfort is affected not just by air temperature but also by heat radiating from bodies and other surfaces, air movement, and humidity. Because air temperature is only one part of the formula, raising the thermostat when we are cold doesn't necessarily provide comfort, although that is what we are accustomed to doing when we want to feel warmer. We constantly exchange heat with the objects around us, including walls and windows. Even if air temperature is a warm 75° F, we still feel chilly if nearby walls and windows are cold. This is because body heat is absorbed by the cold surfaces. This radiated heat loss explains why insulating walls and installing insulating window coverings makes us feel more comfortable even at a lower air temperature.

Air movement is another factor. It speeds evaporation—a process that makes us feel cooler both summer and winter. Heat is lost because evaporating moisture carries heat away from the body. This evaporative cooling effect is desirable during the summer and undesirable in the winter.

Air movement can be managed to our advantage. In the summer, we can raise the thermostat on the air conditioner, using considerably less energy but staying as comfortable by creating some air movement with a small room fan. With a dry air temperature of 85° F and a breeze from a typical small fan, the perceived temperature may be only 78° F. Similarly, eliminating drafts in winter helps us feel warmer.

Humidity also affects comfort. Too little moisture in the air increases the rate of moisture loss from the body, carrying away heat and making us feel colder in winter. Too much humidity slows the rate of moisture loss from the body and inhibits this cooling effect in summer. House plants can increase indoor humidity, as can a humidifier. Dehumidifiers require a great deal of energy and are less efficient than air conditioning in most situations.

ADDING A ROOM

Many growing families feel both the pinch of high energy costs and the squeeze of a house too small for their needs. Adding more space, or remodeling to make more effective use of existing space, can help relieve *both* problems if you use the construction process to make practical and cost-effective energy improvements. If you have decided to remodel, or to add a bedroom, family room, or other living area, you can achieve energy savings at a small additional cost either by making the new rooms energy efficient or by designing them to capture solar energy.

Energy savings should be a part of your project from the beginning. If you plan to alter your house, determine which energy investments make sense at the outset. The starting point for energy measures in a home addition should be the same as for any project: Level I. The basics, such as insulation, weatherstripping, and a furnace tune-up, still make the most economic sense, and they can be accomplished with less mess and less cost as part of a larger project.

Level II and III projects are more ambitious, but they make it possible to use your climate to greater advantage for heating and cooling, increasing both your comfort and savings. Chapters 6, 7, and 8 will help you understand the costs, benefits, and design opportunities available. By making your home addition energy conscious, you can provide a living space that is warmer in winter, cooler in summer, lighter, cheaper to operate, and easier to sell.

ENVIRONMENT AND SECURITY

Much of the literature on energy conservation—and much of this book—deals with economics. In theory, economics provides a general signpost toward the right decisions and away from a wasteful allocation of time, money, and resources.

In practice, though, most economic analyses set up an uneven contest by considering only direct costs and not such indirect costs as federal tax incentives, research funds, support facilities, and other subsidies. Coal, nuclear power, the electric utilities, and synthetic fuels, for example, have received billions of dollars in federal subsidies. Only in recent years have conservation and solar investments received state and federal support, but these incentives go only partway toward balancing the scales.

Most economic analyses use the direct (subsidized) fuel cost charged by fuel suppliers as a benchmark for comparing energy investments. This type of comparison may be appropriate for decisions involving the household budget, but it distorts judgments about the total costs and benefits to the nation.

Traditional economic analysis has another weakness. There is a range of benefits that don't enter into economic models or analyses because they are difficult to quantify. Energy, because of its importance to our economy, its influence on our natural environments, and its role in global politics, cannot be measured strictly in dollars and Btu's.

Environmental quality is the classic example of a value that defies precise measurement. Energy has shaped economic and technical development in this century, but it has also created a host of problems in its wake. The burning of coal to make electricity contributes a large share to the acid rain problem, and the strip mining of that coal displaces farms and ranches, competes for scarce water, and creates permanent scars on the landscape. Oil burning contributes to urban air pollution, to the need to drill in sensitive offshore areas, and to an increased risk of oil spills. All these activities have health and economic effects that are real but—because they are difficult to pinpoint—seldom weighed adequately in the decision process. By reducing the demand for conventional fuels, conservation investments lessen environmental effects and stretch existing resources further.

Economics is also a poor guide when it comes to the question of risk and security. Security is both personal and global. On the personal level, we rely on a highly centralized system of pipelines, powerlines, and power plants for energy delivery. This system is vulnerable to disruption in time of war, from sabotage, or from natural disasters. In California a winter storm recently knocked down two large transmission towers and cut off most of the state's electricity supply. Events like these are common and provide sharp reminders of our crippling dependence and vulnerability.

Investments in energy conservation help alleviate this situation by reducing both the vunerability of our energy systems and our dependence on conventional fuels. By reducing demands for electricity, natural gas, or oil, efficiency measures lessen the strain on the systems that deliver these fuels, decreasing the likelihood of disruption. At home, an energy-conserving or solar house may only drop to 60 or 65° F inside when winter heating fuels are disrupted—even if outdoor temperatures fall below freezing.

These intangibles don't have a place in conventional economic analysis or on a life cycle cost worksheet. But they are significant aspects of our energy production and consumption. And energy efficiency investments—particularly at the household level—are an important part of the cure. If these values are important to you, the best advice is to let economics guide you without excluding other possibilities. Don't let economics persuade you not to do what you know is right.

Estimating Yourself: Time, Stress, Skills

A realistic appraisal of your *personal* resources is as important to a successful energy project as well-defined goals. How much of your time and energy do you want to commit to the project? What are you willing to give up?

Home improvement and expansion projects are often portrayed in the pages of Saturday newspaper supplements and glossy magazines as tasks anyone can manage easily. Have you ever wondered why they show photographs of finished projects and never seem to show the construction phase? Some simple energy conservation measures can be installed with little mess or disruption, but most Level II and III measures involve significant construction. Let's be honest. A building project in your own home is messy, time consuming, and disruptive.

The human element is a crucial factor in the home improvement/energy retrofit equation. For large projects, there are inevitable frustrations as you discover that it might have been worth your money to have hired a professional to complete the task, that your home improvement project coincides with overwork at the office, or that something unanticipated causes agonizing delays. What you choose to do and how you do it will be based on personal questions: How much time do you have to contribute to the project? How well do you work under different types of pressure? What skills do you bring to the project?

Different people place different values on time. If you have plenty of time but not a lot of money,

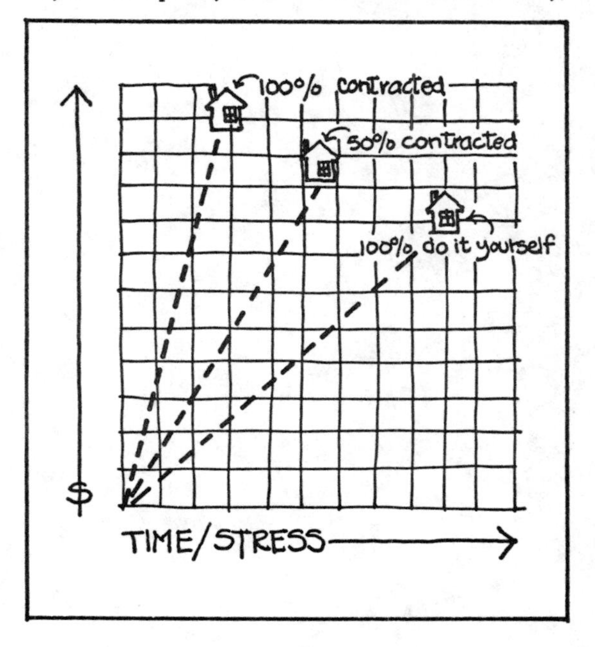

you are very likely to install many of the Level I and II measures yourself. Depending on your skills, you may decide to do it all yourself or hire a contractor to do some of the basic structural work, leaving other tasks for you to finish.

The less time you have to commit, the more money you have to spend. It may not be worth it to you to undergo the stress of completing your own energy remodel; you might be better off taking out a home improvement loan and eliminating the stress by hiring a contractor.

Controlling how long a project takes to complete is difficult, particularly when you are remodeling. It is important to try, though. Develop a detailed schedule before you begin, using the estimates of a contractor or the experience of friends as a starting point. But be prepared to miss your targets. Even skilled contractors find surprises they didn't anticipate as walls are torn out and new aspects of a house are revealed.

Clearly, stress is unavoidable in a home renovation project—ask anyone who has completed one recently. Why is stress a factor to consider? Because a careful look at personal tolerance levels can add realism to the planning process. If you have a low tolerance for this kind of stress, don't plan to do an extensive solar retrofit if all you want to do is save a little energy. Match your construction goals to your personal skills and tolerance level. Don't overcommit either your financial resources or yourself. And be sure you develop a *realistic* timetable for construction.

Your skills, like the amount of time you have to give, shape the project and the way you carry it out. Your skills deserve careful evaluation before you embark on a construction project. If you are eager but not confident, most community colleges or learning exchange programs have short home repair and construction courses that can give you an idea of how you measure up to the tasks you have planned.

The skills you need depend on the type of project. Most Level I projects can be accomplished by anyone with common sense who is handy with basic tools. Level II projects require plumbing and electrical skills and an understanding of the structural elements of a house. Adding onto a house —Level III—requires a lot of time, a full commitment, and a wide range of skills.

After you understand what you want, how much you want to be involved in the project, and what you can spend, embark on a careful inventory of your house. These questions need answers expressed in *numbers*: What is the energy savings potential? What are your energy bills and how much can they be reduced? What is the potential for modification? The answers to these questions begin with a survey of your home and an energy audit.

Chapter Three
Assessing Your Energy Use

Assessing Your Energy Use

You need to understand how energy is used in your home before you devise ways to use it more efficiently or augment it with solar energy. The first part of this chapter looks at basic household energy uses and the major factors, such as climate, that affect how much energy you use. Here you will learn how to use your utility bills to estimate how much your heating and cooling system, hot water, and major appliances use. This information will point you toward the greatest opportunities for energy conservation in your home.

After you've reviewed the first part of this chapter, consider getting an energy audit. The second part of this chapter looks at different types of audits and tells you how to arrange one and what to expect. Whether you get a professional energy audit —as we recommend—or rely on your own home energy survey, this chapter will prepare you for choosing among the investment options described in Chapters 4, 6, and 8.

Understanding Home Energy Use

The average family spends over $1200 annually to heat, cool, and light its house and operate appliances. This amount varies considerably depending on the nature and location of the house, the habits of the occupants, and local energy prices. The greatest amount of energy is used for space heating and cooling, followed by water heating and appliances. Table 3-1 shows exactly how these uses are distributed in an average household.

These generalizations are useful because they point you toward areas of greatest potential savings, but it helps to know something about your own patterns of energy use in order to make the best decisions. To get a clear picture, take a close look at your energy bills, consider the effects of your local climate, and learn how your home is built.

UNDERSTANDING YOUR UTILITY BILLS

Your fuel bills will tell you a lot about how you use energy. They should indicate the type of energy you purchase, the cost per unit, and how many units you used. Some utilities send summaries of energy use over the past year with each bill to help you keep track of your conservation efforts. Home heating oil is sold by the gallon, and the price per gallon is indicated on the bill. Natural gas is sold by the therm or cubic foot; electricity is sold by the kilowatt-hour. If the price per unit does not appear on the bill, call the utility or heating oil company to get that figure. Many utility bills include fixed charges to cover metering, billing costs, and other expenses. These fixed charges, which vary from utility to utility, are generally not affected by your conservation efforts. Additionally, some utilities offer lifeline rates for customers who use less than a certain amount of energy. Your conservation efforts may allow you to qualify for this lower rate.

Some household energy uses are largely independent of season, local climate, or the shape and size of the building. Other energy uses are determined by climate and the condition of the house. To understand more about your yearly pattern of energy use, your energy costs, and how to reduce them, you will find it useful to graph the changes in your monthly energy costs over a year.

Make a chart for each fuel you use in the space provided on the Home Energy Survey and Checklist (Table 3-2) or on a separate piece of paper. Note

TABLE 3-1
HOW ENERGY IS USED IN AMERICAN HOMES

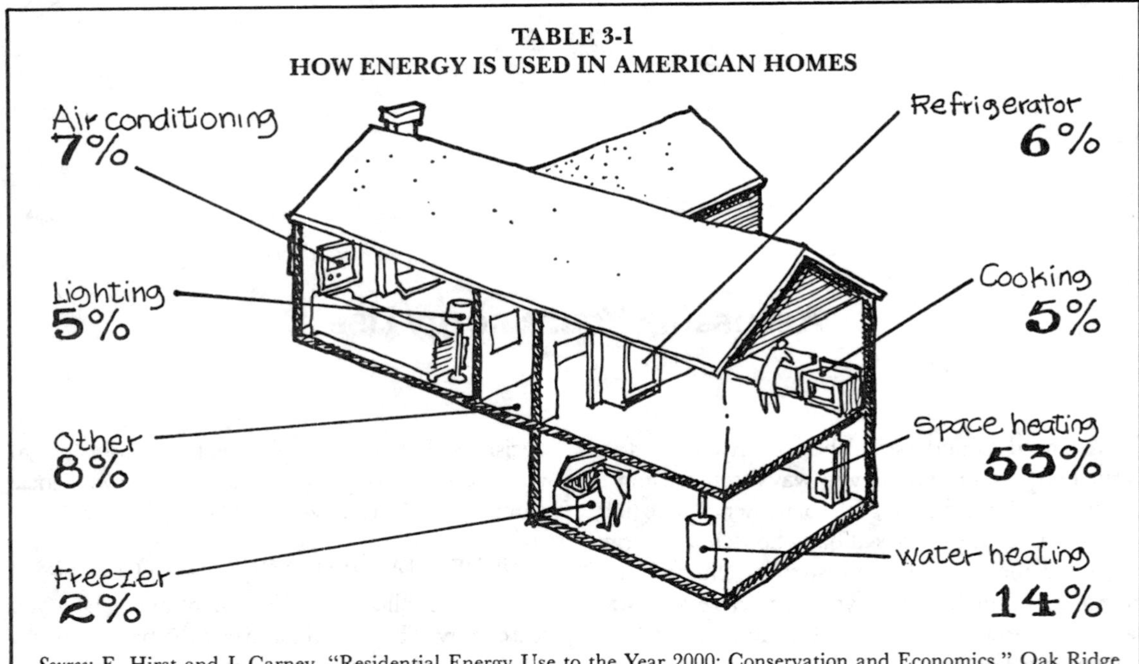

Source: E. Hirst and J. Carney, "Residential Energy Use to the Year 2000: Conservation and Economics," Oak Ridge National Laboratory, ORNL/CON-13, September 1977.

that the vertical axis represents dollars, while the horizontal axis lists the months of the year. Put a dot at the point at which a vertical line drawn up from the month column and a horizontal line drawn over from the cost column would meet. When you connect the dots, you will have charts that look something like the graphs for our sample Washington, D.C., house in Box 3-1. If you have bills going back two or more years, graph them on a separate piece of paper to see the effects of weather patterns, cost increases, and changes in personal habits. If you get bills that cover more than one month, divide the amount of energy used by the number of months covered by the bill to get an average cost per month. Then place dots on the chart at the points corresponding to the months and average costs.

Under each graph, list the major uses for the fuel you have profiled, as we have done in Box 3-1. If you have filled out the Home Energy Checklist and Survey (Table 3-2), you already have much of the information you need to make this list. Make sure you account for each of the five largest household energy uses: space heating, water heating, air conditioning, appliances (including refrigerator, stove, and clothes dryer), and lighting. These items consume 95 percent of all energy used in U.S. residences. If you leave your furnace pilot light on through the summer, list it as an item under the furnace fuel graph.

As you compare the month-to-month variation of your fuel costs, note that space heating and cooling needs—the largest energy uses in households in almost all parts of the country—peak around January and February and again in July and August. Household energy uses, such as lights, appliances, and water heating, are less influenced by climate and remain relatively constant throughout the year. Your hot water energy use is determined by the number of people in the household and the efficiency of the system. Your appliance energy use is determined primarily by the type and efficiency of your models and how you use them. The change in seasons affects lighting energy somewhat, as do the number, patterns of use, and efficiency of the lights in the house.

The graphic pattern of your bills will give you some idea of your energy consumption in these

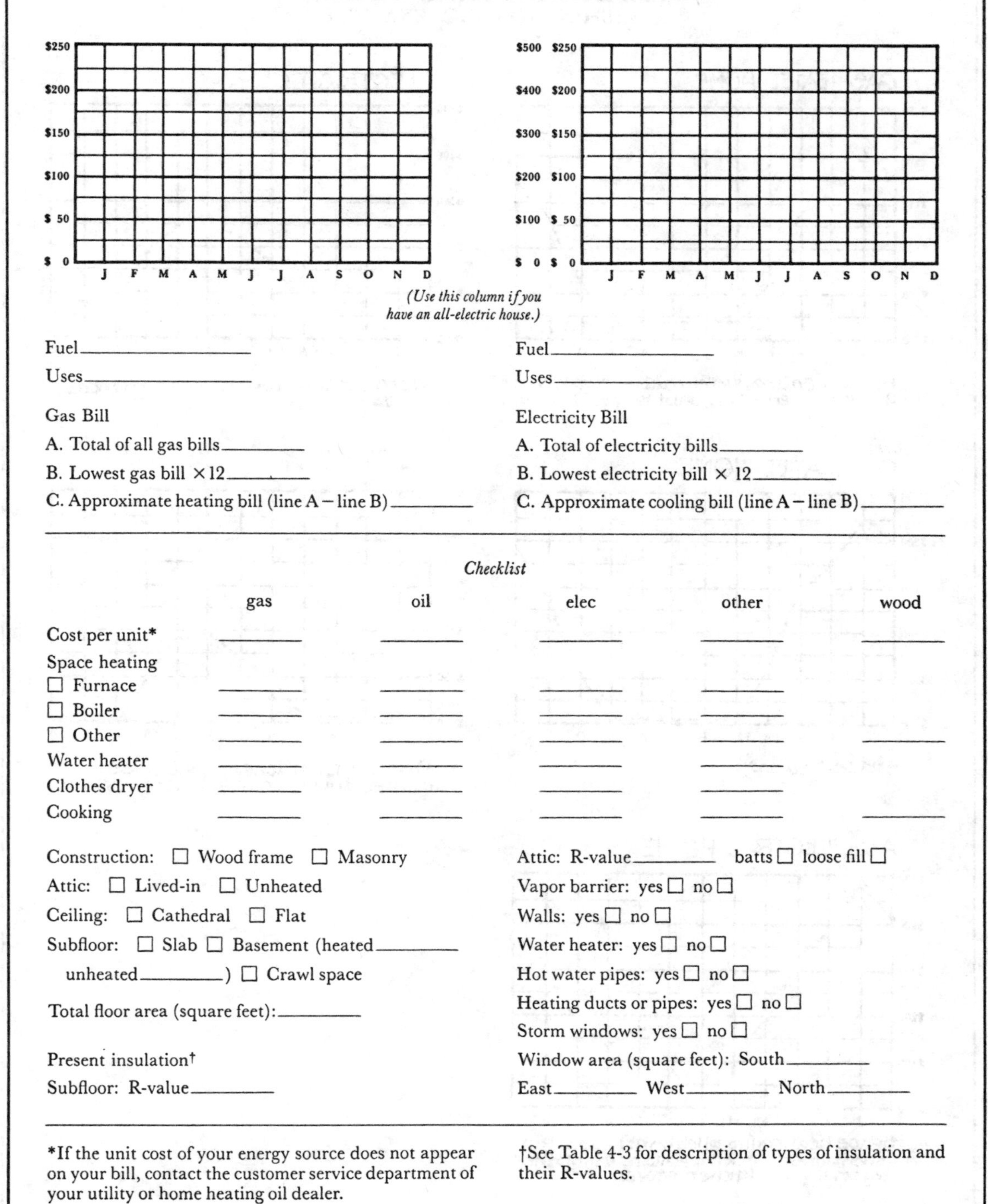

TABLE 3-2
HOME ENERGY SURVEY AND CHECKLIST

(Use this column if you have an all-electric house.)

Fuel________
Uses________

Gas Bill
A. Total of all gas bills________
B. Lowest gas bill ×12________
C. Approximate heating bill (line A – line B)________

Fuel________
Uses________

Electricity Bill
A. Total of electricity bills________
B. Lowest electricity bill × 12________
C. Approximate cooling bill (line A – line B)________

Checklist

	gas	oil	elec	other	wood
Cost per unit*	____	____	____	____	____
Space heating					
☐ Furnace	____	____	____	____	
☐ Boiler	____	____	____	____	
☐ Other	____	____	____	____	____
Water heater	____	____	____	____	
Clothes dryer	____	____	____	____	
Cooking	____	____	____	____	____

Construction: ☐ Wood frame ☐ Masonry
Attic: ☐ Lived-in ☐ Unheated
Ceiling: ☐ Cathedral ☐ Flat
Subfloor: ☐ Slab ☐ Basement (heated________ unheated________) ☐ Crawl space

Total floor area (square feet):________

Present insulation†
Subfloor: R-value________

Attic: R-value________ batts ☐ loose fill ☐
Vapor barrier: yes ☐ no ☐
Walls: yes ☐ no ☐
Water heater: yes ☐ no ☐
Hot water pipes: yes ☐ no ☐
Heating ducts or pipes: yes ☐ no ☐
Storm windows: yes ☐ no ☐
Window area (square feet): South________
East________ West________ North________

*If the unit cost of your energy source does not appear on your bill, contact the customer service department of your utility or home heating oil dealer.

†See Table 4-3 for description of types of insulation and their R-values.

BOX 3-1
GRAPHING YOUR ENERGY BILLS:
A WASHINGTON, D.C., EXAMPLE

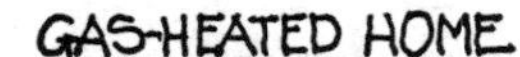

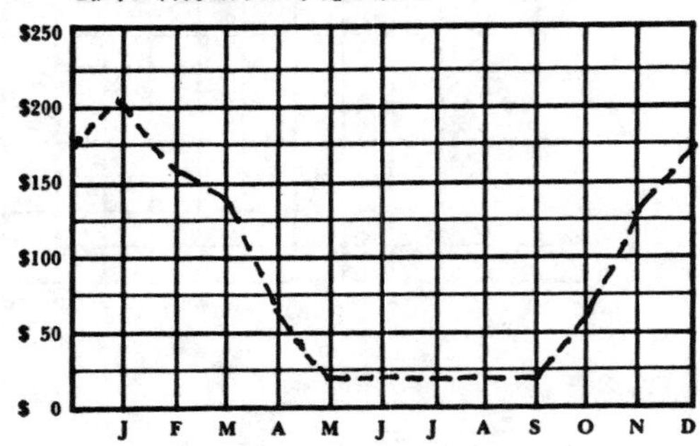

Space heating, water heating, clothes dryer, kitchen stove (pilot light off)

ELECTRICITY

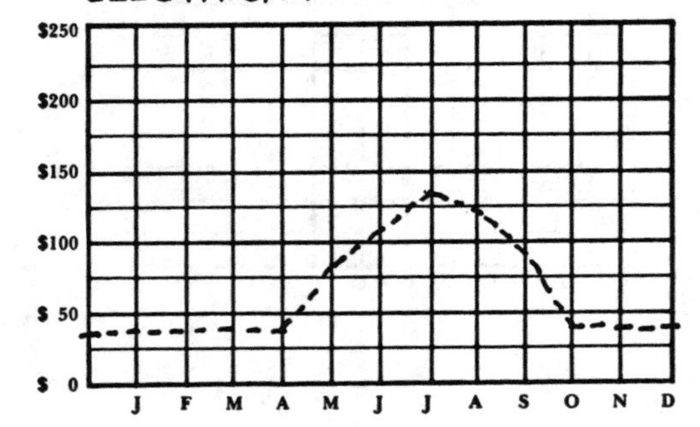

Room air conditioner, small appliances, lights

OIL-HEATED HOME

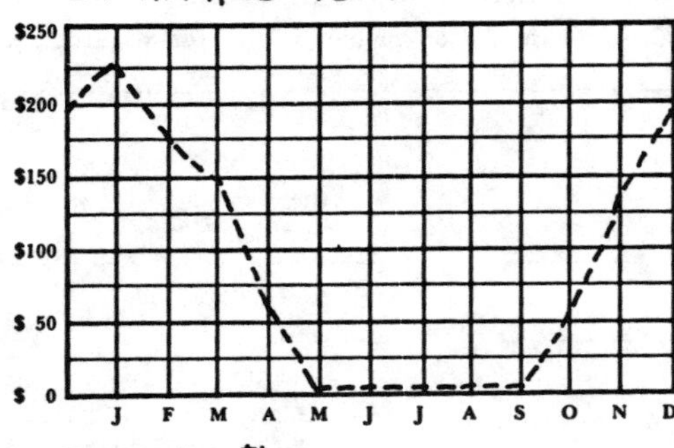

Space heating

ELECTRICITY

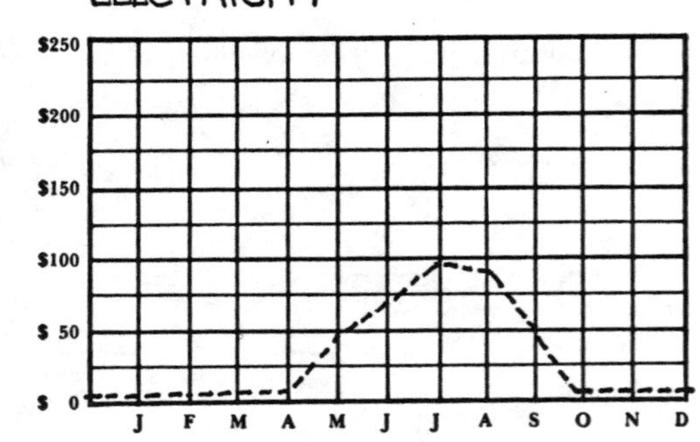

Room air conditioner, appliances, clothes dryer, lights, kitchen stove

ALL-ELECTRIC HOME

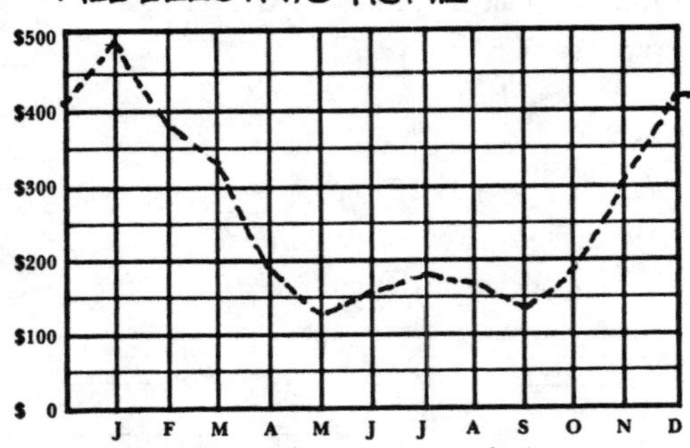

Space heating (no pilot light), room air conditioner, small appliances, clothes dryer, lights, kitchen stove

major categories. In Box 3-1 we show the bill pattern for a family of four living in a 1225-square-foot house in Washington, D.C. The family living in this house uses natural gas for space and water heating, the clothes dryer, and the stove; electricity runs the air conditioning, appliances, and lights. The house has R-11 attic insulation and its thermostat is set at 68° F in winter and 75° F in summer.

Take a close look at the peaks and valleys in the graph for our sample home and for yours. Your lowest monthly total will be for a month in which you don't need to heat or cool your home. The energy uses in this month are hot water, lighting, appliances, and a furnace pilot light if it's operating. This is your baseline energy use (which may include fixed monthly utility charges). To chart your baseline use (appliances, lights, and hot water), draw a horizontal line through the lowest points of the curves as we did in the example.

For the Washington, D.C., house in this example, the lowest monthly bill is $36 for electricity and $22 for natural gas. Since these baseline uses change very little in response to changing weather, multiplying by 12 will give an approximate total annual cost for these uses. In the example, therefore, annual electricity costs for running lights and appliances total $432. Similarly, annual natural gas baseline costs for water heating, clothes drying, and cooking total $264. Of this latter amount, nearly 90 percent is for water heating.

If you do not have records to chart your bills, you can use a rule of thumb for estimating the cost of water heating. Assume that you use 160 kwh (if you have an electric water heater) or 8.5 therms (if you have a natural gas water heater) per month for each person in the household. Multiplying your cost per therm or kilowatt-hour by 8.5 or 160 and then again by the number of people in your household will give your approximate monthly cost for water heating.

What about heating costs? If you heat with natural gas, you can determine roughly what you paid for heating by totaling all your natural gas bills for a year and subtracting your twelve-month baseline costs for the other uses. In our example, this heating component is $770. The Washington, D.C., household turned off its pilot light at the end of the heating season. Gas pilot lights add $2 to $5 to monthly bills.

To determine your cooling costs, if you have an electric air conditioner, you can perform a similar calculation using twelve months of electricity bills. Do the same thing if you also use electricity for heating. To establish your baseline costs, pick a time of year when you do not heat or cool. The additional winter costs above baseline are for heating. In summer the additional costs above baseline are for cooling. If you use oil to heat your home, simply add your fuel bills for a year to find your heating costs.

These numbers are important as a basis for estimating how much you will save from a certain combination of energy investments and deciding how much it makes sense to spend. In Chapters 5 and 7 we calculate savings from various energy investments in sample houses. The results are shown in graphs like the one you have just made. These case studies will be more useful to you if you have already charted and thought out your energy uses, costs, and bill patterns.

TAKING YOUR CLIMATE INTO ACCOUNT

Local climate affects both the size of your energy bills and the range of energy investments that make economic sense for you. If you live in a very cold climate, your bills are high, even if the unit cost of energy is low, and a broad range of efficiency measures is probably justified. If you live in a mild climate, your bills are low and your potential savings are modest—unless you live in an area with very high energy costs.

Climate directly affects the feasibility and economics of many energy investments. Obviously, solar space heating systems won't perform well if you have a short heating season characterized much of the year by fog or cloud cover. (See Chapter 6 for information on solar radiation.) If winters are long and clear, on the other hand, solar heating may be a good choice.

Climate is both a regional and a local phenomenon. Diverse elements combine to make up a climate: sun, wind, temperature, humidity, solar radiation, precipitation, evaporation, and temperature swings between night and day and from season to season. All these elements are influenced by local and regional geographic features, oceans and lakes, cloud patterns, cities, air pressure, altitude, and other forces.

One method of distinguishing the heating and cooling needs of different climates is the "degree-day" concept. Heating degree-days is a figure that represents the number of degrees per day each year that the temperature drops below 65° F. Cooling degree-days represent the number of degrees per day the temperature rises above 75° F.

Degree-days indicate the average heating and cooling requirements of a certain climate. The higher the number of heating degree-days, the greater the heating needs in that climate. The higher the number of cooling degree-days, the greater the cooling requirement in that climate.

Heating and cooling degree-days form the basis for the climate zones in the case studies of Chapters 5 and 7. We have used seven climate zones that are derived from the heating and cooling degree-day weather zones established by the National Weather Service. Box 3-2 shows these climate areas.

While degree-days are a good indication of heating and cooling needs, there are two major climate features that affect energy use but are not indicated in degree-day measurements. These are wind and humidity, and they vary greatly within climate zones.

Humidity is moisture in the air. Relative humidity is a measure of the amount of moisture in the air relative to the amount of moisture it can hold and is expressed as a percentage. When humidity levels are high, there is less evaporation of moisture on the skin, which creates the feeling of mugginess. When humidity levels are low, evaporation takes place very easily with the subsequent sensation of cooling.

Look at Climate Zone 4. It spans the country from Virginia and the Carolinas to New Mexico and Arizona. Because of the high humidity, an 85° F day can seem quite uncomfortable in North Carolina. In dry southern New Mexico, however, an 85° F day may seem quite pleasant.

Wind too affects comfort because air movement evaporates moisture on the skin more quickly and

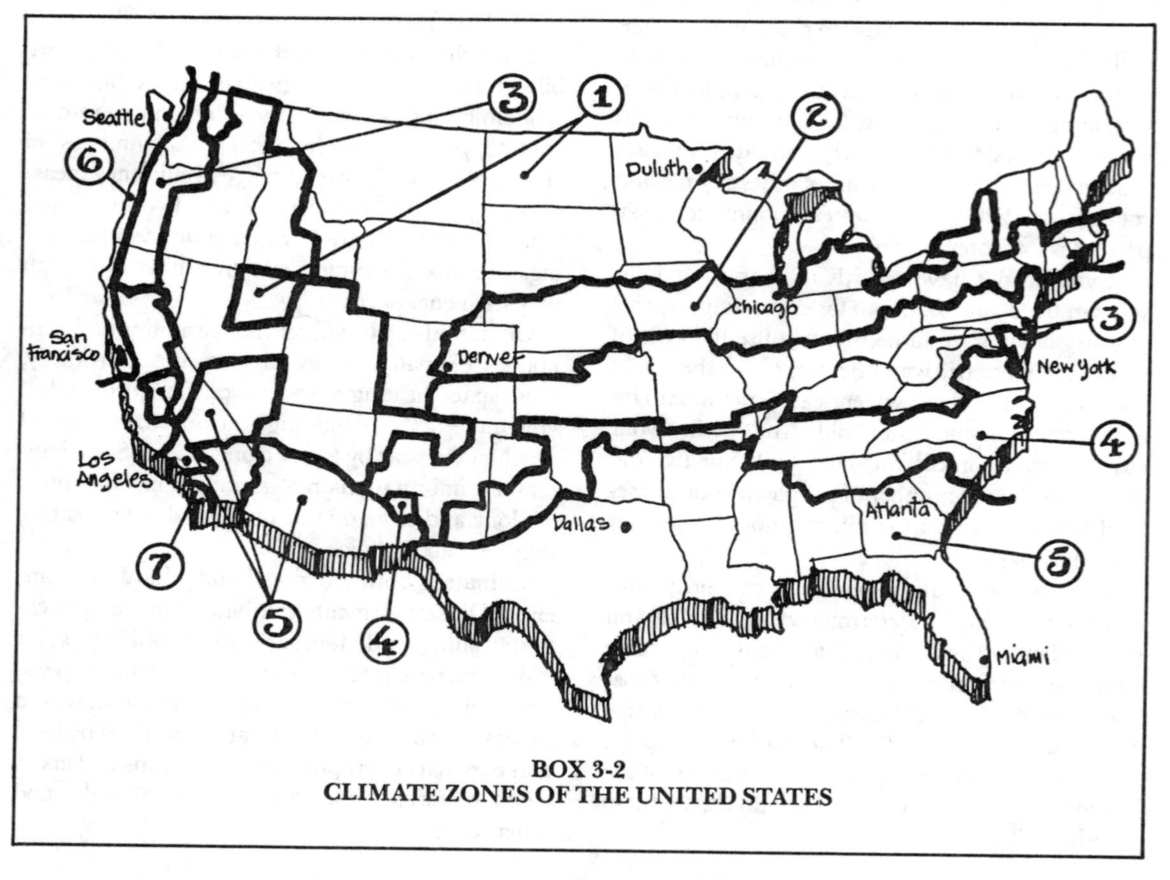

BOX 3-2
CLIMATE ZONES OF THE UNITED STATES

carries heat away from the body. This movement of heat being carried away from the body creates the wind chill factor. On a 40° F day when the wind is blowing at 15 miles per hour, you perceive a temperature of 22° F. This is one reason why it is important to understand the direction and force of the wind and protect yourself against it by landscaping and weatherizing your house—something we discuss in Chapter 4.

Wind speed and humidity can differ widely within a single climate zone. Wind, in particular, can be a local phenomenon because of variations in terrain, location of trees, and other factors. As you look at the case studies in Chapter 5, consider how wind and humidity will affect your energy-saving strategies. People living in areas with high humidity have a greater need for air conditioning and other cooling techniques than those in drier areas. Since achieving tolerable comfort on hot summer days will be more difficult, more energy is used and a greater investment to save cooling energy is warranted.

People living in areas with high winds should focus on protecting their house from winter wind with landscaping and window treatments and making it weathertight by insulating, weatherstripping, caulking, and blocking thermal bypasses. In summer, winds can be used to your advantage for natural ventilation.

Some climate variables can be used to your benefit. One is daily swings in temperature. If you live in an area characterized by warm days and cool nights, you can use natural ventilation to cool your house during the summer, minimizing your air conditioning needs, and design passive solar approaches that heat during the day, storing heat for nighttime use (see Chapters 6 and 7).

TAKING YOUR BUILDING INTO ACCOUNT

In almost all parts of the country, space heating and cooling are the largest energy uses in households. Heat is gained and lost through the house's envelope: the floor, walls, windows, and ceilings that separate heated spaces from the outside or from unheated areas. Differences in housing type and construction affect the rate of heat loss and gain through the envelope. The critical factors are the amount of roof, wall, and window area exposed to the climate.

BOX 3-3 MATCHING THE MEASURES TO YOUR BUILDING TYPE

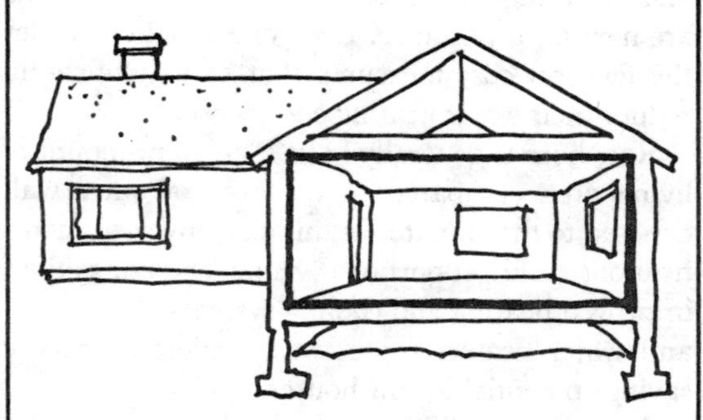

Single-Family Homes. Extensive envelope area (windows, outer walls, and roof) relative to living area. Heating and cooling systems are not shared. Focus should be on the entire range of Level I measures.

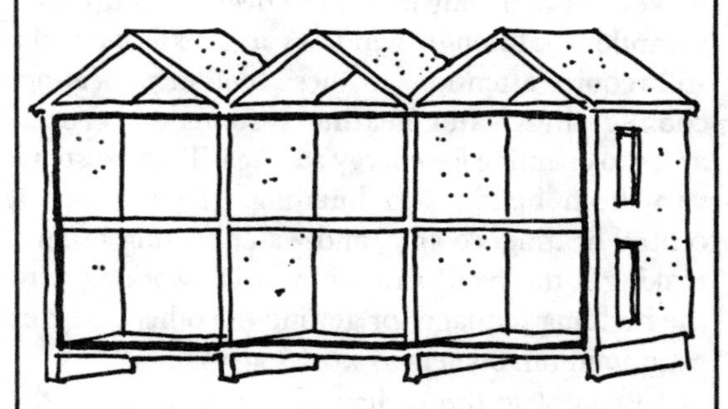

Row Houses. Less envelope area compared to living area. Heating and cooling systems, water heating, and appliance efficiency become increasingly important to achieving savings. Minimize heat loss and gain through windows.

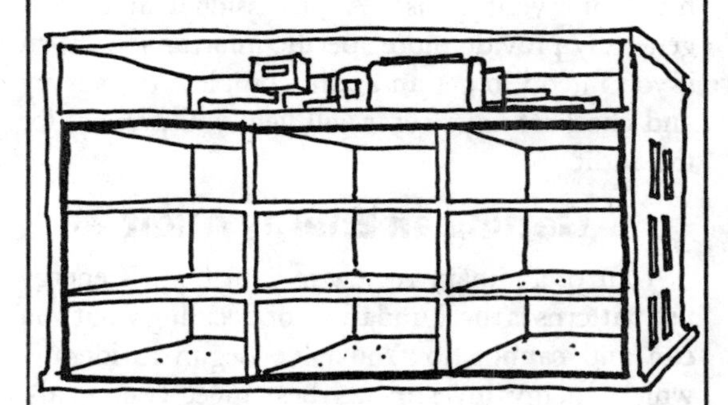

Apartments. Little wall, ceiling, and floor area exposed to climate since most are shared. Focus on heating and cooling system, water heating, and appliance efficiency. Prevent heat loss and gain through windows.

Single-family detached houses have large outer wall, window, and roof areas. Changes in the building envelope usually offer substantial energy savings. Heating and cooling system improvements are next in importance. Everyone should consider the few low-cost measures that can significantly reduce their water heating energy use.

Row houses generally have a greater amount of living area compared to the area of outer wall exposed to the climate. In this case envelope modifications yield proportionally smaller savings than improved heating and cooling systems. Appliances and water heaters represent considerable energy savings potential in row houses.

Apartment buildings, cooperatives, and condominiums present a different set of energy conservation choices. Because walls, floors, and ceilings are shared with other units, the building envelope makes less of a contribution to overall energy consumption—although windows and exterior walls still require attention. In these buildings, heating, cooling, and water heating systems are crucial areas to examine for energy savings. These systems vary from building to building. If yours has a central heating, cooling, and water heating system, making it more efficient will involve working with the building manager or getting the other co-op or condominium owners to work together.

To complete the review of your house, use the Home Energy Survey and Checklist (Table 3-2). The survey and checklist, together with the information in Chapters 4 and 6, will help steer you toward a cost-effective package of energy improvements for your house. A professional audit will generally provide more specific information. Even if you intend to get an audit, complete the survey and checklist anyway; it will help you prepare for the audit.

Getting an Energy Audit

Your preliminary review of your home's energy use patterns is the foundation for deciding what you can and cannot do. You have begun to identify which energy investments best meet your goals. Now is the time to consider getting a professional home energy audit. An audit is not essential, but an expert auditor will give you a more accurate picture of your home's conservation potential. An auditor who is familiar with your local climate and local energy prices will know what has worked for other people in your area.

An audit is a systematic examination of a house: its space heating, cooling, and water heating systems, its insulation and appliances, and the energy use habits of its occupants. The audit results in a set of recommendations for additional energy efficiency measures, together with an estimate of their costs and savings.

Audits are provided by local utilities or heating oil distributors and in some areas by contractors or commercial firms. Most utility audits take one to three hours and cover only basic energy conservation measures—what we call Level I energy investments. A private auditor may come equipped to evaluate the solar heating and cooling potential of your home, test the efficiency of your furnace and make some adjustments, and perform some of the necessary caulking and weatherstripping work. For a Level II or III energy project, you may have to turn to a heating and cooling or solar specialist.

If you choose not to get an energy audit, or if neither a utility audit nor a private professional audit is available in your area, you should do your own audit. The reference section at the end of the book lists sources that include forms and worksheets for doing a detailed self-audit.

USING YOUR UTILITY

Your local utility is the logical place to look for expertise and assistance in energy conservation. Utilities know local conditions and most have large trained staffs. An advantage of using a utility audit is that most utilities are not in the business of selling or installing energy conservation equipment.

Utilities are not always regarded as a customer's best friend, though, and utility conservation programs vary in quality and sincerity. Why should you trust an energy corporation to tell you how to get by with less of it? The best answer is a question: Who else can you trust? People who sell conservation services are equally likely to overstate your needs and exaggerate your benefits. Obtaining another viewpoint is valuable for balance, and many utilities perform this function well. More important, utilities are changing as a result of shifts in the economic environment. As the costs of new power plants and new fuel supplies keep rising steeply, utilities no longer profit as they once did from your increased consumption. Today, paradoxically, conservation often makes utilities more financially sound and gives them a better public image. Most utilities now have conservation departments with dedicated personnel and the support of the corporation. Not all utilities perceive their role this broadly, however; Box 3-4 will help you judge whether your utility's conservation program is worth using.

Large utilities are required by federal law to provide free or low-cost audits (up to $15) to homeowners who request them. This program is called the Residental Conservation Service (RCS). The RCS legislation requires large utilities and some heating oil dealers to offer home energy audits. Congress has specified minimum standards for audits and requires states to supervise audit programs within their borders. Table 3-3 lists the measures that are evaluated in an RCS audit.

Two types of audits are offered under the Residential Conservation Service. Those performed in person by a trained auditor are called Class A audits. The auditor will arrange to visit your home and spend two to four hours making detailed observations and measurements. If personal service is not wanted or not possible, the utility provides material for a Class B self-audit. In a Class B audit, the utility sends the customer a form with questions about the house and the household's patterns of energy use. The utility will then recommend conservation strategies based on its computer's analysis of the responses.

GETTING THE MOST FROM AN AUDIT

Auditing practices depend on the commitment of the utility, the involvement of state and local governments, and the professionalism and experience

BOX 3-4
QUESTIONS TO ASK ABOUT AN ENERGY AUDIT

Ask the utility the following questions to determine whether its energy audit will meet your needs. Some of these same questions should also be helpful when you're working with a private auditor or one from a heating oil company.

1. Will an auditor visit your house? The best audits are based on a detailed survey of your house —possible only if a professional comes by.

2. Will the audit cover a full range of conservation and solar measures? Compare the measures the utility surveys to the list in Table 3-3.

3. How much will the audit cost? Normally, utilities may charge no more than $15 for an RCS audit; a private auditor will charge more.

4. Will the auditor measure furnace efficiency with testing equipment? A furnace tune-up, modification, or replacement may be your best energy investment. If the utility does not test furnaces, plan to have a furnace professional test and tune it at the same time.

5. Will the audit focus on both heating and cooling costs? This can be important. In hot climates, for example, insulating drapes save more summer cooling than winter heating.

6. Will the audit fully consider measures involving fuels sold by other companies? An auditor from a gas utility may be inclined to discount the benefits of a measure that would save electricity.

7. Will the utility help you arrange for installation and conduct an inspection afterward? If the answer is yes, ask the representative to spell out what recourse you will have if something is improperly installed. If the answer is no, plan to do the quality control yourself.

8. Does the utility or heating oil company have a financing plan? Many provide low-interest loans (see Chapter 9); get the specific interest rate and the payback schedule. If the utility has no financing plan, will it refer you to lenders who will finance the conservation measures?

9. If the utility has a financing program, what cutoff will it use when determining which measures to finance? Ideally it should finance measures that repay their cost within their useful lifetime; ten years is a good compromise. A payback standard that is arbitrarily short (five years or less) will exclude a number of measures that will contribute savings and comfort to your life.

10. What fuel escalation rate does the utility use in determining cost effectiveness? Fuel escalation rates that are conservative will make the conservation measures appear less cost effective. Check the utility's estimates and see if they correspond to the energy price increases you have already experienced.

11. Can the utility tell you which measures are eligible for federal or state tax credits?

If you are satisfied with the answers you get to these questions, it will make sense for you to use the utility's energy audit.

TABLE 3-3
MEASURES EVALUATED IN AN RCS ENERGY AUDIT

Conservation measures

—ceiling, attic, wall, and floor insulation
—storm or thermal windows and doors
—furnace maintenance and efficiency modifications
—oil furnace burner replacement
—caulking and weatherstripping
—clock thermostats
—load management devices
—duct, pipe, and water heater insulation
—heat-reflecting or heat-absorbing window or door materials
—evaporative coolers
—whole-house fans
—heat pump water heaters
—swimming pool covers
—replacement of central air conditioners with higher-efficiency units
—water flow reducers for showers and faucets
—sealing leaks in pipes and ducts
—raising thermostat settings in summer and reducing them in winter
—reducing hot water temperatures
—efficient use of shading

Wind and solar energy measures

—wind energy systems to generate electricity
—solar domestic water heating
—active solar space heating systems
—combined active solar space heating and solar domestic water heating systems
—passive solar heating and cooling
—solar swimming pool heating

of the individual auditor. There are, however, certain things to look for. There are four steps in a basic energy audit.

Step 1 is an interview. The auditor asks you questions about your patterns of energy use. Although the auditor is likely to have a record of your fuel bills with that utility, you should gather past bills for other fuels if you have saved them. This information provides a foundation for calculating the cost effectiveness of energy measures. Take this opportunity to discuss your goals with your auditor. Auditors can be more helpful if they know you're considering a certain type of project or level of investment.

Step 2 is a survey of your house. The auditor takes measurements in and around your home to get wall, floor, and window dimensions and to determine your insulation levels. The auditor should also look for areas where air is likely to infiltrate, check for vapor barriers, examine the condition of caulking in cracks and joints and weatherstripping around the windows and doors, check for insulation on your warm air ducts and steam and hot water pipes, and possibly test the efficiency of your heating system. Some utilities add a "hands on" component to the audit. The auditor may install an insulating blanket on your water heater, turn down your water heater, and put low-flow devices in your sinks and showers if necessary.

Step 3 is computation. The auditor combines the information about your house with the information about your fuel bills and the costs and paybacks of energy conservation measures. Some utilities provide their auditors with computer terminals that connect through your phone line with a central computer which analyzes your potential energy savings.

Step 4 is the discussion of the results. The auditor presents the utility's conclusions, beginning with a description of the present condition of your house, and emphasizes the factors that affect your energy consumption. The core of the presentation consists of a list of recommended actions, in order of priority, along with estimated costs and savings. The auditor may leave information with you about energy conservation measures, materials and suppliers, and methods of financing. If this information isn't routinely provided, ask for a copy of the audit worksheets and recommendations.

At this point, ask the auditor about the underlying assumptions in the utility's analysis of your home energy use. How fast do they think gas or electricity or home heating oil prices will rise? Consider whether this rate makes sense in relation to the price increases you've experienced recently. Ask also about the payback period the utility uses in selecting cost-effective measures.

Ask about other services the utility provides. Do they have a low-interest financing program? If not, will they help you arrange conventional financing? Will they arrange the installation of conservation measures and conduct an inspection afterward? Ask as well whether tax credits are available. The auditor should know which measures, if any, qualify in your state. (For more on utility financing programs and tax credits see Chapter 9.)

As you ponder the audit conclusions, keep in mind that these recommendations are based strictly on economics. If other values are important to you, you must do the weighing yourself. Will an energy-efficient house be an advantage when it comes time to sell? How important is comfort to you and your family? Is saving energy important to you for political or environmental reasons?

Are there any reasons not to use your utility's audit program? Utility and heating oil distributor audits are free (or cheap), but they are not uniformly comprehensive in all parts of the country. Some utilities are cutting corners to reduce the time of the home visit and keep program costs down. RCS audits are supposed to consider a home's potential for using solar and wind energy, for example, and to test furnace or boiler efficiency, but these questions are frequently downplayed or even ignored.

Box 3-4 will help you assess the value of an audit in relation to your goals. If there are a number of "no" responses to these questions, consider one of the specialized private audit services described in the next section.

OTHER AUDIT APPROACHES

You may not be able to get a utility audit, or you may decide that the audit available is incomplete. If this is the case, consider seeking the services of an independent auditor, a technical consultant, or a house doctor (see Box 3-5). You'll have to spend more money for a private audit, but it may prove well worth the expense. Private audit services are not always available in all parts of the country. To find out what your choices are, look in the Yellow Pages under "Energy Conservation Services" or "Energy Management."

You may also determine that your goals require more than a standard audit. This will be the case if you want a superefficient house, if you have decided to carry out a major solar addition or remodeling job, or if you are considering an overhaul or replacement of your heating and air conditioning system. Unless you are technically skilled and will-

BOX 3-5
A HOUSE DOCTOR FOR ENERGY ILLS

"House Doctoring" is an innovative approach to evaluating and improving your home's energy efficiency. Developed by researchers at Princeton University, it relies on home visits by trained technicians. The house doctor method differs from standard audits in three respects: in the use of sophisticated instruments to detect heat leaks; in an emphasis on often-overlooked but major thermal defects in the envelope of the house; and in the use of the house doctor to perform many low-cost conservation measures at the time of the visit.

The house doctor comes armed with three tools: a "blower door," an infrared scanner, and a device that analyzes flue gas. The blower door is a fan mounted on a piece of plywood to cover your entry door opening. The fan produces a slight pressure within the house, exaggerating air leaks and making them easier to detect. Gaps or cracks can be caulked as they are discovered. The blower door is calibrated to ensure that homes do not become so airtight that they create indoor air quality problems.

The house doctor uses an infrared scanner to find warm spots in exterior walls or the attic. The scanner detects gaps in insulation that allow heat to escape directly. Scanners are particularly helpful in finding *thermal bypasses*—places where the construction allows heat to travel around insulation from a heated area to an unheated area. Bypasses are often located beside flues, vents, and chimneys.

Finally, house doctors come equipped to analyze furnace flue gas composition and temperature and to calculate overall furnace efficiency, items not usually included in a Residential Conservation Service audit.

House doctors normally spend up to a day finding and plugging leaks and evaluating the status and effectiveness of home insulation. They also measure hot water temperature and flow (another item that is often ignored in an RCS audit).

The house doctor method is more thorough than an RCS audit, and it provides a far better payoff, but it is also more expensive. The Princeton researchers estimate that a thorough house doctor treatment, requiring two professionals for a full day, would cost \$500 to \$600. In terms of cost effectiveness, a house doctor's visit usually pays for itself in short-term savings. And there is little doubt that the information you gain will help you make better choices. For the names and addresses of house doctors near you, write:

Princeton Energy Partners
P.O. Box 1221
Princeton, NJ 08540

ing to do the necessary research, you should consult experts before planning these major investments.

Strictly speaking, people who specialize in solar energy or heating systems are not auditors, but most will offer advice for a fee or even without charge, hoping you will do business with them. These specialists can be used in the same way as auditors according to their areas of specialty. A word of caution, however: Specialists often are selling a product. Get at least a second opinion before you buy. And review the sections on furnaces in Chapters 4 and 6 and the solar sections of Chapters 6 and 8 to get a sense of the issues and your options before you contact a salesperson or technician.

Be as skeptical about choosing a private audit service as about using a utility audit program. Ask the firm the same questions you asked your utility, particularly the most important one: How much will it cost? Be sure to ask for references and call them.

Chapter Four
Level I: The Basics of Energy Conservation

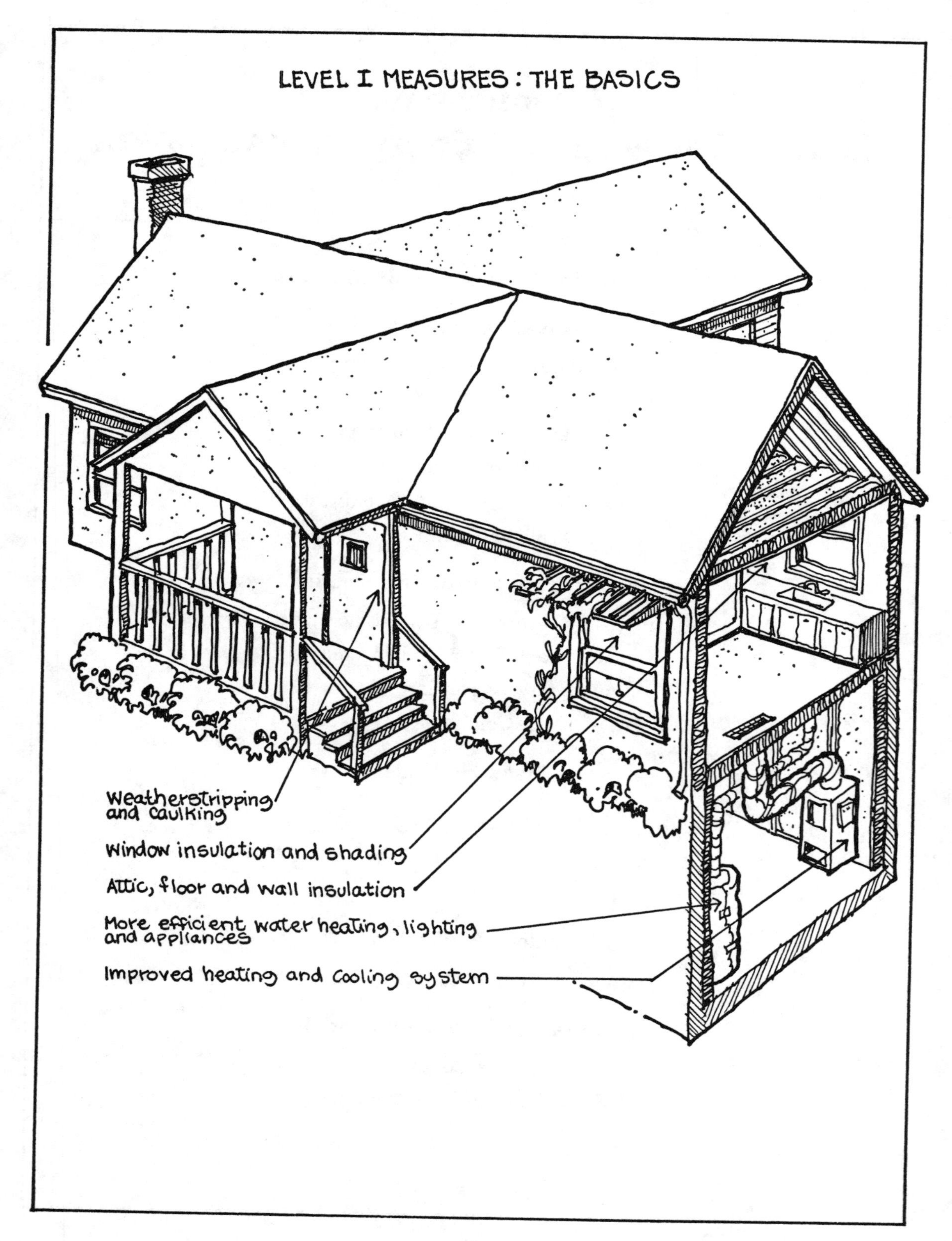
LEVEL I MEASURES : THE BASICS
Weatherstripping and caulking
Window insulation and shading
Attic, floor and wall insulation
More efficient water heating, lighting and appliances
Improved heating and cooling system

Level I: The Basics of Energy Conservation

Level I measures can cut many home energy bills by one-third or more. These basic energy-saving techniques require no structural changes, yield the greatest savings for your investment, and provide a foundation for the types of investments described in Chapters 6 and 8. Even if your house has some of these measures already in place, you will find that many opportunities remain. And even if you don't own your own home there are sensible steps you can take (see Box 4-1).

This chapter surveys the specific measures of a Level I investment. Here you will find basic information about each conservation investment—enough to decide if it makes sense for you. We've grouped the measures into four categories according to the part of your household energy system that is affected:

1. The building envelope—the building surfaces that separate heated from unheated spaces, including the ceiling, floor, outer walls, and windows

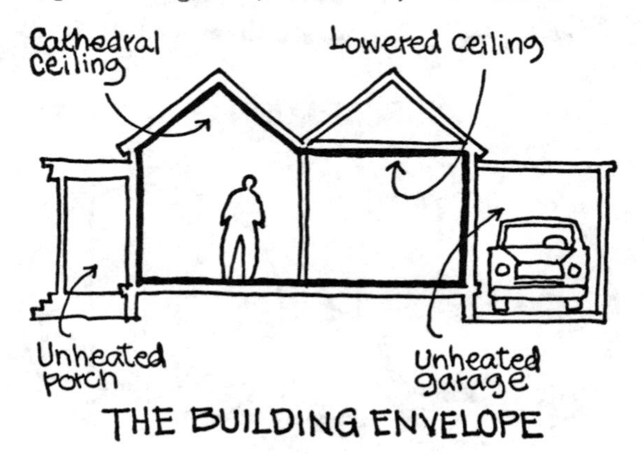

2. The heating and cooling systems
3. The water heating system
4. Appliances and lighting

In each of these categories we describe options, the materials available, how they will help you reach your project goals, and some special problems you may encounter.

The second part of the chapter turns to a problem related to home energy efficiency that warrants increasing attention: indoor air quality. The final section offers guidelines for choosing and working with a contractor if you don't plan to do the work yourself.

The Building Envelope: Reducing Heat Losses and Gains

Over 50 percent of the energy used in residences nationwide is used for space heating. Another 6 percent of the energy is used for air conditioning. How much energy is actually needed to be comfortable? The answer depends on the temperature to which you heat and cool, the rate at which heat (or coolness) is lost to the outside, and the severity of the climate. Energy used to heat and cool provides the largest opportunity for savings and deserves the greatest attention.

The two most significant types of heat loss through the house's envelope are *infiltration* and *conduction*. Infiltration (or convection) means the movement of heated air through holes in walls, floors, and ceilings. Stopping infiltration is a matter of finding and plugging the holes that let outside air in and inside air out.

BOX 4-1
TIPS FOR RENTERS

Most renters are mobile and don't want to invest much in energy conservation. If you are paying the utility bills, there are some things you can do to lower your costs. This checklist indicates the simple and low-cost measures that renters can take. Although limited, these measures will reduce your energy bills by up to 30 percent.

1. Reduce your water heater temperature to 120°F.
2. Insulate your water heater with a water heater blanket.
3. Put aerators in your faucets. These can reduce water flow from 50 to 70 percent.
4. Install a low-flow showerhead.
5. Weatherstrip and caulk doors and windows.
6. Keep your thermostat at 65°F in winter and 78°F in summer.
7. Turn off the gas furnace pilot light in summer and clean furnace and air conditioner filters regularly.
8. Clean the coils of the refrigerator.
9. Turn off gas stove pilot lights, saving up to 33 percent of your natural gas use.
10. Install light switch and outlet gaskets to prevent air leaks through electrical outlets.
11. Install low-cost plastic storm windows.
12. If you live in an apartment or cooperative with a balcony, plant trees in barrels to help shade the windows.
13. Install fluorescent lights.

Many of the materials involved in these low-cost measures are also portable. You can take them with you when you leave. If you'll be in your present rental for a long time, both you and your landlord can benefit from many of the improvements described in this chapter—particularly storm windows, insulation, and thermal drapes.

Conduction means the transfer of heat through materials which, although solid, absorb and transfer heat. A spoon placed in a cup of tea quickly conducts heat from the liquid to the spoon handle until it becomes too hot to touch.

Heat conduction can be slowed by placing a barrier that is a poor conductor—in other words, insulation—between the space you heat or cool and the outside. The measure of insulation's effectiveness in slowing conduction—resisting heat transfer—is its R-value. R-value is based on the heat-resisting properties of wood. One R equals the resistance to heat transfer of a 1-inch-thick piece of wood. The higher the R-value, the greater the insulating value of the material: 5½ inches of fiberglass batt insulation has an R-value of 19; 2 inches of rigid foam board insulation (isocyanurate) has an R-value of 18.

WEATHERSTRIPPING AND CAULKING

Stopping infiltration is the first line of defense against energy waste and a way to have a more comfortable, draft-free house. Most houses have many small holes and cracks that allow air to enter and escape with little or no resistance. The procedures for weatherstripping and caulking to stop infiltration are simple and require no special tools. Weatherstripping and caulking can be done by anyone who is moderately handy, and the materials to complete the work are available at hardware and

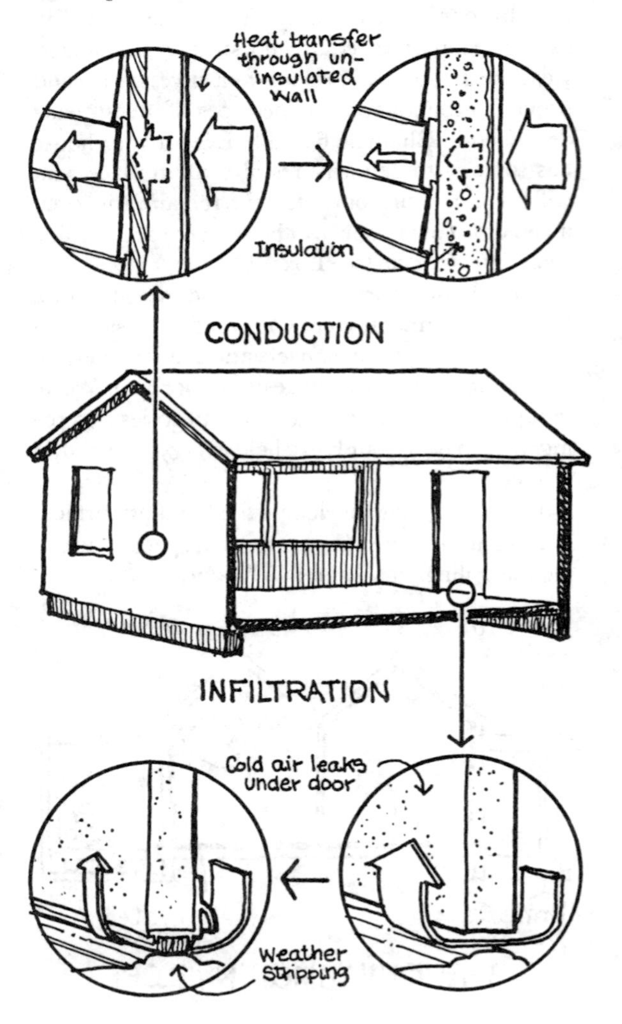

home improvement stores. If there are visible cracks and holes in the house's ceiling, roof, floor, and walls or around doors, or the house has loose windows, don't postpone these measures. Even in a well-insulated house, infiltration adds to your fuel bills, particularly if you live in a windy area.

Table 4-1 lists common caulking materials and Table 4-2 lists some common weatherstripping materials available to plug the leaks. Most are relatively inexpensive. The work is usually easy to do but calls for some detective work: You must seek out and seal all the obvious cracks and leaks. The work also calls for some attention to detail: Poorly applied caulk and poorly installed weatherstripping are not much better than none at all. Common points of infiltration are shown in the illustration on page 44. With careful searching you will be able to find and seal many of these holes.

Weatherstripping and caulking should start with the attic hatch and other cracks, thermal bypasses, and holes in the ceiling and roof. Next is the subfloor over basements or crawl spaces, then windows and walls, unless there are cracks and visible holes or windows and doors are loose. Having the work done by a contractor adds considerably to the cost. Weatherstripping and caulking materials for a door will cost $15 to $20, for example, but a contractor will charge at least $50. If you have a contractor weatherstrip and caulk the entire house, the cost will be as high as $750 for a house that has had no previous work done to it. If windows and doors are in good condition and you only need to do the attic and subfloor, contractor costs will be in the range of $275 to $450.

If you want the most thorough approach to weatherization—including weatherstripping, caulking, insulation, and other measures—you will need the help of a professional using a blower door to pressurize your house and an infrared heat scanner to detect heat loss. (See Box 3-5 in Chapter 3.) This extra effort pays off in energy saved, though, because the technique helps locate hidden cracks and thermal bypasses: gaps in wall, attic, or floor insulation, air spaces within walls that provide avenues for heat escape, and building materials that carry heat away from living areas. (See Box 4-2 for more on thermal bypasses.)

In your thorough search for points of heat escape, don't neglect the big ones. Chimneys, vents, attic hatch doors, and other large openings in the envelope should be insulated (if possible) and closed off tightly when not in use. Remember to seal off ventilating fans (unless in a kitchen or bathroom) and cover the room air conditioner during the heating season.

ATTIC INSULATION

Attic insulation is one of the simplest and most effective energy conservation measures available. Properly installed attic insulation—including extra

TABLE 4-1
SOME COMMON CAULKING MATERIALS

Material	*Cost per 11-oz Tube**	*Comments*
Acrylic based (acrylic/latex)	$3.00	Best for interiors. Surface priming required. Can be painted. 5–10 year life. Curing time depends on product.
Butyl based	$2.10	Some types can be painted. 10–15 year life. For interior and exterior use. Priming not required. Long curing time—up to a week.
Latex based	$1.70	Best for interiors. Can be painted. Tends to wrinkle and shrink. Short life of 2–5 years. Rapid curing time.
Oil based	$1.50	Lowest cost, least durable. Can stain surfaces. Short life of 1–5 years. Can be painted. Poor for exterior uses.
Polyurethane based	$5.20	Good for interiors and exteriors. Requires careful priming. Long life. Cures in 1 hour to 2 days depending on product.
Silicone	$4.60	Good for metal and glass. Long life. Cannot be painted. Fast curing.

* Dollar amounts taken from 1983 *National Repair and Remodeling Estimator* plus 20 percent.

TABLE 4-2
SOME COMMON WEATHERSTRIPPING MATERIALS

Type	*Cost per Linear Foot*	*Use and Comments*
Metal tension strips (aluminum, bronze, brass)	30¢–40¢	Windows and door sides. Best where cracks are uniform. Long lasting.
Tubular gasket (hollow or foam-filled, vinyl or rubber)	10¢–15¢	Windows and door sides. Works where cracks are uneven. Long lasting.
Reinforced gasket (aluminum and vinyl)	45¢–65¢	Windows and door sides. Works where cracks are uneven. Same as tubular gasket but with aluminum flange. Long lasting.
Felt	10¢–15¢	Windows and door sides. Low cost. Does not wear well. Easy to install. Put bead of caulk underneath to ensure seal.
Reinforced felt	35¢–40¢	Windows and door sides. Low cost. Moderate wear. Easy to install. Same as plain felt but with metal reinforcing strip. Put bead of caulk under strip to ensure seal.
Foam strip	20¢–25¢	Windows and door sides. Low cost. Can seal nonuniform cracks. Staple or tack self-adhesive foams for longer life. Does not wear well, but fine for seldom-used doors or windows.
Outlet gasket (foam)	25¢–30¢ each	Install behind cover plates of outlets and switches. Buy only nonflammable material. Low cost. Long lasting.
Door sweep (aluminum with rubber or plastic)	$7–$10 each	Door bottoms. Easy to install. Heavier version available for garage doors. Durable.
Door shoe (aluminum and vinyl)	$10–$12 each	Door bottom. Requires even threshold. Door may have to be removed to install properly. Durable.
Threshold gasket	$10–$12 each	Door threshold. Good replacement threshold. Door may have to be removed to install properly. Gasket will wear but can be replaced.

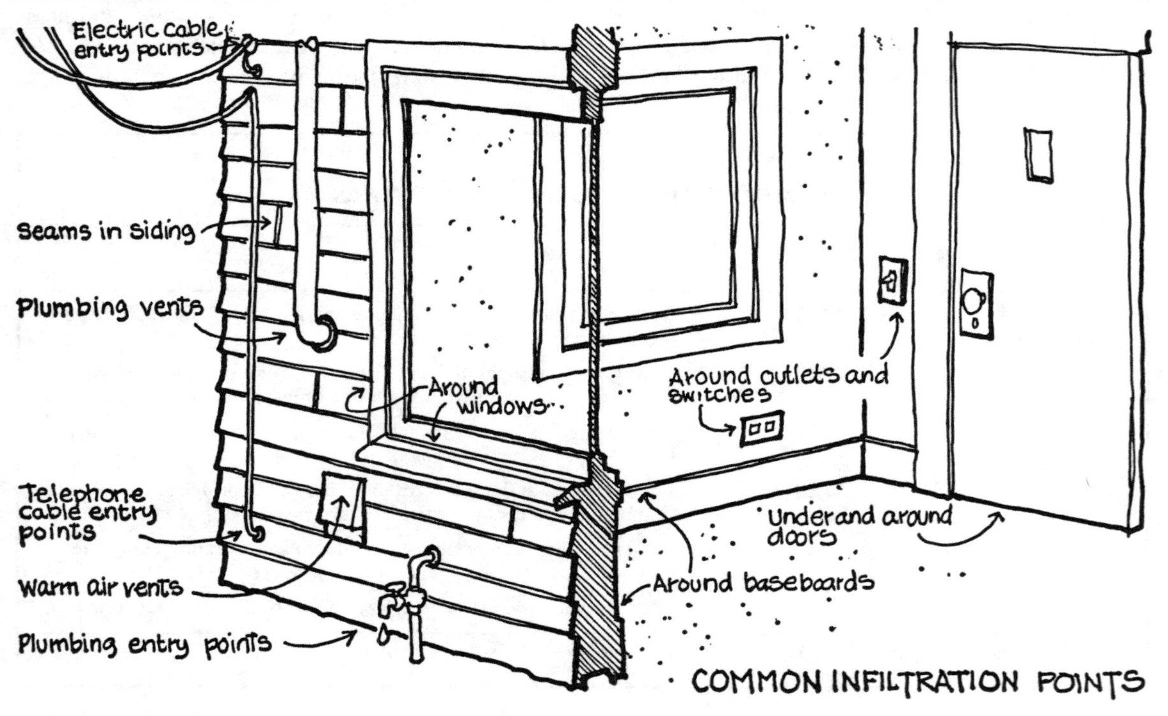

steps to block thermal bypasses—can be counted on to cut heating energy loss by up to 12 percent even if you already have R-11 in your attic. If you have no insulation now, you can cut these losses by 40 percent or more. Table 4-3 lists some common insulating materials along with their R-value and use.

How much insulation you need depends on your climate zone, your fuel costs, and the construction of your house. In most climate zones, any attic in a house with heating or air conditioning should be insulated at least to R-30; the case studies in Chapter 5 recommend the best insulation levels for various climate zones, along with the savings you can expect from your investment. Table 4-4 will give you a good idea of various insulating costs per square foot.

If you have some attic insulation in place already, even if less than currently recommended for new homes, adding more may not be your best energy conservation buy. In a warm climate, as a rule of thumb, if you have one-third or more of the recommended level, you should invest your money in other Level I measures before you add more

BOX 4-2
THERMAL BYPASSES AND BRIDGES

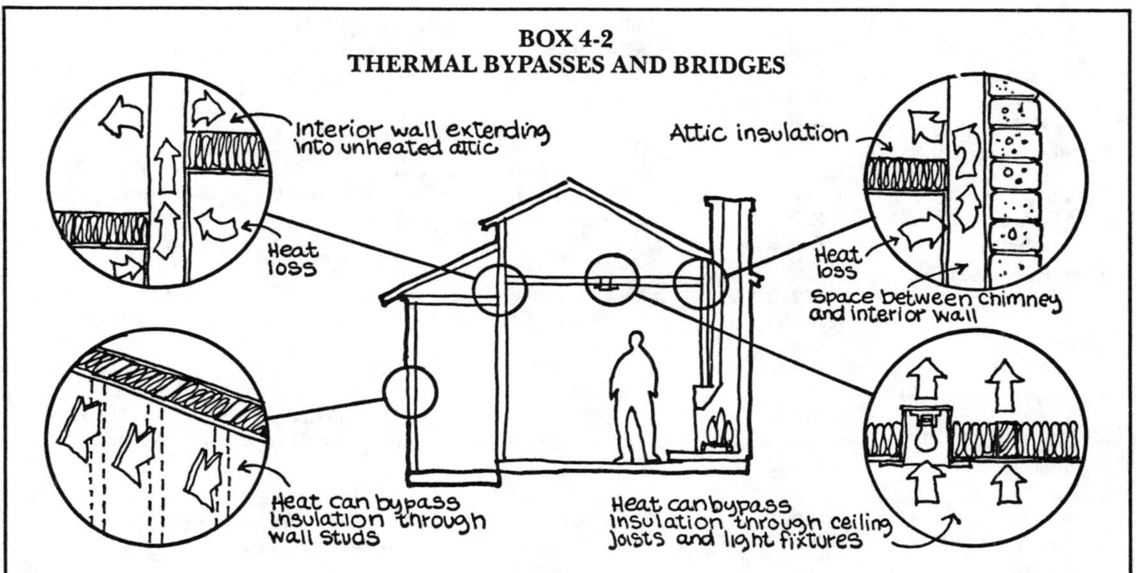

A thermal bypass is a place where the construction or design of the building envelope provides an opportunity for heat to escape around the layer of insulation. Thermal bypasses can result in significant energy losses.

Examples of thermal bypasses include the gaps or air passages next to furnace flues, chimneys, plumbing, and electrical wiring. Thermal bypasses are also created when gaps in exterior or interior walls allow heated air to move upward. Even walls without gaps or cracks can be pathways for heat loss. If, for example, an interior wall extends into an attic or other unheated space, there may be a convective loop within the wall. Heat from the house warms the air within the wall, causing it to rise and be replaced with air cooled through contact with the cold surfaces of the unheated attic or subfloor.

If left unchecked, these bypasses can contribute to heat loss even in a well-insulated home. When you insulate your crawl space, basement, or attic, look closely at any point where the house's envelope was penetrated to make way for a furnace flue, a vent (such as a stove exhaust vent), the chimney, plumbing, and electrical wiring. Plumbing and wiring entries can be sealed easily: Stuff insulation into the big holes; use rope caulk or a caulking gun to seal cracks.

Thermal bridges are another source of heat loss. They commonly occur where wood studs or ceiling joists interrupt the layer of wall or ceiling insulation. Unless you use interior or exterior sheathing, little can be done to correct this problem in walls. When insulating attics, place one layer of insulation between the ceiling joists and the second layer perpendicular to it, across the joists. Be sure to place only fireproof materials near electrical boxes, chimneys, and furnace flues. Also, if you are unsure of the fire codes, check with your local building department.

TABLE 4-3
SOME COMMON INSULATING MATERIALS

Material	*R-Value*	*Use and Comments*
Fiberglass (batt/blankets)		
1 inch	R-3.1	Attics, exposed frame walls, subfloor. Comes with or without vapor barrier. Vapor barrier faces heated rooms. Fire resistant.
3½ inches	R-11	
6 inches	R-19	
9½ inches	R-30	
Rockwool (batts/blankets)		
1 inch	R-3.7	Attics, subfloor, and exposed frame walls. Comes with or without vapor barrier. Vapor barrier faces toward heated space. Fire resistant.
3 inches	R-11	
5 inches	R-19	
8 inches	R-30	
Fiberglass (loose fill)		
1 inch	R-2.5	Blown or poured into attics or walls. No vapor barrier. Can settle with age. Install separate vapor barrier if possible. Fire resistant.
3½ inches	R-8.8	
4½ inches	R-11	
7½ inches	R-19	
12 inches	R-30	
Cellulose (loose fill)		
1 inch	R-3.7	Blown or emptied into attics and walls. No vapor barrier. Buy only material treated with fire retardant. Can settle with age. Install separate vapor barrier if possible.
3½ inches	R-13	
5 inches	R-19	
8 inches	R-30	
Rockwool (loose fill)		
1 inch	R-2.7	Blown or poured into walls or attic. No vapor barrier. Install separate vapor barrier if possible. Fire resistant.
4 inches	R-11	
6½ inches	R-19	
10 inches	R-30	
Fiberglass (rigid board)		
1 inch	R-4.5	For cathedral ceilings, exposed frame walls, or roofs if reroofing. Can be used below ground when insulating slab floor. Fire resistant.
2 inches	R-9	
3 inches	R-13.5	
Isocyanurate (rigid board)		
1 inch	R-9	For cathedral ceilings, exposed frame walls, or roofs if reroofing. Flammable. Must be separated from living space by sheetrock. Moisture resistant.
2 inches	R-18	
3 inches	R-27	
Polystyrene (rigid board)		
1 inch	R-3.5 to R-4.5	Best for insulating slab floors below ground. Highly combustible.

attic insulation. In a cold climate, upgrade your insulation to the recommended levels (or above) if you have less than 50 percent of the suggested level.

In an unused attic, use either fiberglass batts or loose-fill insulation. Batts have the advantage of being easy to remove. If you plan to rewire in the attic at some point in the future, batts will make the job easier and less messy. To achieve R-30 will require a layer of R-19 insulation and a layer of R-11. Place the first layer between the ceiling joists and the second layer crosswise over it. This pattern will slow heat conduction through the wood joists.

If you have a flat roof with no crawl or air space or attic, or a cathedral ceiling, insulating becomes a more difficult and expensive proposition. One approach is to insulate from the inside. An interior ceiling in a flat-roofed house can be lowered to accept rigid foam board insulation or batt insulation. The ceiling must then be resurfaced. Rigid foam board with vinyl facing is available and can be pressed between the beams of a cathedral ceiling. An alternative is to fill the spaces with insulation and refinish the interior with sheetrock, covering the beams. Both these approaches usually mean

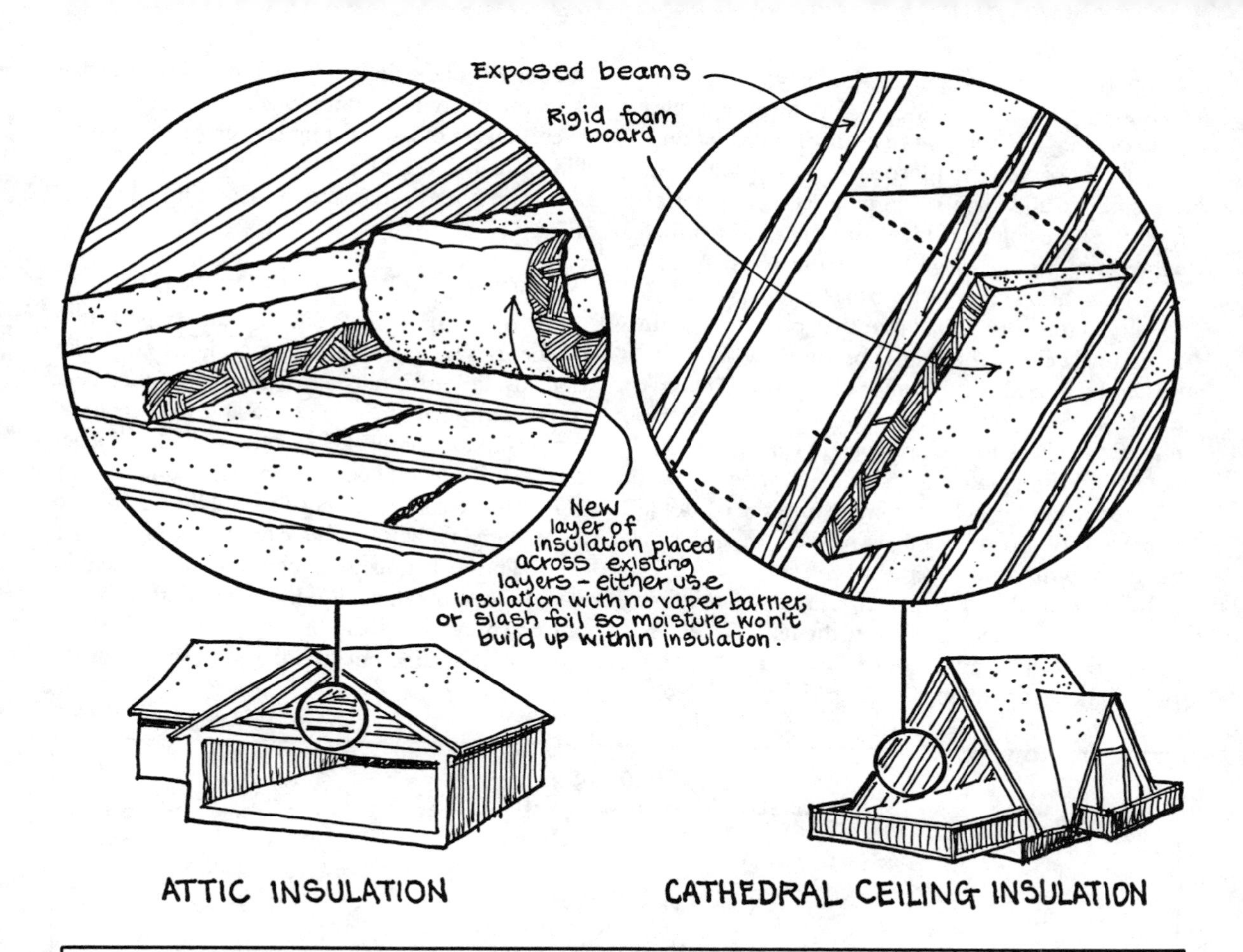
Exposed beams
Rigid foam board
New layer of insulation placed across existing layers - either use insulation with no vaper barrier, or slash foil so moisture won't build up within insulation.
ATTIC INSULATION
CATHEDRAL CEILING INSULATION

TABLE 4-4
INSULATING COSTS PER SQUARE FOOT

Type of Insulation	*R-Value*	*Materials Only*	*Installed*
Wall (blown in)	R-10 to R-13	15¢–30¢	50¢–$1.00
Attic (batts)	R-11	15¢–20¢	45¢–55¢
	R-19	20¢–40¢	60¢–70¢
Attic (blown in)	R-11	10¢–20¢	30¢–40¢
	R-19	20¢–30¢	45¢–55¢
	R-30	30¢–40¢	50¢–65¢
Fiberglass board*	R-4.5 (1 inch)	35¢–45¢	60¢–$1.50
	R-9 (2 inches)	55¢–70¢	85¢–$1.75
	R-13.5 (3 inches)	80¢–90¢	$1.10–$1.95
Isocyanurate*	R-9 (1 inch)	35¢–45¢	55¢–$1.40
	R-18 (2 inches)	60¢–70¢	75¢–$1.80
	R-27 (3 inches)	$1.10–$1.30	$1.30–$2.00
Vinyl-covered rigid insulation	R-10 (1½ inches)	55¢–80¢	85¢–$1.50
Exterior sheathing	R-9 to R-18 (2 inches)	80¢–$1.05	$1.30–$2.00

* Installation costs range considerably, depending on finish required and location of insulation (cathedral roof, exposed frame wall, and so forth).

compromising on aesthetics, but if your heating bills are sky-high the trade-off may be acceptable.

If you have a flat roof or cathedral ceiling and plan to reroof, you can place rigid foam panels over the subroof and then place new roofing material over the rigid foam. (Make sure the rigid foam is sufficiently strong to withstand the tread of the roofers.) Various new foam-based and rigid board roofing systems are available that provide a high insulating value. They must be sprayed on or attached by a roofing contractor using special equipment. These products are relatively new to the market, so check to be sure you are getting a product with an adequate warranty. In either case, you will be paying for both insulation and the cost of a new roof. If you need a new roof anyway, this is your best opportunity to insulate.

Because insulating an attic is usually straightforward, many homeowners do it themselves. When you work with fiberglass or other insulating materials, make sure you're suited up right for the job. Use goggles and a mask with a filter to keep the fine fibers out of your eyes and lungs. Wear gloves and several layers of loose-fitting clothing to keep your skin from coming in contact with the insulation. Box 4-3 outlines the basics of insulating a lived-in attic.

FLOOR AND BASEMENT INSULATION

Floors and basements offer another opportunity for energy savings, although at a higher cost than attic insulation. Uninsulated floors conduct heat away from heated rooms above and lead coolness away from air-conditioned rooms. An added benefit of well-insulated floors is increased comfort.

The most common way to insulate floors is to place fiberglass batts, foil side up, between the floor joists. The batts must fit snugly and can be held in place with wires stapled to the joists. Remember to caulk to prevent infiltration where there are cracks or where two different building materials join together.

BOX 4-3
INSULATING A LIVED-IN ATTIC

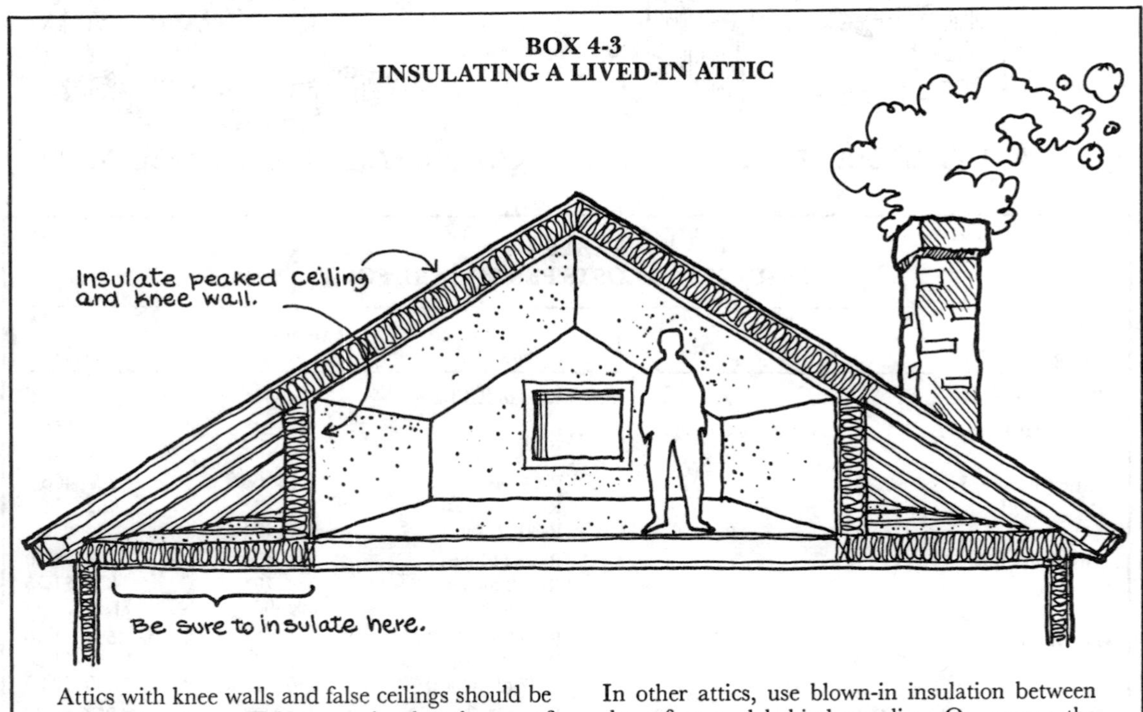
Insulate peaked ceiling
and knee wall.
Be sure to insulate here.

Attics with knee walls and false ceilings should be insulated as shown. Take care to insulate the area of ceiling between the bottom of the knee wall and the exterior wall. Provide a vapor barrier where necessary (see Box 4-5).

In other attics, use blown-in insulation between the rafters and behind paneling. Or remove the sheetrock or paneling, insulate with batts, install a good vapor barrier, and replace the paneling.

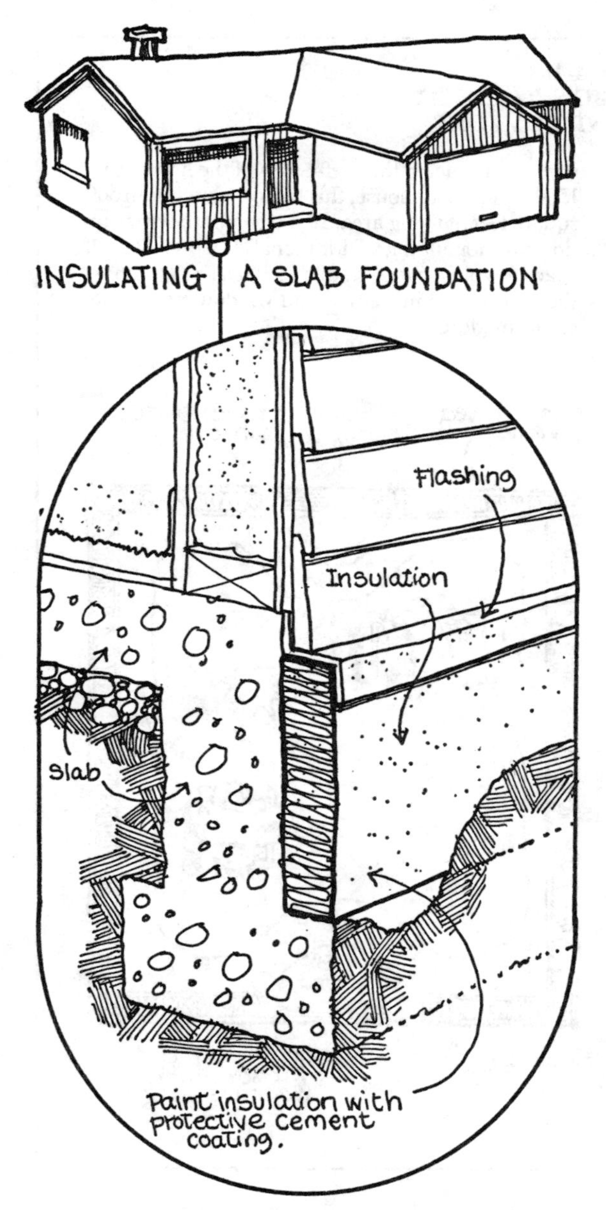

If you have an unheated basement, insulating your floor is usually a straightforward task whether you do it yourself or hire a contractor. If you have a small crawl space, though, working in it can be a most unpleasant task, and you may not be able to gain access to all of your subfloor.

Slab foundations present different problems. In cold climates, the cold or frozen ground around the house will draw a significant amount of heat out of the slab. To reduce this effect, insulate around the foundation perimeter with rigid foam board such as polystyrene. The material you pick must be weatherproof and resistant to water absorption. Any insulation left exposed above ground should be protected by flashing and a cement coating or other impermeable material. Extend the insulation below ground level at least 24 inches. While this measure can yield savings, it involves a lot of work, it disturbs existing vegetation, and, unless you do it yourself, it is expensive.

Remember that carpeting has some insulating value, particularly if there is a thick pad underneath. It can reduce conduction—especially important with slab floors—and slow infiltration. If you plan to install or replace wall-to-wall carpeting, install a thick pad for best insulating value. A thick pad is not a substitute for well-insulated floors, however.

WALL INSULATION

Wall insulation has more than dollar and energy benefits. It increases comfort by slowing the overall loss of heat, eliminating cold areas near exterior walls, and reducing the amount of street noise that enters the house. Wall insulation also helps reduce indoor noise levels. For low- and mid-range frequencies, an insulated wall reduces noise transmission by 5 to 40 percent, depending on the frequency of the noise.

When outside temperatures are 40° F and the indoor air temperature is 68° F, the inside surface of an uninsulated wood frame wall is about 60° F. Bodies give off heat to these cold surfaces. To feel comfortable in spite of this heat loss the indoor air temperature needs to be higher. If you are near an uninsulated wall, the air temperature must be over 80° F for you to feel an effective temperature of a comfortable 70° F.

The temperature of an insulated wall, by comparison, is 67° F when the temperature outside is 40° F and the temperature indoors is 68° F, allowing you to feel comfortable at a lower room air temperature. The higher surface temperature of the insulated wall significantly reduces the conductive chill you feel and allows you to keep the room temperature lower.

In addition to drawing heat from the body, the cold wall or window sets up a convection pattern. Heated room air next to the window cools and sinks, drawing warm air past the window. This

BOX 4-4
WALL INSULATION, THERMAL WINDOWS, AND COMFORT

The cold inner surfaces of uninsulated walls and single-glazed windows draw heat from the adjacent air, creating cold zones near walls and windows. Well-insulated rooms don't have these cold zones, as you can see in the illustration.

To increase their sense of comfort, most people will sit further away from an uninsulated wall and window, reducing the useful area of the house. In a 1500-square-foot house, this loss can amount to 300 square feet of living area. If you compare construction costs for adding an additional 300 square feet of space to your house—at $25 to $50 a square foot—the cost of wall insulation and window treatments seems modest.

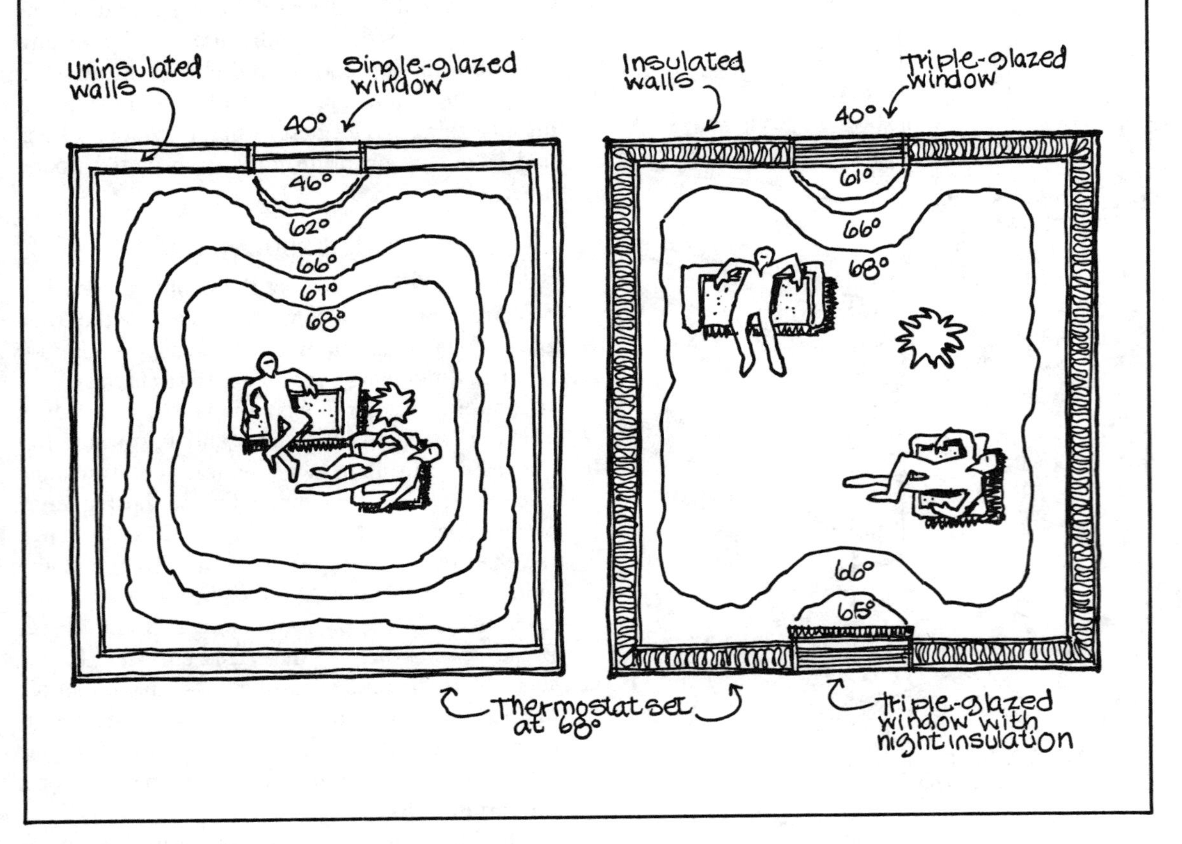

pattern of air movement is the draft you feel sitting next to a window or wall on a cold night. Box 4-4 explains how wall insulation contributes to greater personal comfort.

Wall insulation is generally installed by a contractor and costs 50¢ to $1 per square foot installed for a wood frame house. The most common way to insulate the walls of wood frame houses is to find the studs, drill holes between them, and blow loose cellulose, mineral wool, or fiberglass into the wall cavities. If the work is properly done, the material is packed so tight that it will not settle. Contractors must take care to fill all wall cavities, paying particular attention to places where there are likely to be fireblocks, diagonal bracing, or irregular studs.

Blown-in wall insulation has no vapor barrier. When you repaint your interior walls, use a paint with a low permeability rating. (See Box 4-5.)

If you are insulating your walls while remodeling and you plan to resurface some interior walls, insulate between the studs with foil-faced fiberglass batts wherever possible. There are several advantages to this approach: You will save on labor costs; you can install a vapor barrier along with the insulation; and you will know that you have completely filled the wall.

The amount of wall insulation installed is generally dictated by the size of the wall cavity. A standard 2×4 frame wall, for example, will accept enough blown-in cellulose insulation to provide an insulating value of approximately R-13. Using fiberglass insulation will bring wall insulation levels up to R-11. If you happen to have 2×6 frame walls, they will accept enough insulation to bring the R-value to 19.

Insulating the walls of existing houses is more cost effective in cold climates than in warmer areas. In Buffalo, New York, for example, wall insulation to R-11 reduces heating bills by 15 to 20 percent, and the measure pays for itself in savings within five years. In Atlanta the payback takes nearly ten years.

If you live in a house with solid brick or masonry walls, you won't be able to insulate with blown-in insulation or batts because there are no cavities to hold insulation. To insulate the walls of a solid masonry home, you can apply rigid foam panels or build a framework for batt insulation on the inside. Once this is done, a new finished surface of sheetrock must be added. This treatment is warranted if the wall surfaces need replacing anyway.

As an alternative, some experts recommend adding a layer of exterior insulation to the brick and covering it with new siding or other finishing mate-

BOX 4-5
VAPOR BARRIERS

Whether you are installing wall or attic insulation, and regardless of the material you use, preventing moisture from building up in the wrong places is worth special attention. A typical family of four produces 2 to 3 gallons a day of water vapor: from showers and baths, cooking, laundry, and other sources. Warm air inside the house holds this moisture, but it condenses as it touches cold surfaces—just like the condensation on the glass of an iced drink. The moisture moves through the building walls and ceiling from the heated house toward the cold outside and condenses on insulation and building materials. This moisture can cause building materials to rot or mildew and insulation to lose much of its insulating value.

Simple vapor barriers—sheets of plastic or tar paper—are routinely installed in new construction to stop the passage of moisture and prevent rot. Your house may not have them. It is worth the time to check with the builder or look under your attic insulation to see if there is a barrier. If the attic had a vapor barrier installed when the house was built, the chances are excellent that the walls have vapor barriers too. To make sure, you can remove the cover plate from an electric receptacle and see if there are traces of plastic, tar paper, or foil that have been stapled to the wall studs.

If you are insulating an attic that is currently uninsulated, place a vapor barrier between the insulation and the heated space. If you are adding to existing insulation, add new insulation without a built-in vapor barrier such as loose-fill insulation or fiberglass batts without foil facing; otherwise the new vapor barrier will trap moisture in the old insulation. To prevent moisture buildup in the attic, make sure that the attic is adequately ventilated. Check local codes for specific ventilation requirements for your climate. A common guide for ventilation is at least 1 square foot of ventilation opening for each 150 square feet of attic floor space. When you paint interior walls and ceilings, use a primer coat or a paint that is also a vapor barrier. Several manufacturers market paints designed to serve as vapor barriers. These products are marked with permeability ratings. Look for paints with a permeability rating of 1.0 or less. If these paints are unavailable, two coats of high-gloss enamel paint will provide an equivalent barrier.

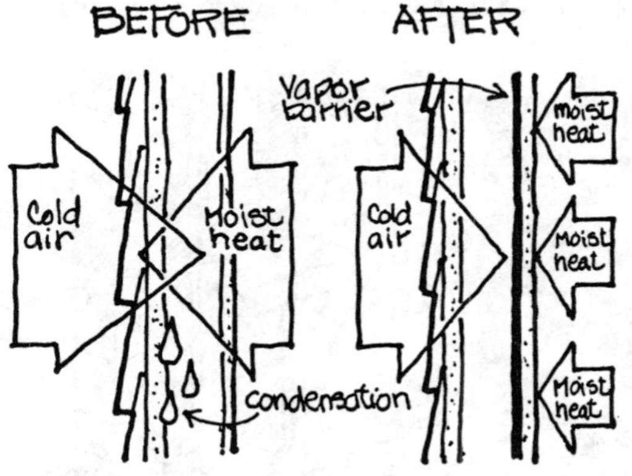

Vapor barrier prevents moisture from reaching cold surface.

rial. This is no less of a major job, though, and it may decrease the value of your brick house if brick is desirable in your community.

Some brick and masonry houses have cores in the brick or cement blocks themselves or there is a space between the brick and the inner wall (brick veneer walls). Insulating these walls, another tricky operation, involves gaining access to the brick or block cores or access to the air space between the brick veneer and interior walls. Special care must be taken to avoid moisture accumulation. This is definitely a job for an experienced professional.

If you decide not to insulate the walls of your masonry house, improve the efficiency of your furnace. Since your heating energy use remains higher than it would if you did insulate the walls, improvements to the heating system are correspondingly more cost effective.

INSULATING A BRICK OR MASONRY HOUSE

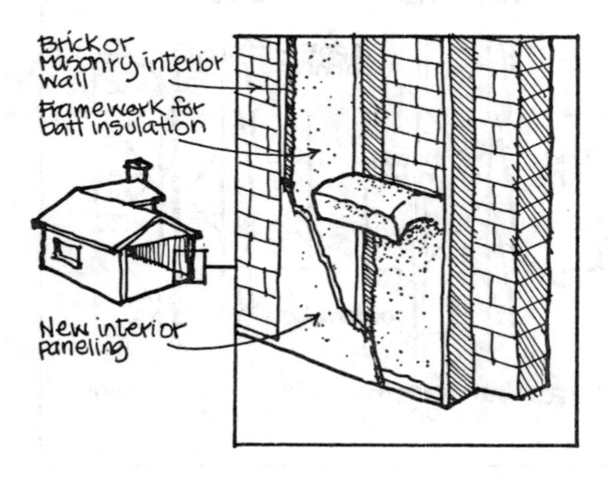

LANDSCAPING FOR SHADE AND WINDBREAKS

One important—and often unrecognized—way of cutting energy demand is through energy-conscious landscape design. Protecting your home from the wind and sun can reduce your heating and cooling needs up to 30 percent. Since savings like this are possible, it makes sense to pay closer attention to how trees, shrubs, vines, and other plantings are placed around your lot. Renters who plan to stay in one house for a long time should also look into the low-cost, high-return benefits of energy-conscious landscaping. Even apartment dwellers with porches or balconies can benefit by using small trees or shrubs in containers to block cold winds, increase humidity, and provide summer shade.

Both summer heat buildup and winter heat loss are affected by the location and extent of vegetation around your house. A house well shaded by trees or vines will gain much less heat on a hot day than an unprotected house. Because of the effects of shading and transpiration, an average full-size deciduous tree—that is, a tree that sheds its leaves—gives a cooling effect outside the home equivalent to five average-sized room air conditioners. That same tree can lower the indoor temperature of a lightly constructed building (such as a garage) by 20° F. Another heat-reducing technique is to plant strips of lawn or groundcover in places where light-colored walkways or gravel reflect the sun's heat into windows. You can also plant shrubs and trees where they will funnel evening breezes toward a home.

Landscaping for cooling can be compared to an investment in window shading. A window shade merely blocks light and heat from a window. A mature shade tree, however, shades walls and roof as well and provides cool air around the house, reducing cooling needs more effectively than window shades. One disadvantage is the time it takes to grow good shade trees. Most trees will take at least ten years to reach their full shading potential. A compromise may be to install moderate-cost exterior window shading that will last until the shade trees are tall enough to block the sun. Vines and most shrubs grow more quickly than trees and provide shade sooner.

Landscaping can also help reduce your winter

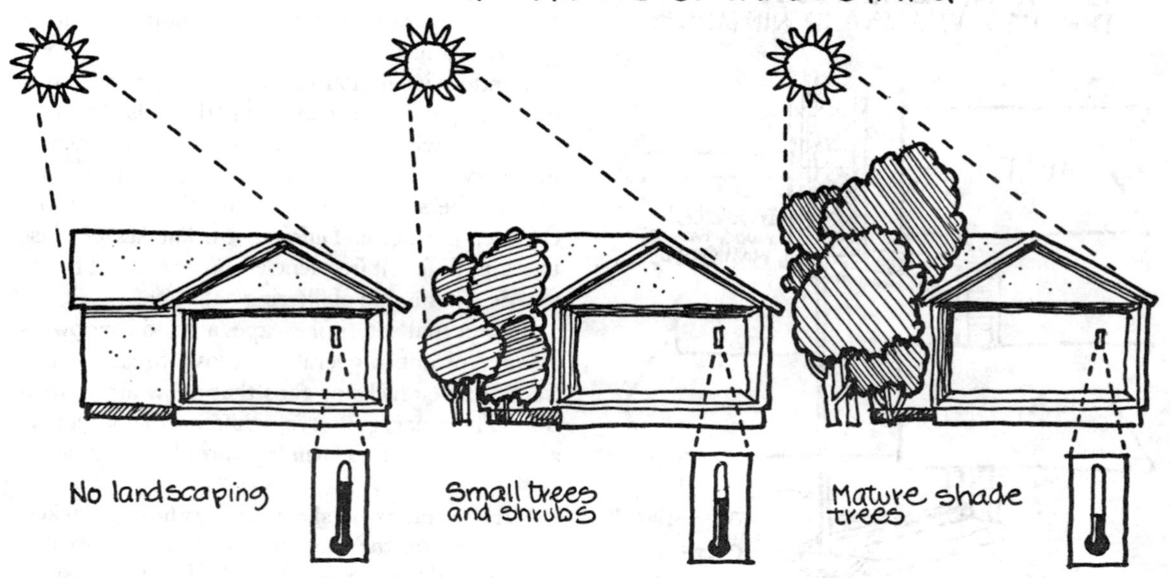

heating costs. Trees and shrubs can be planted where they prevent winter winds from striking a house. Wind velocity affects the rate of infiltration —each time the wind speed doubles, the rate of infiltration into a building *triples*. Carefully planted shelterbelts divert winds away from the house and create dead air spaces that act as a buffer zone. This effect not only decreases infiltration but also lowers the wind chill factor immediately around the house.

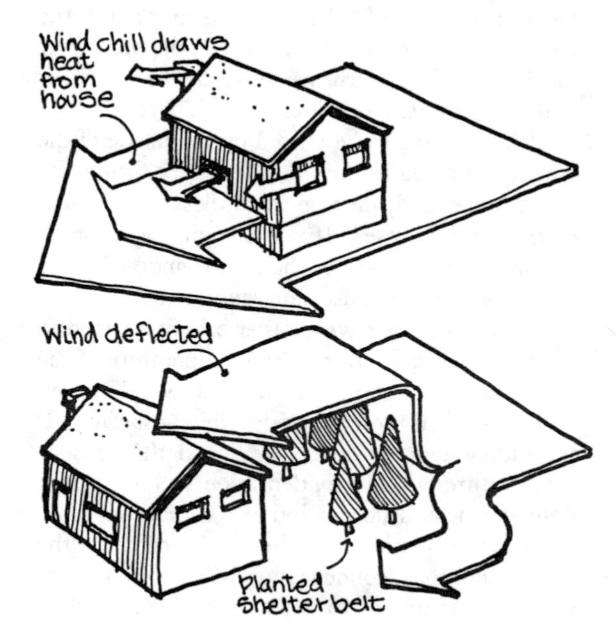

Care should be taken in placement of trees, however, to ensure they don't shade southern windows that catch winter sun. Even deciduous trees that have lost their leaves can block significant amounts of sun.

As with any energy investment, do some research into energy-efficient landscaping before you plant. Different climate zones require different planting strategies. Start your research with the reference section on energy-efficient landscaping at the end of the book. Local nurseries, garden clubs, and arboretums will also be able to help you make your selections.

To reduce the time and effort you'll have to put into landscaping over the years, pick native plants and others that have proved themselves hardy in your area. Also consider varieties that require little water or fertilizer. Deciduous plants on the south side of your dwelling will shed their leaves and let you take advantage of winter sun. Fast-growing varieties will yield energy benefits sooner.

Savings from landscaping are difficult to quantify, but good landscaping will nearly always pay for itself in energy savings and increased resale value. A mature shade tree, for example, will increase property value by at least $500 in many areas of the country. If you like gardening and yardwork, landscaping for energy savings can, in the long run, be one of your best strategies.

COMPARATIVE HEAT LOSS THROUGH WALLS AND WINDOWS

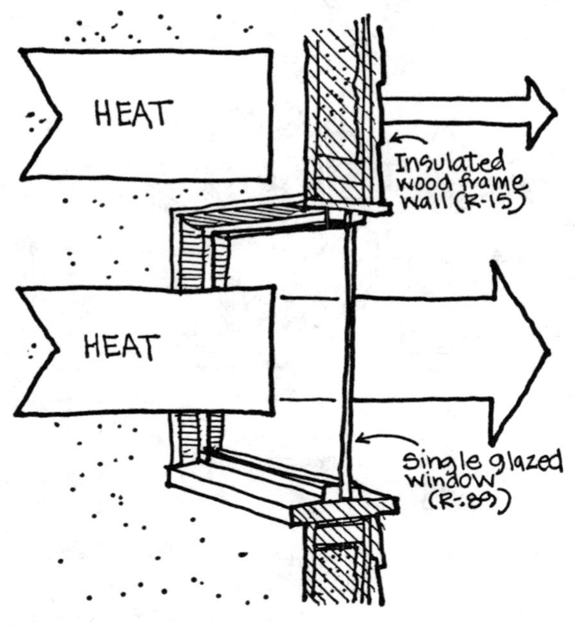

WINDOW TREATMENTS

Windows contribute to energy waste in three ways: They have a very low R-value and thus allow a lot of heat loss in winter; they are sources of infiltration; and they let in unwanted summer heat (heat gain).

Most windows provide very little resistance to heat flow. A single-pane window has an R-value of 0.9, compared to R-5 for an uninsulated frame wall. This means that heat flows out of a square foot of glass more than five times as fast as it does out of a square foot of frame wall. Even though windows account for only 10 to 25 percent of the total wall area in most houses, the conductive heat loss through the windows of a typical house exceeds the heat loss through all the walls. Moreover, improved windows will increase interior comfort by reducing radiation to cold window surfaces and eliminating the cold drafts they generate.

The inside surface of a single-glazed window, for example, has a temperature of 46°F when the outside air temperature is 40°F and the inside is 68°F. This cold surface chills people up to 4 feet away. By contrast, the inside surface of a triple-glazed window is 61°F under similar conditions. And if the single-glazed window has R-9 night insulation, the inside surface temperature is 66°F. These higher surface temperatures reduce the distance at which a person is chilled.

Window insulation can also lower noise transmission into the house by 5 to 10 decibels. Thermal and storm windows with the same glass thickness help very little in reducing noise because they resonate at the same frequency and therefore simply conduct the noise. Different thicknesses of glass transmit different frequencies, however, and therefore do a better job of filtering out noise.

The air that enters or escapes around windows is also important in overall heat loss. Most window frames have cracks or gaps that allow air infiltration. These energy losses, while normally moderate, can be high if the windows are old, ill-fitting, or broken.

Various tapes, gaskets, and adhesive-backed foam strips on the market can be used to weatherstrip windows (see Table 4-2). If you are installing a storm window outside an existing leaky window, weatherstrip the existing window anyway to eliminate condensation between the two. Windows you don't use can be weatherstripped and then sealed with a caulking gun and compound.

Storm windows have been the traditional first line of defense against harsh winters. Two window layers have an R-value ranging from 1.6 to 2.5, roughly twice that of a single layer. Three layers yield an R-value of 2.4 to 4.5. Up to a point, the greater the air space between layers, the higher the insulating value. Storm windows can be plastic or glass, permanent or removable. There are also models designed to be placed on the inside of the window. As long as the window is tight-fitting, the benefits are nearly the same regardless of the design or the material used. If you use air conditioning during the summer, leave the storm windows on the windows that aren't used for ventilation.

Storm windows have another benefit apart from energy savings. By raising the temperature of the inside pane, a storm (or thermal) window will reduce condensation on inside window surfaces. If the indoor temperature is 70°F and the outdoor temperature is 30°F, condensation will form on a double pane and storm window combination when the relative humidity reaches 70 percent. In the same conditions, condensation will form on a single-pane window at 35 percent relative humidity.

Storm doors serve the same purpose as storm windows. Most storm doors are tight-fitting aluminum frames with a glass insert and are designed for easy installation and removal. Alternatively, you can use insulated doors: hollow doors with insulation inside or solid wood doors. These doors save 1 to 2 percent in heating bills when properly weatherstripped. An added benefit is that they can reduce by half or more the noise of a hollow-core door.

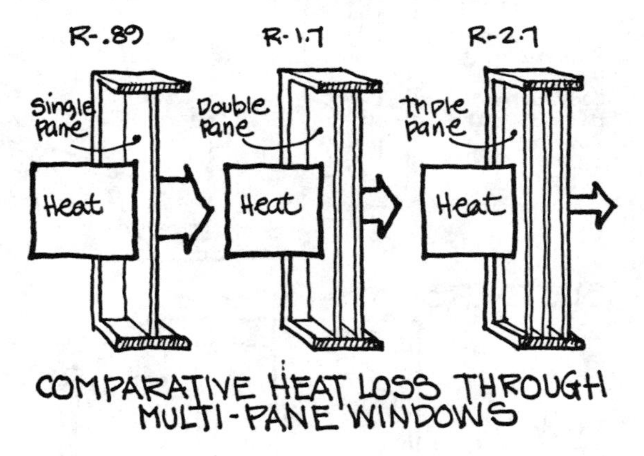

COMPARATIVE HEAT LOSS THROUGH MULTI-PANE WINDOWS

Replacement thermal windows (double or triple pane) are an alternative to storm windows. Multiple-pane windows are manufactured with two or three closely set layers of glass separated by thin air spaces. They involve replacing the existing window entirely and are more expensive than storm windows. Thermal windows are appropriate if the climate is moderate to cold and if the original windows are in poor condition. Thermal windows have the advantage of convenience: They do not need to be taken on and off, and there is no more maintenance than that required by an ordinary window.

Some thermal windows incorporate materials that inhibit the transfer of heat. These "transparent insulations" only reduce slightly the amount of solar radiation allowed through the window, while holding heat inside the house. Some of these windows have a greater insulating value than night window insulations and have a R-value greater than triple-pane glass. Table 4-5 lists costs and R-values of various window treatments.

TABLE 4-5
STORM WINDOWS, THERMAL WINDOWS, AND WINDOW INSULATION

	Cost Range per Square Foot	*R-Value*
Standard single-pane		0.9
Storm windows (window only)		
Exterior glass (openable)	$5–$10	1.7*
Exterior glass (fixed)	$4–$7	1.7*
Interior glass (openable)	$3–$6	1.7*
Interior acrylic	$3–$6	1.7*
New thermal windows		
Double glazed:		
Windows only	$6–$10	1.7
Windows plus installation	$12–$16	1.7
Double glazed with internal transparent insulating film:		
Windows only	$20–$40	3–4
Windows plus installation	$26–$46	3–4
Triple glazed:		
Windows only	$10–$15	2.7
Windows plus installation	$16–$22	2.7
Window insulation		
Roman blinds with magnetic seal, multilayer fabric:		
Materials only	$2.50–$5	4*
Finished only	$5–$7	4
Finished and installed	$8–$13	4
Shutters or set-ins with 1½ inch vinyl-covered foam board	$1–$5	11*

* R-value with single glazing. To obtain the total R-value when used with double glazing, add 0.9 to the value given; for triple glazing, add 1.8.

Storm or thermal windows are not the only way to reduce heat loss through your windows. Tight-fitting interior blinds, drapes of multilayer fabric, or shutters made of rigid foam can provide a greater insulating value than standard double-pane windows. In contrast to conventional curtains, the fabric made for insulating windows contains layers to reflect heat, insulate against heat transfer, and provide a vapor barrier.

Conventional curtains do not do much to slow heat loss or gain, and often they can actually increase summer heat gain. This happens when the heated or cooled air between the glass and curtain rises or falls into the rooms, creating a regular convective loop. To remedy this problem, insulating blinds and shutters are designed to fit tightly against the window on all sides, by means of a track or magnetic strip, thus eliminating infiltrating drafts and preventing hot-air convection currents from warming the house.

Installed costs for insulated shutters and blinds can range from $4 to $20 per square foot depending on the product and whether or not they are custom made. Some foam-core shutters are relatively inexpensive, fit a variety of window types, can be installed without undue trouble, and can provide a high insulating value. Apart from their higher cost, insulated shutters and blinds have certain other disadvantages. Both are opaque so they must be raised during the day when you need light . . . and, of course, they only pay off if you use them.

Heat absorbed from outside air, direct sun through windows, and infiltration can also contribute to summer heat buildup. Just a few unshaded windows can drive up air conditioning costs and dramatically reduce your comfort.

All these window treatments—storm windows, thermal windows, insulating curtains, shutters—will help keep your home more comfortable in summer, but they are not as effective as simple, low-cost measures designed to keep the sun from hitting your south, west, or east windows. Any of the following tactics will serve this purpose:

1. Vegetation may be the best solution. Deciduous trees or vines trained on a trellis are a low-maintenance way to shade windows. Plants cool the air around them through transpiration, and they allow sun through the windows after they shed their leaves.

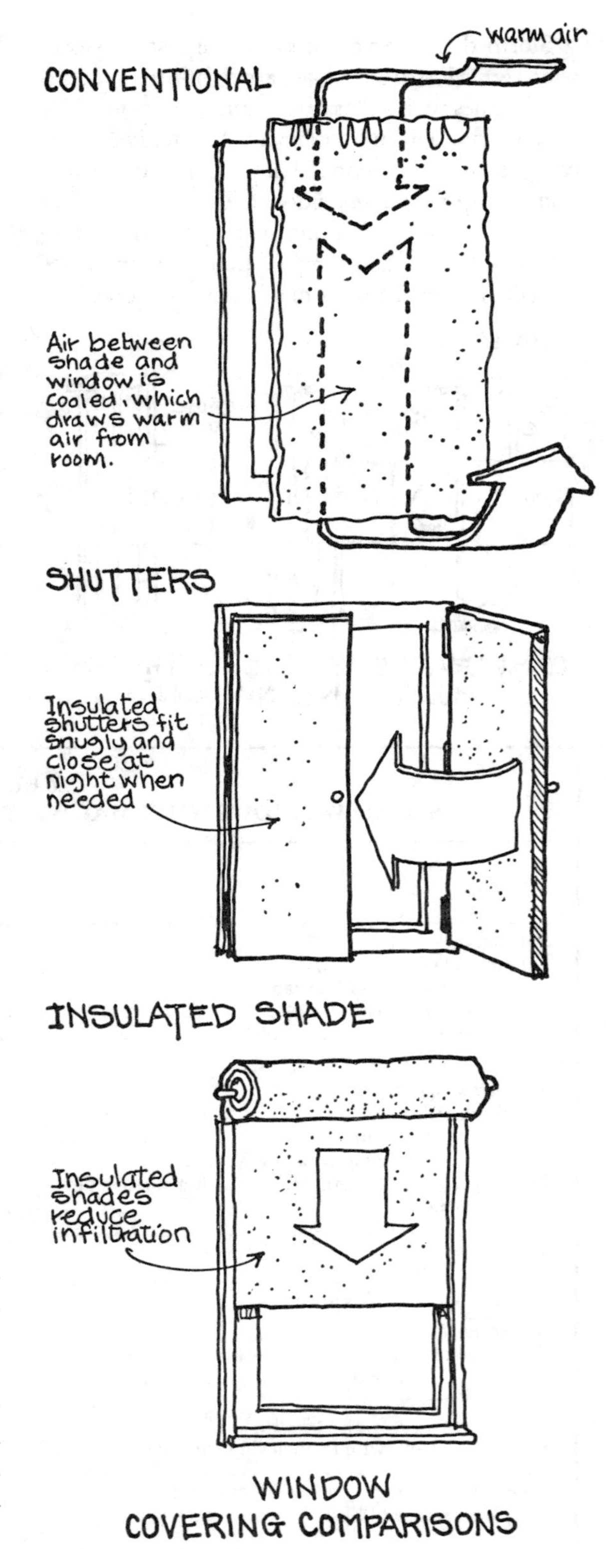

warm air
CONVENTIONAL
Air between shade and window is cooled, which draws warm air from room.
SHUTTERS
Insulated shutters fit snugly and close at night when needed
INSULATED SHADE
Insulated shades reduce infiltration

WINDOW COVERING COMPARISONS

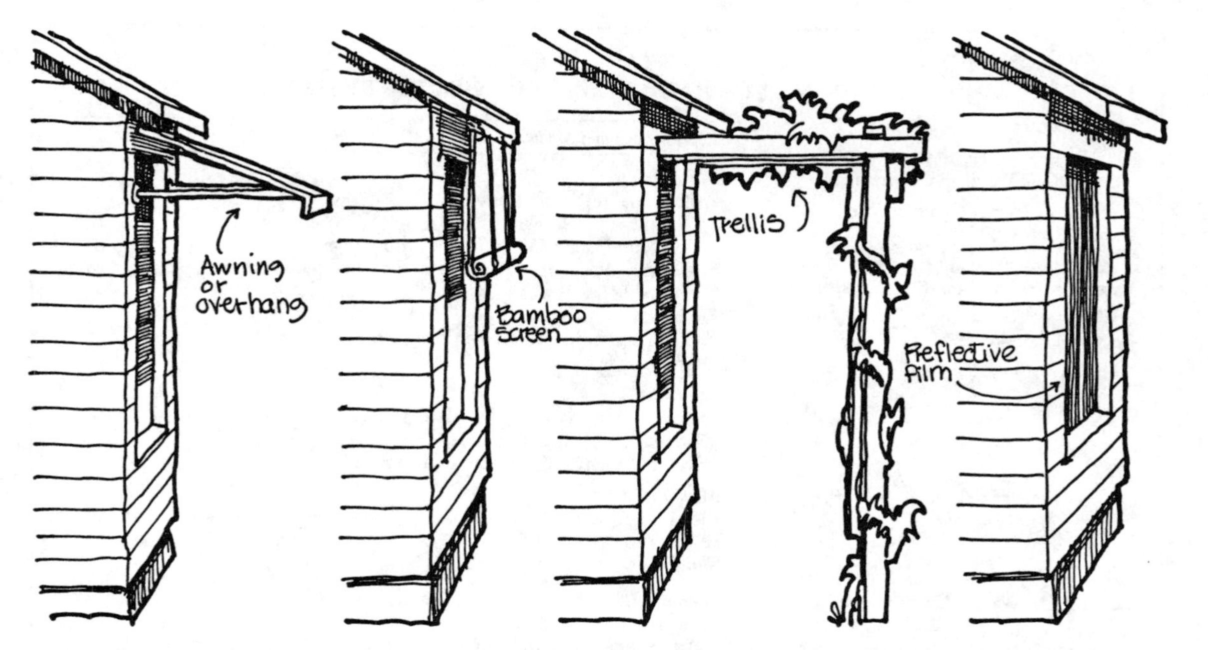

2. Awnings are another solution. Almost any design and any durable, weatherproof material will work. Awnings should have ventilating slits to prevent heat buildup next to the window.

3. Bamboo screens are another workable, low-cost approach. Commercially available fiberglass sunscreens are only slightly less effective than an opaque material and are easy to install. They are designed to replace the insect mesh in your window screens.

4. Adhesive reflective films applied to the inside of the glass will reject some heat while preserving your view. Some films discolor, though, and they must be carefully installed to prevent warping and peeling.

5. A final way to prevent the sun from striking the walls or windows of a house is an overhang, an alternative discussed in Chapter 6. In hot climates, however, an overhang will not be sufficient and additional shading techniques may be required.

If it's impossible to shade roof and walls to protect yourself from summer heat, one way to prevent excessive heat buildup and cut down on air conditioning costs is to paint the exterior walls of the house white and use a light-colored roofing material next time you reroof. Light surfaces, because they reflect sunlight, absorb about half as much heat as dark surfaces. Your house stays cooler as a result.

More Efficient Heating and Cooling

Improvements are possible in each part of the heating and cooling system: in the thermostatic controls; in the network of pipes or ducts that carry heated air, water, or steam; and in the operation of the heating or cooling unit itself. Typically these improvements can save 10 to 30 percent in your heating and cooling bill. Table 4-6 summarizes these measures. As with most measures in Level I, your decision should not be whether to do them, but when and how. These steps are particularly important if you cannot insulate your roof and walls.

Turning the thermostat down (or up during the cooling season) at night or when the house is unoccupied saves fuel without sacrificing comfort. This step alone can save 5 to 15 percent on annual heating bills depending on where your thermostat was previously set. Clock thermostats cost from $40 to $200. They can be programmed to turn the temperature down at night and up in the morning before you arise, as well as down or off if you are not home during the day and back on before you get back. Most clock thermostats come with instructions and can be installed by the purchaser.

In most heating systems, hot or cold air, steam, or hot water are distributed to the living space through a network of ducts and registers or pipes

TABLE 4-6
IMPROVING YOUR HEATING AND COOLING SYSTEMS

Type	*Improvements and Modifications*
Central Gas Warm-Air Furnace Average seasonal efficiency with standing pilot: 60%* Average seasonal efficiency with improvements and modifications: 82% Best new models: 95%	*Improvements* Professional test and tune-up: Oil and adjust blower, fans Check and clean gas orifice for proper operation Measure flue gas temperature and carbon monoxide/oxygen and carbon dioxide levels Check flue damper Clean and adjust thermostat contacts Change air filter Distribution system: Check for air leaks and insulate ducts Vacuum and clean registers Remove obstructions from registers *Modifications* Electric ignition Automatic flue damper Smaller gas orifice
Central Oil Warm-Air Furnace Average seasonal efficiency: 66% Average seasonal efficiency with improvements and modifications: 81% Best new models: 85%	*Improvements* Professional test and tune-up: Adjust and clean oil burner Clean combustion chamber Perform smoke test Measure flue temperature and carbon dioxide/oxygen levels Adjust flue damper Downsize oil burner nozzle Change oil and air filter Check oil pump Clean and adjust thermostat contacts Oil and adjust blower and fans Adjust fuel/air ratio Distribution system: Same as for gas furnace *Modifications* Flame retention burner Automatic flue damper
Gas-Fired Boiler Average seasonal efficiency: 63% Average seasonal efficiency with improvements and modifications: 80% Best new models: 92%	*Improvements* Professional test and tune-up: Check and clean gas orifice Measure stack temperature and carbon dioxide/oxygen and carbon monoxide levels Check flue damper Clean and adjust thermostat contacts Drain and clean boiler yearly Steam distribution system: Balance system Remove obstructions from radiators Keep radiators dust free Check for leaks and insulate pipes Check radiator traps Place reflectors behind radiators Water distribution system: Same as steam except: Check and service pumps Check and use bleed valves

Type	*Improvements and Modifications*
	Modifications Sediment trap Electronic ignition Smaller orifice Automatic flue damper Outdoor temperature aquastat (water distribution only)
Oil-Fired Boiler Average seasonal efficiency: 65% Average seasonal efficiency with improvements and modifications: 82% Best new models: 87%	*Improvements* Professional test and tune-up: Check and clean oil burner Measure stack temperature and carbon dioxide/oxygen levels Check flue damper Check and clean pump Check oil filter Downsize burner nozzle Drain and clean boiler yearly Steam distribution system: Same as for gas boiler Water distribution system: Same as for gas boiler *Modifications* Automatic flue damper Sediment trap Flame retention burner Outdoor sensing aquastat (water distribution only)
Central Air Conditioner Average seasonal efficiency: 6.5 SEER Best new models: 14.0 SEER	*Improvements* Shade the unit Check refrigerant Clean and check thermostat controls Replace disposable filter or clean permanent one monthly Disconnect compressor pump heating element after cooling season Distribution system: Keep grill clean and free of debris Check for leaks and insulate ducts Remove obstructions from registers Balance the system
Room Air Conditioner Average seasonal efficiency: 6.4 SEER Best new models: 11.0 SEER	*Improvements* Shade the unit Vacuum the condenser coils Check refrigerant Change or replace filter yearly Remove unit at end of season or caulk and weatherstrip around edges and cover during winter
Heat Pumps Average efficiency (cooling): 5–8 EER Average seasonal efficiency (heating): 1.7 COP Best new models (cooling seasonal efficiency): 11.0 SEER Best new models (heating): 2.6 COP	*Improvements* Change the filter Check for leaks and insulate ducts Shade the unit in summer Balance the system

* Equipment efficiencies are given according to their various standard ratings. For definitions of these ratings, see Chapter 6 and the glossary.

and radiators. Hot exhaust containing combustion gases is vented separately through a chimney called a flue. There are a number of steps you can take to make sure the distribution system is efficient. These are listed in Table 4-6 under improvements. Some of these measures are inexpensive do-it-yourself projects that the homeowner and renter can do.

There are several types of conventional heating systems. Furnaces use oil, gas, or electricity and sometimes coal or wood as the heating source and deliver hot air through a network of ducts and registers to the rest of the house. Boilers too use oil or gas, but they heat water or steam that is delivered to the living areas through pipes and radiators or baseboard conductors.

Another major type of heating system employs baseboard electric resistance heaters and central electric furnaces. In recent years, electric heat pumps—more efficient than electric resistance heating—have been installed in many homes. If you have an electric resistance central furnace, insulate your ducts; there are no real efficiency improvements you can make short of replacing the system. See Chapter 6 for more information on replacing furnaces and boilers.

We have divided the steps you can take to improve your furnace or boiler into three categories:

1. Efficiency improvements that are routine maintenance chores and low-cost, do-it-yourself projects (Level I)
2. Modifications that require the help of a technician (Level I)
3. Replacement—a big but often warranted expense (Level II)

This chapter covers efficiency improvements and modifications. Table 4-6 shows recommended efficiency measures and improvements according to the fuel source and type of heating system. This

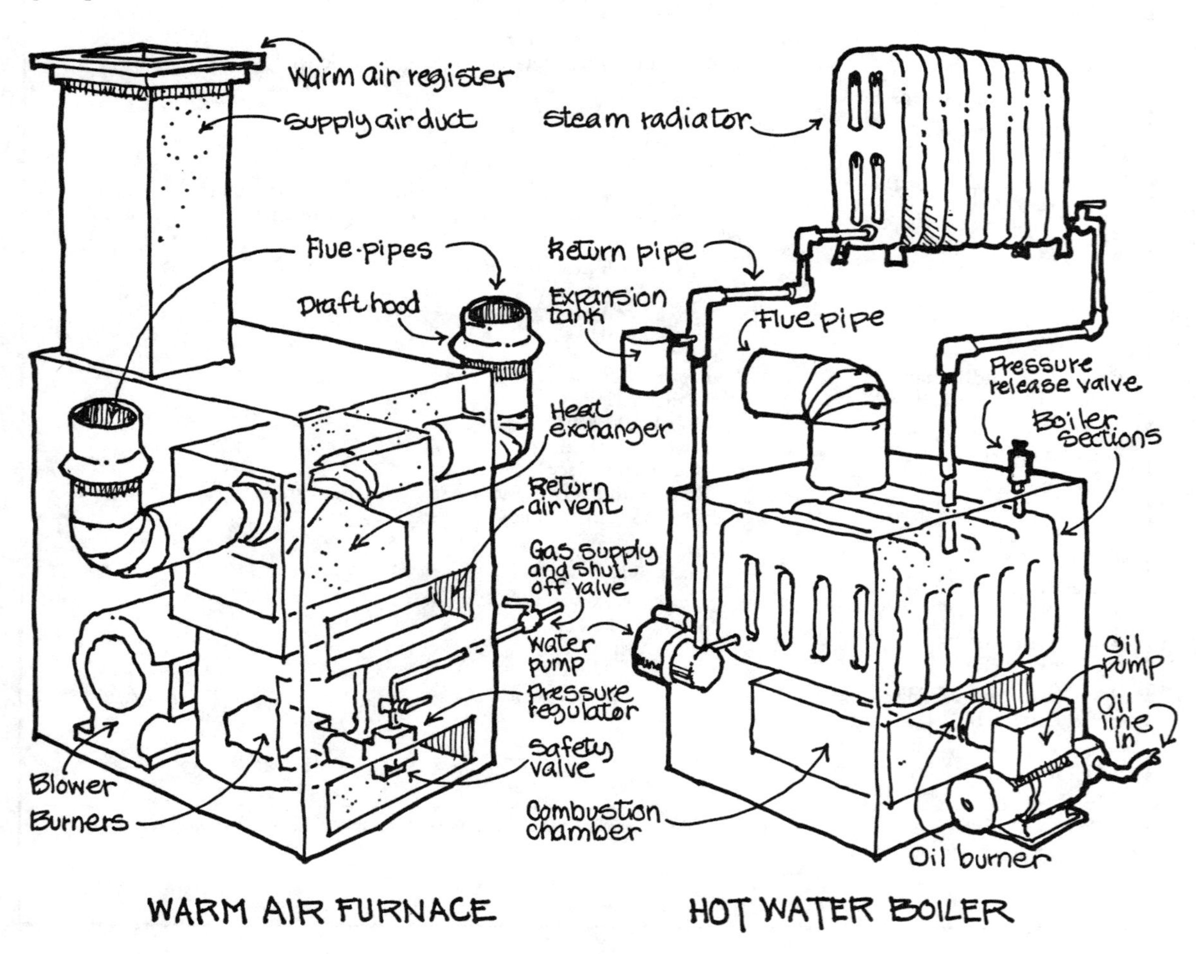

table will give you guidance on the steps to take, when to take them, and when to seek the help of a professional.

In Chapter 6 we survey some of the new super-efficient furnaces now on the market, and Chapter 7 shows you a way of calculating the economics of furnace replacement. If your heating bills are over $700 a year or you have electric space heating, review the section of Chapter 6 on furnace replacement before you spend time and money on efficiency improvements or modifications. You may have a candidate for replacement.

IMPROVING FURNACE AND BOILER EFFICIENCY

Improvements should start with a measurement of your furnace or boiler's current combustion (steady state) efficiency. This step requires the help of a professional. If your heating oil or gas supplier cannot do the test, look in the Yellow Pages under "Heating Contractors" or "Heaters: Sales and Service" or "Furnaces."

When you call a heating and cooling specialist, make sure you understand what the technicians will do when they arrive at your home. Most companies charge by the hour, and that hour may include travel time to and from your house. Some will charge this base hourly rate just to come give you an estimate; others will actually perform some work while they're there.

To test your furnace or boiler's efficiency, a technician measures the temperature of the exhaust gases in the flue (sometimes called a vent). If temperatures are high, too much heat is traveling up the flue and a tune-up is called for.

The technician also measures the amount of smoke and carbon dioxide or oxygen in the exhaust, if you have an oil system, and the amount of carbon dioxide or oxygen and carbon monoxide in the exhaust of a gas system. These readings and the temperatures in the flue indicate how completely your furnace or boiler is using the fuel.

These tests measure the steady-state efficiency of your heating system: how much of your fuel's energy value is being converted to useful heat. Levels of 60 to 75 percent are common. A tuned-up furnace or boiler will have an efficiency of 75 percent or higher. *Steady state* means that efficiency is measured as if the furnace or boiler were running all the time, which it does not. To get an estimate of what is called *seasonal efficiency*, the technician factors in additional heat losses as the unit cycles on and off to maintain the house's temperature.

If, for example, your gas-fired warm-air furnace with no flue damper and a pilot light has a steady-state efficiency of 70 percent, the unit may have a seasonal efficiency as low as 53 percent. True efficiency is considerably lower if you factor in heat losses that occur as the warm air travels from the furnace to the registers in the room. Adding a flue damper and an electric ignition to this furnace increases seasonal efficiency to 63 percent.

You can estimate the steady-state efficiency your furnace was designed to attain by checking the name plate on the furnace. If the efficiency isn't listed on the plate, divide the output number, sometimes called a *bonnet*, by the input number given. This should give you a number like 0.80 or 80 percent. The furnace, as designed, will not be able to achieve efficiencies greater than this. If you have a gas furnace or boiler, look at the color of the flame. It should be bright white and yellow with some red, but only a little blue color.

Typical ways of improving your furnace's efficiency include insulating the warm air ducts, adjusting and cleaning the gas orifice or oil nozzle, adjusting and oiling the blower and fans, changing air filters, cleaning registers, inspecting pumps and changing oil filters (oil furnace), adjusting the registers for proper airflow, and checking to make sure the flue damper (if there is one)is working properly. Finally, the distribution system is balanced to ensure that the right amount of heated air is delivered to each register.

You can improve your boiler's efficiency by cleaning and adjusting the fuel burner, adjusting the flue damper, blower, and fans, flushing out the boiler each year, checking for scale buildup in pipes and in the boiler, repairing system leaks, and insulating pipes.

FURNACE AND BOILER MODIFICATIONS

Furnace modifications require a greater investment than the improvements just discussed and involve some choices that are determined by the type of heating system you have. Here we'll consider modifications of gas-fired and oil-fired furnaces and take a brief look at boiler modifications.

Gas-Fired Warm-Air Furnaces. If you have a gas-fired warm-air furnace, consider these changes: installing electric ignition, reducing the size of the gas orifice if possible, and installing an automatic or electric flue damper.

Electric ignition is also referred to as automatic or pilotless ignition. It involves replacing the pilot light, a major source of energy waste, with an electric sparking device that lights the furnace when heat is called for. Adding one to your gas furnace costs $50 to $250 but can save up to 10 percent of your heating bill depending on the length of the heating season and how often heating is required.

Reducing the size of the gas orifice, called *derating*, limits the amount of gas that reaches the burner, so the burner stays on longer to achieve the temperature setting on the thermostat. This means the furnace burns more efficiently at close to steady-state performance with less heat loss up the flue. You will get varying opinions from furnace technicians about the feasibility of this change. Some will perform the modification and some will not.

A third change to consider is adding an automatic flue damper to prevent the escape of heated air up the flue after the burner has turned off. An automatic flue damper consists of two or more "wings" that fold down to block the flue when the furnace is off and fold up to release exhaust when the furnace is on. Some flue dampers are wired to the ignition mechanism and fold up and down when the burner goes on and off (both oil and gas). Others fold up as the blades of the damper heat up (gas only). We refer to this type as an electric flue damper in the Chapter 5 case studies.

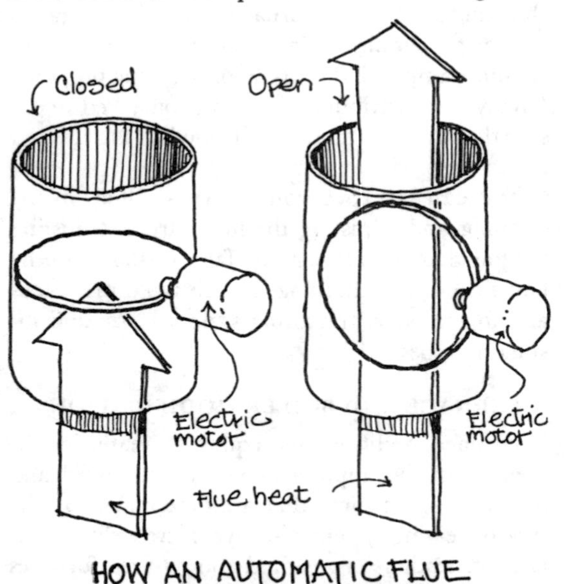

HOW AN AUTOMATIC FLUE DAMPER WORKS

Costs and savings of flue dampers vary greatly. They are most cost effective if the furnace and flue are oversized (likely if you have thoroughly weatherized the building envelope) and you live in a cold climate. Automatic flue dampers must be approved by the Underwriters Laboratory or the American Gas Association, and installation must meet local codes.

Oil-Fired Warm-Air Furnaces. If you have an oil-fired warm-air furnace, consider replacing the oil nozzle with a smaller one (called *downsizing*), installing an automatic flue damper, and putting in a new flame retention burner. The options in flue dampers are the same as those described for gas-fired warm-air furnaces.

Downsizing to a smaller oil nozzle of conventional design costs $50 to $100. It can be done by a homeowner, but it is best to consult a heating contractor. A more efficient but more expensive option is downsizing with a new flame-retention burner. This device, which combines a smaller nozzle size with a more efficient burning technique, costs $300 to $400.

Boiler Modifications. Many of the furnace modifications are also possible for gas or oil-fired boilers. Moreover, you can have a professional install a sediment trap in the water lines to prevent flow restriction.

Gas or oil boilers that deliver hot water to conductors or registers can be modified by replacing the aquastat with one that senses outdoor temperatures and adjusts the water temperature accordingly. Most aquastats are set to deliver water steadily at a high temperature; the high temperature increases heat loss and is not always needed to maintain comfort. Boilers with water and steam distribution systems benefit most from efficiency improvements. These improvements are listed in Table 4-6.

WOOD HEATING

Fireplaces are the least efficient means of home heating. Fires draw heated air into the fireplace and straight up the chimney. In an unweatherized

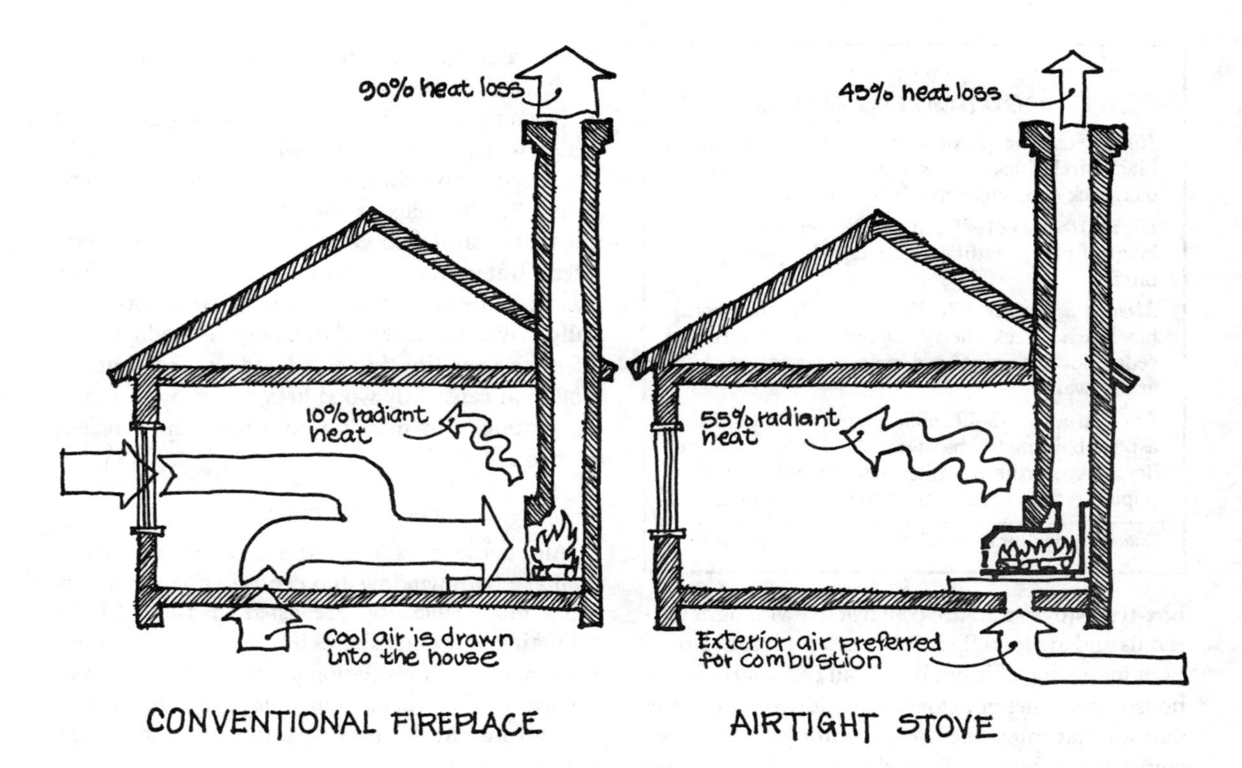

house, this draft pulls cold air into the house, stealing more heat than the fire gives off to the house. Only 5 or 6 percent of the heating value of wood burned in a typical fireplace gets delivered to the dwelling as useful heat. If you are paying for wood you know it is too expensive to waste.

Glass screens and tubular grates help make a fireplace more efficient. Together they can increase the fuel efficiency of a typical fireplace to between 10 and 20 percent.

Fireplaces are also a source of heat loss when they're *not* in use. An open or ill-fitting flue damper provides a large pathway for heat loss. Warm air from the house rises easily up the chimney, creating a constant energy drain. Glass screens help eliminate this problem.

The woodburning stove is an efficient alternative to the conventional fireplace. Wood stove inserts are shaped to fit into a fireplace opening and designed to use the existing chimney. A well-built iron fireplace insert will increase fuel efficiency up to 40 percent. Steel inserts yield smaller but still significant savings.

If you do not have a fireplace but are thinking about a woodburning stove as a primary source of heat, consider several factors. Wood is readily available and inexpensive in some areas, costly in others. Wood prices can make the difference between a wood stove that saves money and one that is a drain on your time and pocketbook. In computing wood costs, consider the energy content of the wood available. Cheap wood may not be a bargain if it has a low energy content. Its heating value is proportional to its Btu content. Moreover, wood with a high moisture content—uncured or green wood—may use up to 50 percent of its heating value just to vaporize the moisture in the wood. As a result, you have to burn more to heat your house. Table 4-7 lists the heating values of various types of firewood.

Consider also the configuration of your house and the possible locations of a new chimney. The stove should be located in a primary living area and close to all the rooms you want to heat. Too many bends or too long a vertical run will increase the deposit of creosote in the flue and magnify the risk of a chimney fire. Outside the house, the chimney must be clear of trees and other obstructions and must be accessible for annual cleaning.

Wood stoves differ widely in cost and come in a variety of designs and efficiencies. They range from

TABLE 4-7
WOOD HEATING VALUES

Highest heat value (27 or more million Btu per cord): black birch, hickory, live oak, locust, northern red oak, rock elm, sugar maple, white oak

High heat value (24–26 million Btu per cord): beech, longleaf pine, southern red oak, white ash, yellow birch

Medium heat value (20–23 million Btu per cord): black ash, black cherry, Douglas fir, eastern red cedar, loblolly pine, red maple, sycamore, tamarack, walnut

Low heat value (13–19 million Btu per cord): alder, aspen, balsam fir, basswood, cedar, cottonwood, hemlock, northern white cedar, ponderosa pine, poplar, red fir, spruce, sugar pine, white pine

Source: Agricultural Handbook No. 72, USDA, 1974.

box-type stoves that are constructed with light materials and are less efficient heaters to airtight stoves built for a long, efficient burn that can heat a whole house. Since airtight stoves have sealed seams, the only air that enters the stove's combustion chamber comes through specially designed inlets. Table 4-8 compares different types of wood and coal heating alternatives.

A wood heating manual can help you fit the size of your wood stove to the space to be heated and your climate. (See the reference section at the end of the book.) Avoid a stove that is too large. It will require more damping to keep your living area from getting too warm, contributing to a creosote build-up in the flue.

A wood stove that is damped frequently can pollute the air inside the house and also contributes to outdoor air pollution. In Portland, Oregon, for example, half the households heat with wood, and the state's Department of Environmental Quality believes that by 1987 pollution from woodburners will be twice that from industrial sources. One solution to this problem is a wood stove with a catalyst. Catalysts—similar to those used in cars—help burn exhaust gases completely, reducing exhaust pollutants and increasing overall efficiency. Wood stoves with catalysts cost about $200 more than similar models without them.

Some wood stoves also serve as water heaters. Plumbing in the stove allows you to use the wood heater either as a water heater or as a backup to a solar water heater during extended cloudy and cold periods.

Not only do wood stoves have the appeal of using a renewable resource, but where winters are cold and wood is abundant they can also reduce conventional heating bills or—if you install the Level I measures suited to your house—even eliminate them. But urban dwellers who now heat with oil or gas should examine the economic trade-offs carefully. Given the cost and difficulty of handling tons of wood, and the increased indoor and outdoor pollution caused by wood fires, you may be better off putting your money into a new superefficient furnace.

AIR CONDITIONERS

Air conditioners, like furnaces, need care. Ways to make both window and central air conditioners work more efficiently are listed in Table 4-6. If your air conditioner shares ducts with your heating system, the duct insulation you've installed to save on heating fuel will also cut your cooling bill. If you haven't insulated your ducts, this is another good reason to do so.

Air conditioner efficiency is measured using the *energy efficiency ratio* (EER), a measure of how well the equipment uses electricity to extract Btu's of heat from the air, or the *seasonal energy efficiency ratio* (SEER), which takes into account efficiency losses that occur through normal use. Nearly all air conditioners are labeled with an EER or an SEER. The SEER is always lower than the EER. When shopping for a new air conditioner, look for one with an EER of at least 8 (preferably 10 or more) and an SEER of 8 or above. If the unit has no efficiency labeling, don't buy it. Any money you save on the initial cost will soon be spent on electricity bills.

There are steps you can take to help your present air conditioner operate more efficiently. Some central air conditioners have a heating element that operates full time to keep moisture from accumulating in the compression pump. You can turn this heater off at the end of the cooling season by disconnecting the circuit that serves the air conditioner. A day or two before you use your air conditioner again, turn the circuit back on or you risk damaging its compressor.

Keep air conditioners free of dust; change the filters in a central system frequently. Wash cooling

TABLE 4-8
WOOD AND COAL HEATERS

*Type**	*Approximate Efficiency**	*Features*	*Advantages*	*Disadvantages*
Simple fireplace (masonry or prefabricated)	−10 to +10%	Open front. Radiates heat in one direction only.	Visual beauty.	Low efficiency. Heats only small area.
High-efficiency fireplace	25 to 45%	Freestanding or built-in with glass doors, grates, duct, and blowers.	Visual beauty. More efficient. Heats larger areas. Long service life. Maximum safety.	Medium efficiency.
Box stoves	20 to 40%	Radiates heat in all directions.	Low initial cost. Heats large areas.	Fire hard to control. Short life. Wastes fuel.
Airtight stove	40 to 55%	Radiates heat in all directions. Sealed seams, effective draft control.	Good efficiency. Long burn times, high heat output. Long service life.	Can create creosote problems.
High-efficiency airtight stove	50 to 65%	Radiates heat in all directions. Sealed seams, effective draft control.	Highest efficiency. Long burn times, high heat output. Long life.	Creosote problems. High purchase price.

* Product categories are general; product efficiencies are approximate.

Source: 1983 *ASHRAE Book of Fundamentals*, American Society of Heating, Refrigerating, and Air-Conditioning Engineers, Atlanta.

coils each season, and have the refrigerant checked regularly.

Shading the air conditioner and allowing good air circulation around the unit will improve performance. If you have a heat pump that also serves as an air conditioner, remove the shading during winter to improve heating performance. Cover room air conditioners in winter to prevent cold air from getting inside the house.

Air conditioning will always be an expensive way to keep cool because it uses electricity. A well-shaded, fully insulated, and weatherstripped house will help control air conditioning costs by preventing the cool air from escaping and by reducing or eliminating the amount of time the air conditioner is on.

In dry climates where mechanical cooling is necessary, a lower-cost alternative to the air conditioner is an evaporative cooler. Evaporative coolers

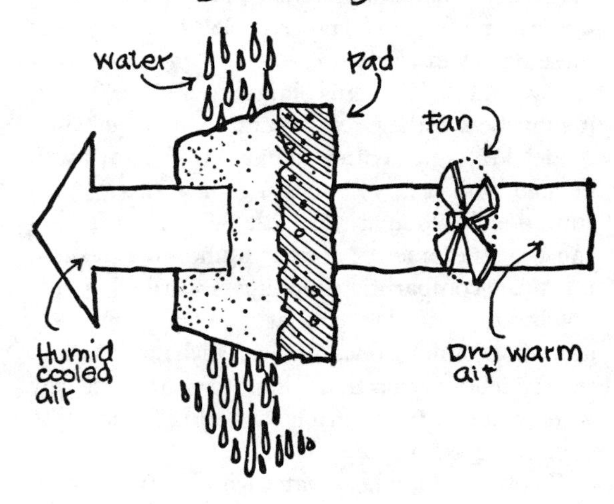
Water is evaporated from pad, cooling the air by absorbing heat
water
pad
fan
Humid cooled air
Dry warm air

HOW AN EVAPORATIVE COOLER WORKS

are located on the roof or at a window and use a fan to blow air through a wet pad where evaporation chills the air and increases its humidity. For the unit to be most effective, windows in the house should be slightly opened to increase air circulation and limit the buildup of humidity in the house. Because evaporative coolers rely on the evaporation of moisture to chill air, they don't work well in humid climates. New evaporative coolers are smaller, need less maintenance, and are more efficient than the unwieldy swamp coolers of the past.

Water Heating

The water heater is second only to heating as the major domestic user of energy, accounting for over 14 percent of the energy used in most homes. Because demand for hot water is not seasonal, like heating or cooling, investments in the efficiency of your hot water system will pay back year-round.

Energy losses in the hot water system occur in four ways: Heat escapes through the jacket of the water heater; heat is lost through the hot water pipes; heat escapes up the exhaust flue; and energy is wasted when you use more hot water than necessary.

Four simple measures can reduce these losses: a water heater blanket; lowering the water heater thermostat setting to 120°F; insulating hot water pipes; and installing low-flow showerheads and faucet restrictors. These measures are inexpensive and they can be installed easily. In most households they will reduce the energy needed for heating water by more than 30 percent. Box 4-6 shows how these strategies work.

If your water heater is old, rusty, and inefficient, it may be worth it to purchase a more efficient model. Water heaters are required by federal law to be sold with a label indicating their energy consumption in comparison with other models. Because of the amount of year-round energy these units use, comparison shopping is worthwhile. Do not buy a water heater that is not appropriately labeled. (For more on appliance efficiency labeling, see the following section.) Plan to wrap your new water heater with an insulated blanket to increase your energy savings.

If you currently heat water with electricity, consider switching to a heat pump water heater or a solar water heater. Both these alternatives will, in the long run, be a good investment. If your water heater uses gas or oil, your choices include installing a more efficient water heater or a solar water heater. For more on the trade-offs involved, see Chapter 6.

BOX 4-6
FOUR TIPS FOR WATER HEATING CONSERVATION

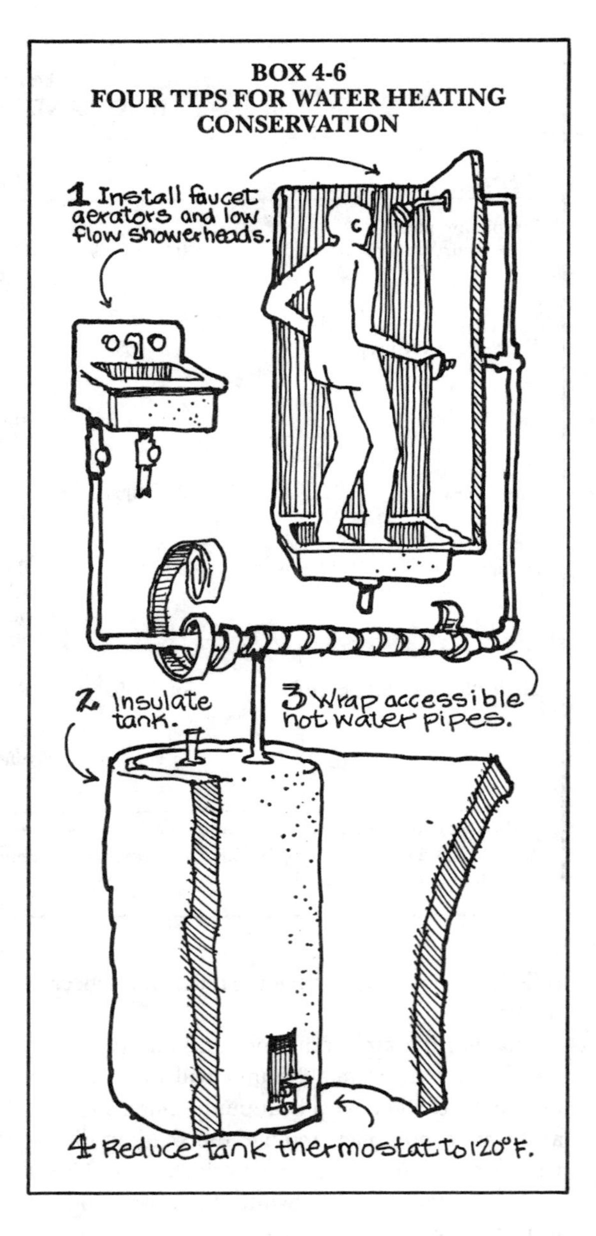

1 Install faucet aerators and low flow showerheads.
2 Insulate tank.
3 Wrap accessible hot water pipes.
4 Reduce tank thermostat to 120°F.

Appliances and Lighting

Appliances and lighting can account for 20 to 30 percent of the energy use in a typical household. Since appliances take the major share, buying efficient models can save considerable energy and, in the long run, money.

EFFICIENT APPLIANCES

Among household appliances, refrigerators and freezers are the largest energy users, and they cover a broad range of efficiencies. This performance range has narrowed somewhat in recent years as regulations in some states have forced less efficient models off the national market. If you bought a refrigerator before 1980, though, it is likely to be using much more electricity than necessary to get the job done. The average refrigerator sold in 1980 uses 40 percent more electricity than many models available today. The average freezer sold in 1980 uses 30 percent more than models available today. The Japanese are now making refrigerators that compare in size and features with our most efficient models but use 40 percent less electricity.

The type of refrigerator and freezer affects energy use, too. Manual defrost units with separate freezers use up to 60 percent less electricity than comparable self-defrosting models.

How can you tell if your refrigerator or freezer is an energy hog? One way is to measure actual performance using your own meter. Call your utility for help or instructions on how to read your meter.

Measure your refrigerator's energy use when your house is vacant for a few days or more. Note your meter reading (in kilowatt-hours) when you leave and when you return, and subtract to obtain a total consumption figure. If you leave any lights on, multiply the bulb wattage by the number of hours burning, divide by 1000 to get kilowatt-hours, and subtract this number from the total consumption figure you obtained from the meter. Divide this number by the number of days you were gone. Multiplying this last figure by 30 will give you a rough estimate of the refrigerator's monthly kilowatt-hour use. You can compare this figure with the energy use of models on the market. This procedure will not work if you leave electric appliances on, however, or if you have more than one refrigerator or a separate freezer.

Another method is to find a guide to energy consumption that includes your make and model. The Association of Home Appliance Manufacturers publishes registries of appliance efficiencies; its address is listed at the end of this section.

When you have established the energy consumption of the refrigerator or freezer, you need only perform a few simple calculations to weigh the benefits of replacing that appliance. Figure the annual cost of operation by multiplying annual consumption (in kilowatt-hours) by the price per kilowatt-hour charged by your local utility. You can compare this figure with what it would cost to operate a new energy-efficient refrigerator or freezer by visiting an appliance showroom and reading the EnergyGuide labels on them. You are likely to find that you can save up to $100 a year depending on the condition and age of your present refrigerator or freezer.

Gas stoves and ranges vary in energy consumption depending on the insulation around the oven and whether they have electronic ignition or standing pilot lights. Pilot lights account for 33 percent of your stove's natural gas use. Self-cleaning gas and electric ovens that rely on a high-heat cycle for cleaning use less energy because the oven box is built with extra insulation to withstand high cleaning temperatures. Poorly insulated ovens and pilot lights also add to cooling costs in the summer, as the air conditioner has to work to overcome the heat they produce.

Natural-gas clothes dryers waste energy—up to $2 each month—if they have a standing pilot light rather than electronic ignition. In most parts of the country, however, a gas dryer has a significant cost advantage over an electric dryer. This is true for most natural gas appliances in most parts of the country.

If you are in the market for a new appliance, it pays to shop around for models that are efficient. Refrigerators, freezers, refrigerator-freezers, room and central air conditioners, gas space heaters, water heaters, clothes dryers, gas cooking appliances—all are required by law to be labeled with energy use information. The labels, called EnergyGuides, contain the information needed to compare the annual operating costs of different makes and models. With this information you can compare the initial and lifetime operating cost (number of years operated times annual operating costs) of the two appliances and then determine how long it will take you to recover your additional investment through energy saved.

If the EnergyGuide label is not on the appliance, ask the salesperson to show you this information. They are required by law to have it, but sometimes they do not want to display the information on the less efficient models they carry. If the sales clerk cannot give you the information, do not buy the appliance.

One drawback of the EnergyGuide is that it only tells you about the model it is attached to. To get a full comparison of the market, you will have to travel to several stores and look at different lines of appliances. Another source of information on appliance efficiency might be your state energy office or utility. Their estimates of operating costs will reflect local energy prices and thus will be more accurate for your situation. If they do not carry lists of appliances and their energy consumption, write to one of the following:

Association of Home Appliance
Manufacturers
20 North Wacker Drive
Chicago, IL 60606

Gas Appliance Manufacturers Association
1901 North Fort Meyer Drive
Arlington, VA 22209

Air Conditioning and Refrigeration Institute
1815 North Fort Meyer Drive
Arlington, VA 22209

LIGHTING

Lights, like other appliances, have been getting more efficient as energy costs rise. Still, lighting accounts for approximately 5 percent of household energy use. Fluorescent lights use 60 percent less energy than an incandescent bulb and last twelve times as long. Fluorescent lights are becoming more attractive, too: New "warm" fluorescent bulbs don't shed the same harsh light as older fixtures. Screw-in fluorescents are now widely available, and you don't have to replace and rewire your current fixtures to use them.

Don't forget to consider energy-efficient lighting for outdoor use, particularly if outdoor lights are on all night for security reasons. The following table indicates the energy efficiency of two types of indoor and outdoor lighting. Two factors are important in selecting a type of lighting: light output (measured in lumens) and energy demand (in watts). The following chart shows some available bulb types and their efficiencies. The higher the number, the more efficient the lighting.

Type	Light Output (in Lumens) per Watt
Indoor lighting	
Standard incandescent	20
Fluorescents	67–83
Outdoor lighting	
Metal halide	85–115
High-pressure sodium	80–140

If you are considering replacing old incandescent fixtures with fluorescents, look first at those areas in your home where lights are used the most. By replacing heavily used incandescent lights with fluorescent lights, and by turning off lights when not in use, you can reduce your lighting costs by 50 percent.

When replacing lights, look for new products. Efficiency improvements continue to appear and these breakthroughs can save you money. For example, a major munufacturer has recently developed an 18-watt fluorescent bulb that has a life of 7500 hours. It sheds the same amount and quality of light as a 75-watt incandescent bulb with a life of 750 hours. The new fluorescent bulb markets for $25. At 7¢/kwh, it will cost $34.45 to purchase and operate the new fluorescent bulb over its lifetime—compared to $44.20 to purchase and operate ten 75-watt incandescent bulbs for the same period of time.

Indoor Air Quality

Caulking and weatherstripping reduce the rate of airflow through a house but can —if done *too* thoroughly—result in a health hazard in some houses by allowing concentrations of unhealthy contaminants in the air to build up. The risks associated with different levels of pollutants are poorly understood. Nor is much known about the health effects of these pollutants when they combine. Experts tend to agree that even in a tight house indoor air pollution will not become serious unless the house has heavy smokers, a portable kerosene heater, particle board (in furniture, cabinets, or floors, for example) or extensive new carpets, poorly vented gas stoves, ovens, or furnaces, or radon present in the soil or masonry.

Indoor pollution raises two general concerns. First, the average person spends about 16 hours a day at home, most of it indoors. As a result, exposure to indoor air pollutants can be significant. Second, many pollutants are odorless and colorless, even in high concentrations. Thus their presence often goes undetected.

UNDERSTANDING THE PROBLEM

The concentration of air pollutants in indoor air generally depends on how fast air flows through the house and how quickly pollutants are released. Air moves through an average house at a rate sufficient to empty and refill it every forty to sixty minutes. In a tightly constructed new home this cycle may take two hours or more. This does not mean all the air in the house is replaced. There may be pockets of dead air in certain areas, where pollutants can accumulate in higher concentrations. The building industry measures this rate of infiltration and ventilation in "air changes per hour." Most experts think that a complete air change every two hours (or one-half air change per hour) is sufficient to maintain healthy air in an average house.

If you weatherstrip and caulk your house conscientiously, filling all the gaps and cracks you can see, you are unlikely to reduce your infiltration rate below this recommended level of one-half air change per hour. In cases such as this, indoor air pollution is not likely to be a serious problem unless the sources of the pollutants are particularly severe. If you have house doctors pressurize your house with a blower door, make sure they have been professionally trained and the blower door is calibrated to determine the exact level of weatherizing that permits a safe number of air changes per hour.

Tightening up your house has significant energy and comfort benefits. To avoid problems with indoor pollutants, it is important to learn something about them, where they come from, and how to prevent them from building up. Box 4-7 explains how to detect the presence of these substances. The following pollutants are present in many houses and merit concern.

Formaldehyde. Formaldehyde is a chemical used extensively in binding agents or as a fungicide and preservative in many products. It is in plywood, new carpets, floor coverings, particle board, and many other household items. Particle board and wall-to-wall carpeting are the biggest sources. These materials give off formaldehyde gas. The rate of emission declines in time; within one to five years, half the gas has been exhausted. Formaldehyde is also a product of combustion and is emitted when gas appliances are in use.

Formaldehyde gas causes skin and eye irritation, nausea, and lethargy in most people at high concentrations and in some individuals at low levels. Long-term effects from slight exposure are suspected but not proved. Urea-formaldehyde foam, common in mattresses and furniture, gives off formaldehyde gas if not mixed or cured properly. In

BOX 4-7
HOW TO MEASURE HARMFUL POLLUTANTS

Most products and services for detecting pollutants are designed for industry, but a few are available for residential use. Formaldehyde monitors are available from:

Occupational Health and Safety Products
3M Center
St. Paul, MN 55144

This monitor is placed in the home for a 24-hour period and then sent back to 3M for diagnosis. The cost of this monitor is $35.

Radon monitors are available from:

Terradex Corporation
460 N. Wiget Lane
Walnut Creek, CA 94598

There is one monitoring service for pollutants in the home environment that will measure radon, formaldehyde, carbon monoxide, and pesticides such as chlordane. This nonprofit research center, called the National Indoor Environmental Institute, will send you information about indoor pollutants to help you decide what needs to be monitored. Then, for $100, they will send you monitoring equipment and instructions for its use. In return you get a full analysis of the results, a confidential report of the results, and telephone assistance on how to reduce the amount of any pollutants you find. Of the total fee, half covers the cost of equipment; the remaining half for the analytical services is tax deductible as a charitable contribution for medical and scientific research. This was the only organization performing this service at the time of publication. Their address is:

National Indoor Environmental Institute
5200 Butler Pike
Plymouth Meeting, PA 19462

1982 the Consumer Product Safety Commission banned its use as an insulating material. This ban has been overturned by the courts, though, and the product is still on the market. Most experts recommend not insulating walls with urea-formaldehyde foam: There are several safe and effective alternatives that do not pose a hazard to your health.

Combustion Products. Wood stoves, kerosene heaters, gas appliances, cigarettes, and cooking oils emit fine particulates, unburned hydrocarbons, oxides of nitrogen, formaldehyde, and carbon monoxide. Even though there are no indoor air quality standards, it is known that nitrogen dioxide levels indoors can exceed health standards established for outdoor air.

Gas appliances that must be vented to the outside (water heaters, clothes dryers, furnaces) do not contribute to indoor air pollution when properly installed. The unvented gas cooking stove is the biggest offender in most houses. The gas stove produces nitrogen oxides and carbon monoxide, which can cause headaches and dizziness at low concentrations and result in nausea or vomiting at higher levels.

Tobacco smoke is the most important source of particulates and complex hydrocarbons in homes occupied by smokers. A growing number of studies suggest that tobacco smoke affects the health of nonsmokers who are exposed to others' smoking.

Portable kerosene heaters have increased in popularity because of their ability to heat one room without the expense of heating the entire house. Several states have banned their use in residences, though, because these heaters can produce quantities of carbon monoxide, carbon dioxide, and nitrogen dioxide that exceed outdoor air quality standards.

Solvents and Cleaning Agents. Aerosol sprays, harsh cleaners, and other household chemicals can cause headaches, depression, rashes, eye injuries, nausea, and other symptoms, particularly if used excessively or improperly. The average American household contains forty-five aerosol products, which contain chemical substances that can cause diverse health problems, particularly for sensitive people. In some cases, the toxicity of these chemicals is not known.

Radon. Radon is a naturally occurring, chemically inert, radioactive gas found in soil, brick, concrete, and groundwater (though rarely). It is not in all these materials everywhere, however, or in the same concentrations. Most building materials are not significant sources of radon, with the exception of building materials made from mine tailings. Higher levels of radon in soils are known to exist in parts of Florida, Maine, Montana, New Hampshire, Colorado, Pennsylvania, and some parts of Texas. Because radon concentrates in ancient geological features such as old streambeds, one house may have high levels of radon while another next door or a block away will not.

Where radon is present in soils, it infiltrates into the house where it decays to another radioactive byproduct. These decay products can attach to airborne particulates (dust, smoke) and, in turn, lodge in the lungs. While high concentrations of radon are rare, the effect of long-lerm, low-level exposure is an increased risk of lung cancer.

Asbestos. Asbestos was once a commonly used insulating material for hot water plumbing and duct work, and it was incorporated into ceiling tiles and plastering and spackling compounds. Some materials containing asbestos become brittle with age and can crack and flake off, releasing asbestos fibers into the air. Asbestos has been linked to lung cancer in workers who were exposed to it. The general public's exposure level to asbestos is not well known, but it appears to be low. Nevertheless, repair or replacement of plumbing, duct work, ceilings, or other areas insulated with material containing asbestos can increase your exposure.

There are several ways to control indoor air pollution. The following tips illustrate ways of protecting yourself without sacrificing energy savings:

1. Use a fan above your gas stove during cooking. If it is a fan that merely recirculates air, replace it with a fan or hood that vents directly to the outside. A fan that exhausts the air above a gas stove will remove 60 to 85 percent of the gaseous pollutants from your kitchen. If your kitchen does not have a vent, consider installing one or a range hood that leads to the outside.

2. Use household chemicals sparingly and with adequate ventilation or use them outside or in the garage if possible. Be especially careful with caustic sprays such as oven cleaners. Use safe chemicals or chemical substitutes where available. The *Household Pollutants Guide* describes the problems with many

BOX 4-8
HEAT EXCHANGERS

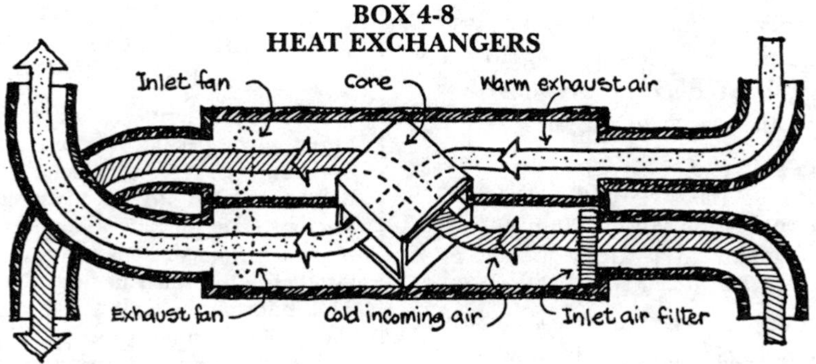

The technical solution to the trade-off between indoor air pollution and energy savings is an air-to-air heat exchanger. Heat exchangers exhaust indoor air and bring in outside air simultaneously. Most models are able to recover about 85 percent of the heat from the outgoing air. The unit can also cool incoming air in the summer.

Air-to-air heat exchangers can be attached to a wall or window in much the same way as an air conditioner. These exchangers are easy to install and plug into a 110-volt standard outlet. Another type of exchanger is integrated into the house's heating and cooling ducts if you have a warm-air furnace. These models are more expensive.

Heat exchangers are widely used in Japan, Europe, and Canada; most are manufactured in these countries but are available in the United States. Prices range from about $100 for a room-size heat exchanger to $400 to $700 for a larger unit.

For sources of information on air-to-air heat exchangers, see the section on Indoor Air Quality in the references at the end of the book. For a list of equipment available in the United States and Canada, write to:

Heat Exchangers
Ventilation Program,
Building 90-3058
Lawrence Berkeley Laboratory
University of California
Berkeley, CA 94720

household substances and suggests alternatives. (See the references at the end of the book.)

3. Never use a portable kerosene space heater or an unvented gas space heater in an unventilated space.

4. Confine tobacco smoking to a room that can be easily ventilated.

5. Install an air-to-air heat exchanger (see Box 4-8).

6. If you plan to modify old plumbing, duct work, or ceilings, contact your local health or building official to see if asbestos was used. If it was, it might be best to leave it alone (if it is not cracking, peeling, or flaking) or to isolate it further if you can by covering it tightly with a sheet of plastic or heavy coats of paint. If it requires work, wear a mask and goggles and seal off areas of the house on which you are working.

7. Controlling radon requires attention to detail. If the source of the radon is soil in the crawl space, some experts suggest covering the soil with a sheet of plastic. Take care that the soil is thoroughly covered and there are no gaps or tears in the plastic. You can also increase ventilation in the crawl space, although the effectiveness of this measure will depend on your local climate. If you can locate a major source of radon in, for example, a basement sump, you can ventilate that area. If none of these measures are feasible and you are certain you have a radon problem, buy an air-to-air heat exchanger to increase ventilation rates while recovering up to 80 percent of the heat in the air.

8. There are several particulate control devices on the market, but take care in selecting one. Recent studies show that the tabletop fan-filters are not effective in reducing particulate concentrations. More expensive devices that use a fan and high-efficiency filter or an electrostatic precipitator (an "electronic air cleaner") are more effective. Prices range from $150 to $400.

9. Some filters that absorb formaldehyde are on the market, but their effectiveness has yet to be proved. Ventilation is one of the best ways to reduce formaldehyde gas levels in the air, but use an air-to-

air heat exchanger if foam insulation is the source of the problem. Some heat exchanger cores appear to transmit certain gases from the outgoing to the incoming airstream, thus reducing the effectiveness of the unit, although research in the area is still incomplete.

In the long run, consumer education may be the best approach to reducing indoor air pollutants. If you're careful in selecting and purchasing home products and furnishings, you can minimize the sources of the pollutants. Sensible use of gas appliances and household cleaning products will reduce the concentrations of the pollutants they emit in your house. Your local health office and building inspector should know whether the local soil or building products contain radon or if the materials in the house might contain asbestos. If they can't answer your questions, urge them to do the research necessary to find out.

Working with a Contractor

A competent and reliable contractor will help make your project a smooth one. Equally important, a conscientious professional will assure that you get high-quality work. Improperly installed materials will erode your energy benefits . . . and dollar savings. If the job is not completed correctly and the contractor doesn't care about his or her reputation, there will be very little you can do to get your money back. Your vulnerability underscores the need to take the time to select a contractor carefully.

The information in this section will help you select and work with a contractor on Level I energy investments. At the end of Chapter 8, we've included additional information about hiring a general contractor and selecting an architect for a more extensive project.

FINDING A CONTRACTOR

Finding a trustworthy contractor takes care and research. You've probably heard the rule about getting three bids and checking references. It's important advice, but it won't completely protect you. Box 4-9 offers valuable tips for hiring a contractor.

Start looking for a reputable insulation contractor with your friends. Word-of-mouth references, if they are based on experience, can reduce the amount of time you spend interviewing contractors. If your friends can't help, contact your utility. Utilities that perform audits often compile lists of contractors for their customers. If your utility can't help, look in the Yellow Pages under "Insulation Contractors."

Most contractors will perform Level I projects for an amount fixed in advance. The bid should list the measures involved, such as wall insulation, attic insulation, or duct insulation. It should also list the R-value to be installed and the total R-value to be attained. The costs of measures such as wall and

BOX 4-9
EIGHT RULES FOR HIRING A CONTRACTOR

1. Prepare a written description of your project, listing each specific task and indicating material requirements. Be sure to include the date the job is to be completed. Present the same list to each contractor so that the bids are based on identical information. Make sure the level of insulation to be installed is specified in both R-value and inches. This information will allow you to corroborate claims of performance for specific materials.
2. Get a written description of the work to be performed and the material used, along with the dollar amount of the bid.
3. Get references from each contractor that responds—and *call* them. Ask if the contractor completed the work on time, cleaned up well, and performed the job accurately and thoroughly.
4. Make sure the contractor is licensed by the appropriate city, county, or state authorities. The contractor should be bonded and insured.
5. Be wary of claims about tax benefits or warnings that they'll soon expire. To check on current credits and measures that qualify, contact your state energy office, your utility, the state taxing authority, the Internal Revenue Service, or the office of your representative in Congress.
6. Watch out for salespeople or contractors who say they represent a utility company. It's not very likely. Check with the utility or ask to see their utility identification card.
7. Expect an accurate assessment of your present insulation, but avoid contractors who resort to scare tactics.
8. Steer clear of salespeople and contractors who make exaggerated claims about savings. If someone predicts exorbitant increases in the cost of energy, ask for documentation and compare it to the price increases you've already experienced.

attic insulation should be expressed on a per-square-foot basis; this will help you compare competing bids.

BEFORE YOU SIGN THAT CONTRACT

Don't make an initial payment until you have received a written contract providing details of the work to be performed and materials to be used and have checked the contractor's references. The contract should specify the quantity of material to be used (the number of rolls of fiberglass batting or bags of insulation, for example), where it will be used, how it will be installed, and the R-value to be achieved. If the contractor uses loose-fill insulation, insist on material certified by Underwriters Laboratories (UL) or the National Association of Home Builders (NAHB) Research Foundation for quality and fire-retarding ability.

The contract should also indicate whether the contractor is to repaint, if necessary, and clean up. It should include a guarantee that extends long enough for you to determine that the job was completed to your satisfaction.

Most contractors will need a down payment on the job to pay for materials. This is a standard practice. Remember to save a generous portion of the payment until after the project has been completed and you have inspected it.

Keep a watchful eye on the progress of your job if you can. This will help guarantee performance as promised. If loose insulation is used, count the number of empty bags to see that all the material you paid for was used, make sure the UL or NAHB Research Foundation certification is on the bags, and check to see that the insulation is evenly distributed and there are no gaps.

After the job is complete, go through your written contract and make sure that everything the contractor agreed to do was completed to your satisfaction.

Chapter Five
The Economics of Level I: Case Studies

The Economics of Level I: Case Studies

How much energy—and money—can you save? Depending on your goals, the answer influences your choice of measures and the order in which you do them. This chapter presents nine energy conservation case studies that show the energy savings that result from installing Level I measures in seven different climates. Seven of these case studies are for single-family detached houses and two are for row houses.

These case studies give you rough estimates of costs and savings for a package of energy-saving measures. They are based on fuel use in different regions of the country and on average national energy costs and house size. The analysis for the case studies was done with the Computerized Instrumented Residential Audit, a computer program developed at the Lawrence Berkeley Laboratory in California. We have correlated these findings with actual experiences involving energy conservation measures in homes.

These case studies should help you in several ways. First, they show you the savings possible from different measures in different climate zones. Second, they illustrate which measures deserve priority and suggest the kinds of savings the entire package of measures can deliver. Finally, the case studies allow you to weigh the savings from a particular measure against its cost.

About the Case Studies

Each case study has five parts: (1) a description of the house, energy prices, and climate zone; (2) before and after graphs of utility bills; (3) a list of conservation measures that can be installed in the house; (4) average contractor-installed costs for those measures and the annual savings that result from their installation; (5) notes to help adapt the case study to your situation.

The heart of each case study is the list of recommended energy conservation measures for the model house. The measures are listed in order of cost effectiveness—those that provide the highest dollar return come first. The cost-effectiveness ranking of a measure is based on how well it performs over a ten-year period. Over this period we assume a modest increase in energy costs greater than the rise in inflation, so your savings are likely to be more. Your own energy use may vary by as much as two times that in the case study, yet the priorities do not change significantly.

Most of the recommendations are Level I measures, but some case studies also include measures from Level II (see Chapter 6) when they are important to the conservation strategy in the model house and when they can be cost competitive with the basic conservation measures. This is the case, for example, in houses with electric water heating. Furnace replacement is another Level II measure that appears in these case studies.

Each case study lists the annual percentage of heating, cooling, or water heating energy saved by each measure. Each savings estimate assumes that the higher priority measures have been installed. Thus you can add the percentages to estimate your total savings from a package of projects. If you have already completed some of the high-priority measures, your percentage savings will not change.

In addition to the list of recommended cost-effective measures, each case study offers alternatives enclosed in brackets. These alternatives help

ANATOMY OF A CASE STUDY

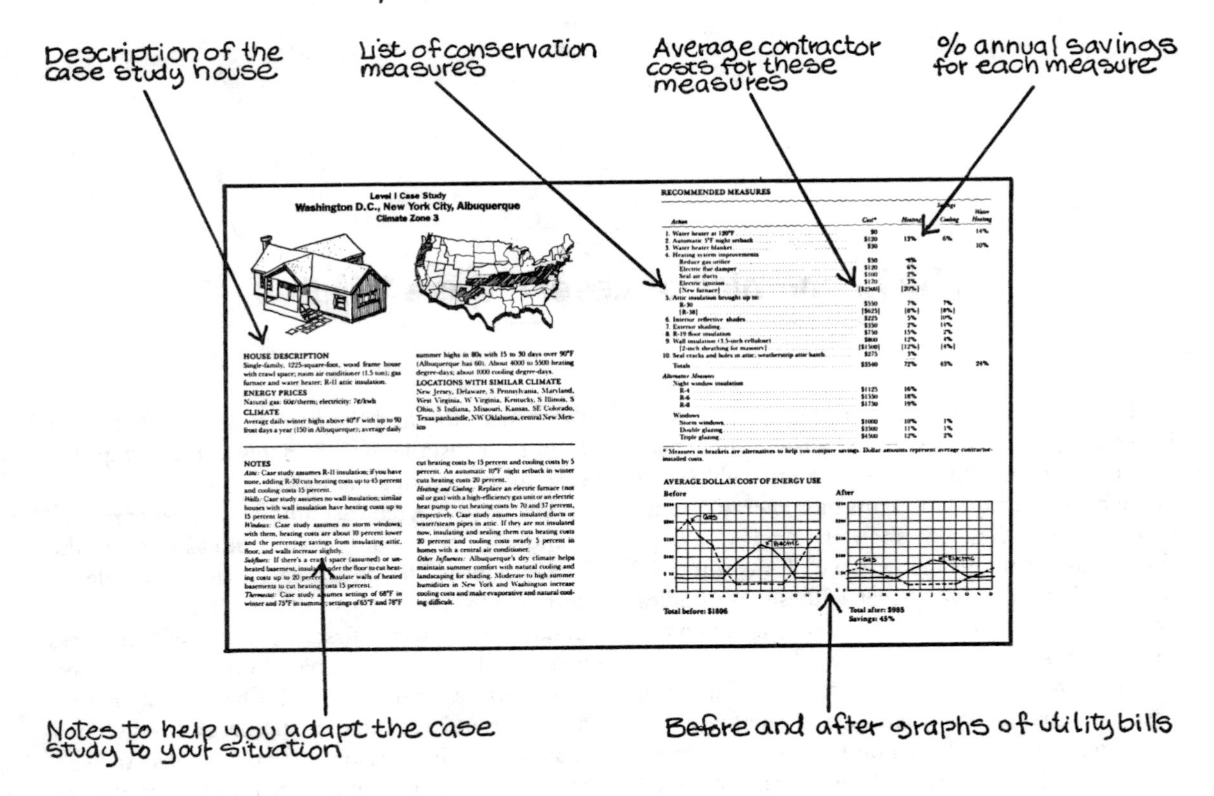

you gauge how savings will change if, for example, you add more or less attic insulation or make investments in addition to those completed in the model house.

If you have less attic or roof insulation than the levels assumed in the case studies and your fuel costs are higher, consider adding more than the recommended levels. Often it pays to add 25 to 50 percent more insulation than the recommended level. Compare your potential savings to local costs of installing the thick insulation.

The model house in the first seven case studies is a detached, 1225-square-foot, one-story wood frame structure. The model for the final two case studies is a two-story row house with basement. The row house has 1225 square feet of living space. Heating systems vary from climate zone to climate zone. Since your house is certain to differ from the model houses, we have included notes that explain the chief ways in which costs and savings change for different types of houses. Lifestyle and personal habits may be the biggest influence on how much your savings vary from those in the case studies.

There are some common assumptions in these case studies. We assume, at the outset, that families heat to 68°F day and night and cool to 75°F in the summer in places where cooling is needed. Savings from lowering or raising your thermostat an additional amount during the heating or cooling season are noted. If your thermostat is set higher for heating or lower for cooling, your savings are correspondingly greater.

The case studies also assume that the total window area is 224 square feet for the detached house and 112 square feet for the row house. Windows have an average fit—they are snug, with no cracks, and do not rattle. Loose windows use 2 to 4 percent more heating. Whenever 2 percent of your total winter heating bill exceeds the cost of installing window weatherstripping and caulking throughout the house, you should install it on loose-fitting windows.

CASE STUDY ASSUMPTIONS

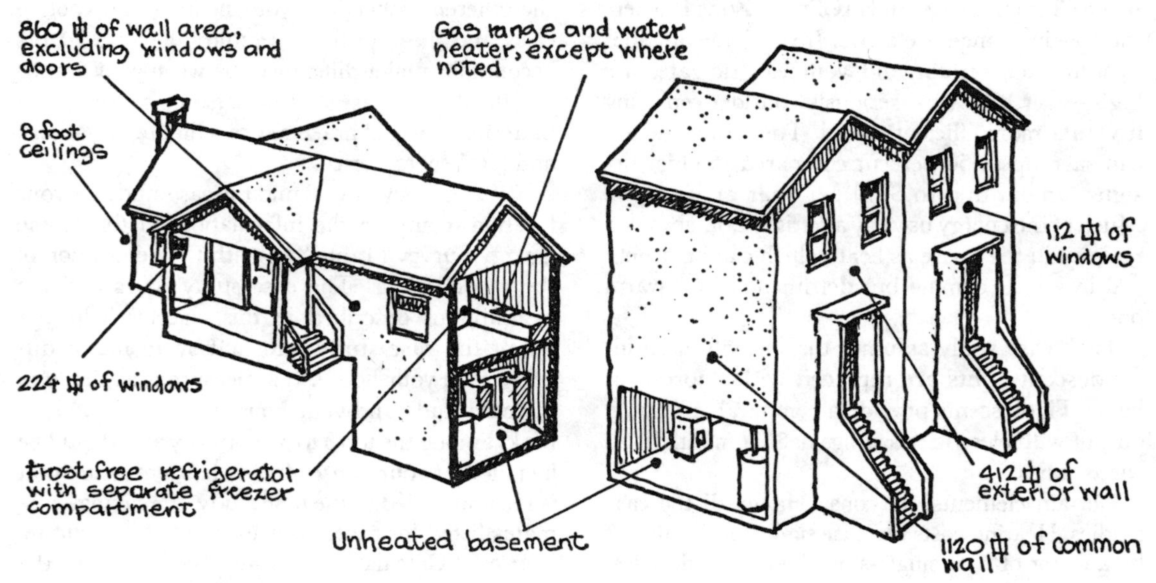

Ceilings are 8 feet high. The detached house has approximately 860 square feet of wall area excluding windows and doors. The row house has 412 square feet of exterior wall area and 1120 square feet of common wall area. If the model house has a basement, it is unheated. Heated basements should be insulated in all but the warmest climates.

The case studies assume that heating and cooling systems are maintained annually, that filters are changed every year, that air conditioner compressors are cleaned annually, that refrigerant is checked routinely, and that all distribution pipes or ducts are insulated. If you haven't done these maintenance measures recently, do them now. They reduce heating costs by 3 to 5 percent and cooling costs from 2 to 3 percent. Insulating ducts saves up to 20 percent on both heating and cooling. We assume that gas pilot lights are turned off after the heating season, saving between $2 and $5 per month or from 1 to 2 percent on heating bills. These case studies do not consider heat loss from fireplaces. In most climates, a glass screen saves up to 5 percent on heating bills if you don't have a tight-fitting damper.

Oil and gas boilers and furnaces are assumed to have a steady-state efficiency of 70 percent and flue temperatures of 350°F. For every 1 percent your furnace or boiler departs from the efficiency of the model house, you can roughly estimate that you are using another 1 percent more or less energy to heat your house.

Even if your furnace or boiler has been tuned up, consider additional efficiency measures. Because most furnaces and boilers are larger than necessary to heat the house efficiently—especially after conservation improvements have been made—reducing the size of the gas orifice or oil burner nozzle and adding a flue damper and electric ignition is generally advisable and can save up to 10 percent of your annual heating bill.

Most of the case studies assume a gas water heater and gas range, so the baseline gas use includes both. The energy used for heating water is generally 80 to 90 percent of the total in these months. The case studies assume that you have already installed flow restrictors in the faucets and shower. Potential savings can be as high as 20 percent but average 5 to 10 percent. If you invest in a new furnace or boiler that also heats water, your water heating savings can be as high as 40 percent.

The model houses have a frost-free refrigerator with a separate freezer unit, an electric dryer, and gas cooking range except in the Minneapolis, Albany, Cheyenne case study (Climate Zone 1) where the cooking range is electric. If you have an older frost-free refrigerator and your electric rates are high—over 15¢/kwh—seriously consider replacing it with a more efficient model. The newer models can save up to 50 percent compared to older designs, amounting to $130 per year at 15¢/kwh. Much of the energy used by a refrigerator, however, remains in the house as heat, which can be beneficial in a cold climate but detrimental in a warm one.

Each case study assumes that heavily used incandescent lights are replaced with fluorescent lights. Fluorescents provide a comparable lighting output with electricity savings of $6 a month in all case studies.

Certain elements are consistent in all the case studies: Heating costs increase significantly, almost by a factor of 2, as single-story house size doubles; increases in hot water use are proportionate to the number of people in the family (case studies assume a family of four); annual percentage of savings for space heating from building envelope improvements is roughly the same regardless of the fuel and heating system. The larger the ratio of window to floor area, the more important are window treatments, but the more costly they are to install.

Making the Case Studies Work for You

Which measures should you select? How much should you spend? The case studies are another tool to help you find the right combination of Level I investments to meet your personal goals. What you now spend for heating and cooling is the baseline for projecting savings from various conservation measures. Chapter 3 showed you how to compute your annual heating and cooling costs by using a twelve-month record of fuel and utility bills. Retrieve that number (or go back and do the calculations now), for it enables you to translate the information in the case studies to your situation.

To use the case studies, follow these steps:

Step 1: Find the case study that most closely matches your climate. Comparing your utility bill graphs to the graphs in the case studies also helps you recognize similarities in climate. Look for the size of your peaks and note when they occur, observe how they vary from year to year, and look at the differences between your heating and cooling costs and those in the case study. Diverse factors account for major differences between your graphs and those in the case studies: personal consumption patterns, house characteristics, climate variations, and local energy prices.

Step 2: Once you've found the case study for your location, compare the information on the Home Energy Survey (Table 3-2) with the description of the model house. The case study notes and the assumptions described in this chapter help you adapt the case study information to major differences in your house. If a measure is assumed in the case study and your house does not have it, it ranks among the top 3 to 5 in priority and should be installed. If your house already has a measure that is recommended in the case study, the savings estimates listed for other measures are still accurate.

Step 3: Calculate the annual savings from the measures you are considering by adding the percentages for heating, cooling, or water heating and then multiplying the total by your annual cost for these uses. Your annual costs should be on the Home Energy Survey and Checklist (Table 3-2).

These percentage estimates need to be adjusted for differences in your house. The notes you made as part of step 2 can help you do this. Keep in mind, too, that the case study estimates are average; your home's performance probably falls within a range of 20 percent above or below the case study estimates.

Step 4: Estimate your total costs. The cost of installing each measure is given in each case study as a rough guide, but to be precise you should rely on a contractor's estimate or on your own estimates derived from the costs in Chapter 4. The costs in the case studies represent average contractor estimates, including labor, for the model house. Check these costs against local prices, which can vary widely.

If you plan to do your own installation, the costs are much less—in fact, labor can account for 50 percent or more of installation costs. You can also use the information in Chapter 4 to estimate the cost and amount of materials needed for your house. If you do the work yourself, you can accomplish more for the same dollar investment. Because your expenses are less, many more measures pay back in energy savings.

HOW TO USE THE LEVEL I CASE STUDIES

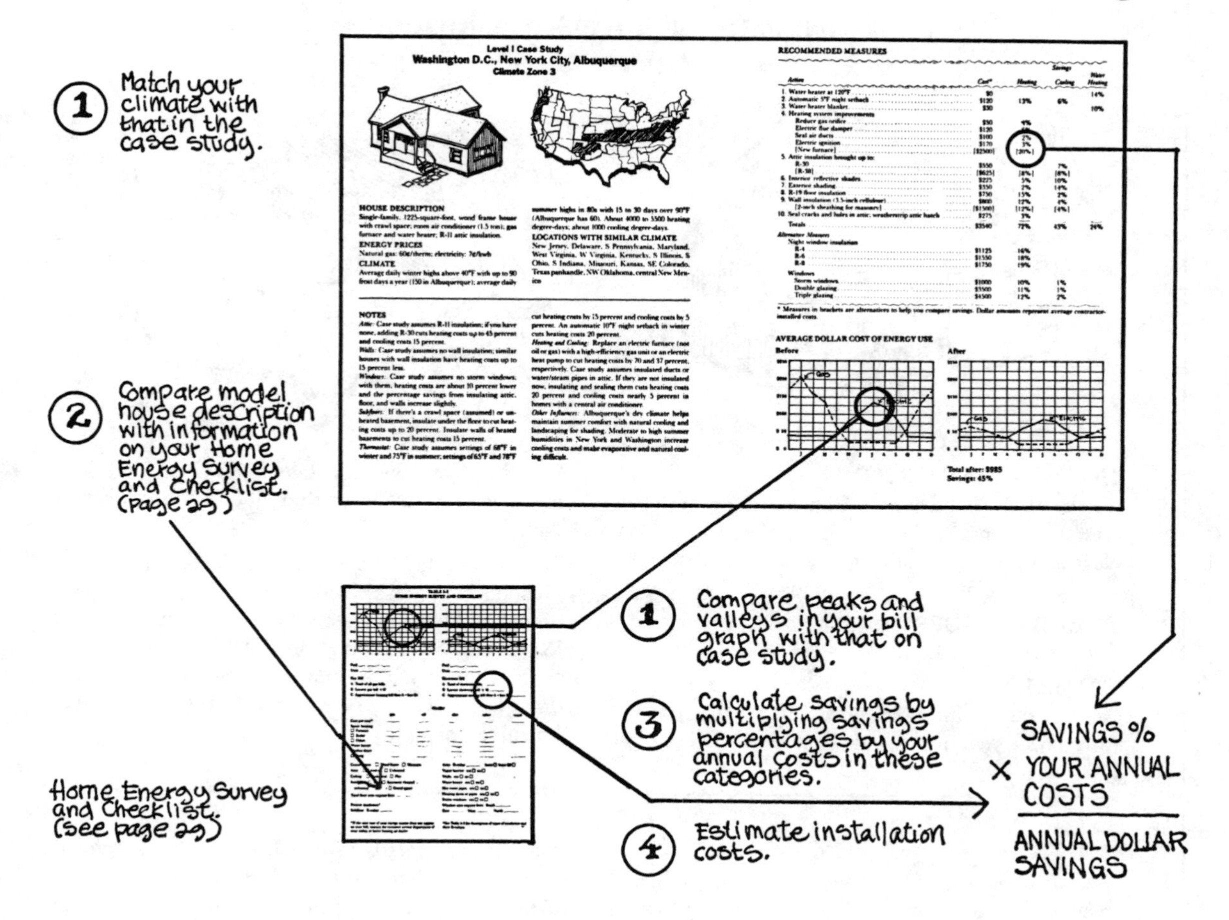

1 Match your climate with that in the case study.
2 Compare model house description with information on your Home Energy Survey and Checklist. (Page 29)
Home Energy Survey and Checklist. (see page 29)
1 Compare peaks and valleys in your bill graph with that on case study.
3 Calculate savings by multiplying savings percentages by your annual costs in these categories.
4 Estimate installation costs.
SAVINGS %
× YOUR ANNUAL COSTS
ANNUAL DOLLAR SAVINGS

Be sure to write down costs and annual savings estimates and the assumptions on which they were based. You may want to use these cost estimates in Chapter 9 when we evaluate the economic performance of your energy investments.

You now have an initial projection of both the costs and the savings of a package of measures for your house. Go through step 3 and 4 using different measures to get a sense of how costs and savings compare for different packages.

Some conclusions can be drawn here and now without going further. Is your total annual energy bill low in relation to the cost of the measures you are considering? Suppose, for example, you spend only $100 a year for heating and cooling. An investment of $3000 in energy conservation measures requires up to thirty years to pay itself back even if it eliminates heating and cooling bills entirely. But if you now spend $1500 a year to heat and cool, an investment of $3000 could be a very attractive proposition even if it reduces your fuel costs by only 20 percent.

If you have other goals, you may be willing to settle for savings that are less than the cost involved. Comfort, noise reduction, or energy self-reliance may be your motive for saving energy. If this is the case, consider including some of the additional measures in your package; these can yield significant savings but will not be as cost effective as the recommended measures.

If you view these measures simply as investments, the financial analysis in Chapter 9 will help you determine which set of measures best meets your investment criteria.

Level I Case Study
Minneapolis, Albany, Cheyenne
Climate Zone 1

HOUSE DESCRIPTION
Single-family, 1225-square-foot, wood frame house with basement; oil boiler with water distribution; electric water heater; no air conditioning; R-19 attic, R-11 wall insulation; storm windows.

ENERGY PRICES
Oil: 95¢/gallon; electricity: 7¢/kwh

CLIMATE
Average daily winter highs up to 30°F with up to 180 frost days a year; average daily summer highs in low 80s with 15 or fewer days over 90°F. Over 7000 heating degree-days; fewer than 1000 cooling degree-days.

LOCATIONS WITH SIMILAR CLIMATE
Upstate New York, Maine, New Hampshire, Vermont, W Massachusetts, N Michigan, N Iowa, Wisconsin, Minnesota, North Dakota, South Dakota, NW Nebraska, Montana, Wyoming, W Colorado, NE Nevada, N and E Idaho, N central Washington

---

NOTES

General: Case study assumes R-19 attic and R-11 wall insulation and storm windows; if they are not in place, adding them reduces your heating bills by 50 percent.

Attic: Case study assumes R-19; if you have R-11 or R-30, wall insulation, and storm windows, insulating to R-47 reduces heating costs by 11 and 4 percent, respectively.

Walls: Case study assumes R-11; if you have none but do have storm windows and R-19 attic insulation, adding R-11 reduces heating costs by 20 percent. Uninsulated masonry homes use about 30 percent more heating fuel than insulated wood frame houses or masonry houses with 2-inch wall sheathing.

Windows: Case study assumes storm windows; if they are not in place, adding them reduces heating costs 13 percent; triple glazing reduces heating costs up to 17 percent.

Subfloor: If you have an unheated basement or crawl space (as assumed), insulate floors; if your basement is heated, insulate walls to reduce heating costs up to 15 percent. Insulate around slab floors to cut heating costs 10 percent.

Thermostat: Reducing the winter setting from 68°F (assumed) to 65°F cuts heating costs 7 to 10 percent. A 10°F night setback lowers heating costs up to 20 percent.

Heating and Cooling: Replace an electric furnace (not oil or gas) with a high-efficiency gas unit or an electric heat pump to cut heating costs 28 to 35 percent. Case study assumes insulated ducts or water/system pipes in basement. Insulating them saves 5 percent in a water/steam system and 10 percent in an air system. Ducts in the basement lose about 5 percent less energy than ducts in the attic. The recommended measures reduce cooling costs about 20 percent.

Water Heating: Replace an electric water (not gas or oil) with solar or a heat pump. Locate heat pump in a place that doesn't freeze.

RECOMMENDED MEASURES

Action	*Cost**	*Savings*		
		Heating	*Cooling*	*Water Heating*
1. Water heater at 120°F	$0			14%
2. Automatic 5°F night setback	$120	7%		
3. Heating system improvements				
Reduce boiler water temperature	$50	4%		
New flame retention burner	$350	10%		
[Electric flue damper]	[$120]	[6%]		
[New boiler]	[$2500]	[20%]		[40%]
4. R-19 floor insulation	$750	20%		
5. Heat pump water heater	$1100			45%
[Solar water heater]	[$2500]			[45%]
[Water heater blanket]	[$30]			[10%]
6. Thoroughly seal cracks and holes in attic, floor, and walls; weatherstrip attic hatch and basement door	$650	8%		
7. Attic insulation brought up to:				
R-47	$700	8%		
[R-38]	[$525]	[6%]		
Totals	$3720	57%		59%
Alternative Measures				
Night window insulation				
R-4	$1125	8%		
R-6	$1550	10%		
R-8	$1750	11%		
Windows				
Interior plastic storm windows	$1000	5%		
Double glazing and present storm windows	$3500	12%		
Triple glazing and present storm windows	$4500	15%		
Two new insulating doors	$350	2%		

* Measures in brackets are alternatives to help you compare savings. Dollar amounts represent average contractor-installed costs.

AVERAGE DOLLAR COST OF ENERGY USE

Before

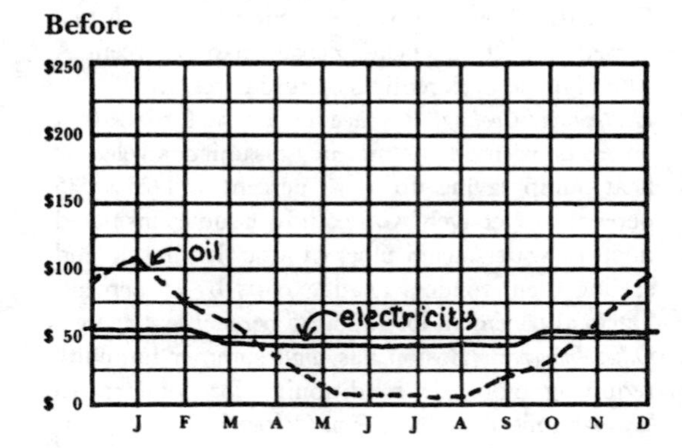

Total before: $2152

After

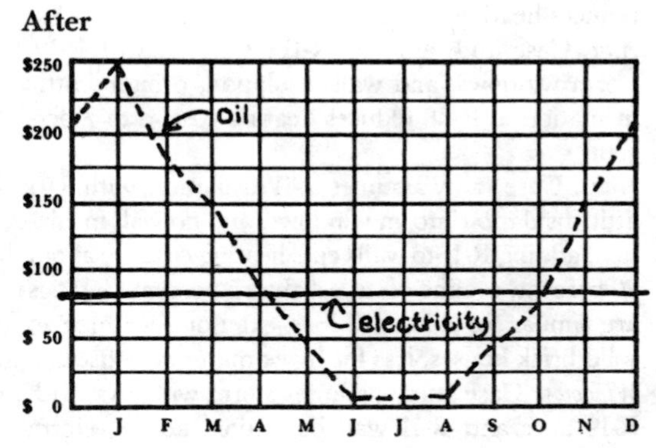

Total after: $1097
Savings: 49%

Level I Case Study
Chicago, Boston, Colorado Springs
Climate Zone 2

HOUSE DESCRIPTION
Single-family, 1225-square-foot, wood frame house with basement; room air conditioner (1 ton); gas furnace and water heater; R-11 attic, R-11 wall insulation; storm windows.

ENERGY PRICES
Natural gas: 60¢/therm; electricity: 7¢/kwh

CLIMATE
Average daily winter highs of 30–40°F with up to 180 frost days a year; average daily summer highs in mid-80s with up to 30 days over 90°F. About 5500 to 7000 heating degree-days; fewer than 1000 cooling degree-days.

LOCATIONS WITH SIMILAR CLIMATE
E Massachussetts, Connecticut, Rhode Island, S and W New York, N Pennsylvania, N Indiana, N Illinois, S Iowa, S Michigan, S Ohio, NW Kansas, Nebraska, NE Colorado, N New Mexico, N Arizona, NW and central Nevada, NE California and high Sierra, E Oregon, Utah, E Washington, central and W Idaho

---

NOTES

General: Case study assumes storm windows and R-11 attic and R-11 wall insulation; if lacking, adding them reduces heating costs up to 50 percent.

Attic: Case study assumes R-11 insulation; with R-19, storm windows, and wall insulation, bringing attic insulation to R-38 reduces heating costs 5 to 7 percent.

Walls: Case study assumes R-11 insulation; with R-11 attic insulation, storm windows, and no wall insulation, adding R-11 to walls cuts heating costs by about 20 percent, cooling costs less than 5 percent. Savings are similar for adding 2-inch exterior sheathing to solid brick houses, less for block masonry houses.

Windows: Case study assumes storm windows; with R-19 attic and R-11 wall insulation, adding storm windows cuts heating costs 10 percent; triple glazing reduces them up to 15 percent.

Subfloor: Insulate floor above heated basement or crawl space or insulate walls of heated basement to cut heating bills 15 percent.

Thermostat: Lowering winter setting from 68°F (assumed) to 65°F cuts heating costs up to 10 percent. A 10°F night setback reduces costs 15 percent.

Heating and Cooling: Replace an electric furnace (not oil or gas) with a high-efficiency gas unit or an electric heat pump saving up to 70 percent and 26 to 35 percent, respectively. Case study assumes insulated ducts or water/steam pipes in attic. Insulating and sealing them reduces heating costs by 15 percent. Ducts in basement lose about 5 percent less energy.

Other Influences: Boston has high summer humidity requiring more air conditioning for comfort. In lower-humidity areas such as Colorado Springs, natural and mechanical ventilation reduces air conditioning costs substantially.

RECOMMENDED MEASURES

Action	Cost*	Savings Heating	Savings Cooling	Savings Water Heating
1. Water heater at 120°F	$0			14%
2. Automatic 5°F night setback	$120	10%	10%	
3. Heating system improvements				
Reduce gas orifice	$50	4%		
Seal air ducts	$100	2%		
Electric flue damper	$120	6%		
Electric ignition	$170	2%		
[New furnace]	[$2500]	[20%]		
4. Water heater blanket	$30			10%
5. R-19 floor insulation	$750	23%		
6. Attic insulation brought up to:				
R-38	$625	12%	3%	
[R-30]	[$550]	[10%]	[2%]	
7. Thoroughly seal cracks and holes in attic and subfloor; weatherstrip attic hatch and basement door	$475	7%		
Totals	$2440	66%	13%	24%
Alternative Measures				
Night window insulation				
R-4	$1125	10%		
R-6	$1550	12%		
R-8	$1750	13%		
Two new insulating doors	$350	2%		
Interior plastic windows	$1000	7%		
Exterior shading or landscaping for all windows	$350		5%	
Windows				
Double glazing and present storm windows	$3500	12%		
Triple glazing and present storm windows	$4500	14%		

* Measures in brackets are alternatives to help you compare savings. Dollar amounts represent average contractor-installed costs.

AVERAGE DOLLAR COST OF ENERGY USE

Before

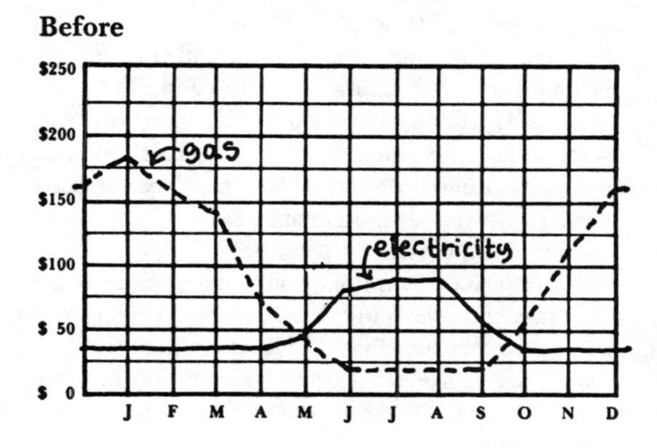

Total before: $1626

After

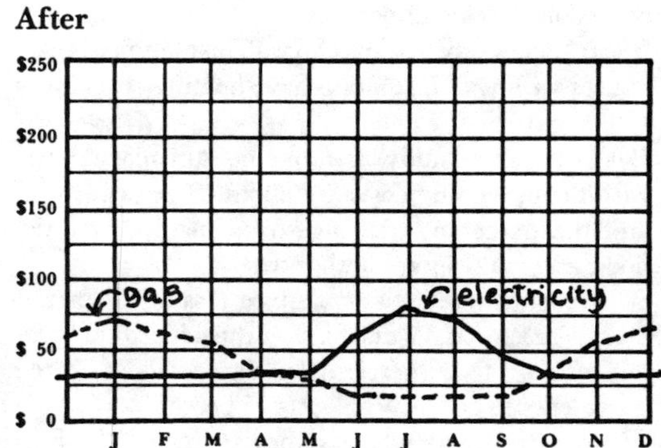

Total after: $980
Savings: 40%

Level I Case Study
Washington D.C., New York City, Albuquerque
Climate Zone 3

HOUSE DESCRIPTION
Single-family, 1225-square-foot, wood frame house with crawl space; room air conditioner (1.5 ton); gas furnace and water heater; R-11 attic insulation.

ENERGY PRICES
Natural gas: 60¢/therm; electricity: 7¢/kwh

CLIMATE
Average daily winter highs above 40°F with up to 90 frost days a year (150 in Albuquerque); average daily summer highs in 80s with 15 to 30 days over 90°F (Albuquerque has 60). About 4000 to 5500 heating degree-days; about 1000 cooling degree-days.

LOCATIONS WITH SIMILAR CLIMATE
New Jersey, Delaware, S Pennsylvania, Maryland, West Virginia, W Virginia, Kentucky, S Illinois, S Ohio, S Indiana, Missouri, Kansas, SE Colorado, Texas panhandle, NW Oklahoma, central New Mexico

---

NOTES
Attic: Case study assumes R-11 insulation; if you have none, adding R-30 cuts heating costs up to 45 percent and cooling costs 15 percent.
Walls: Case study assumes no wall insulation; similar houses with wall insulation have heating costs up to 15 percent less.
Windows: Case study assumes no storm windows; with them, heating costs are about 10 percent lower and the percentage savings from insulating attic, floor, and walls increase slightly.
Subfloors: If there's a crawl space (assumed) or unheated basement, insulate under the floor to cut heating costs up to 20 percent. Insulate walls of heated basements to cut heating costs 15 percent.
Thermostat: Case study assumes settings of 68°F in winter and 75°F in summer; settings of 65°F and 78°F cut heating costs by 15 percent and cooling costs by 5 percent. An automatic 10°F night setback in winter cuts heating costs 20 percent.
Heating and Cooling: Replace an electric furnace (not oil or gas) with a high-efficiency gas unit or an electric heat pump to cut heating costs by 70 and 37 percent, respectively. Case study assumes insulated ducts or water/steam pipes in attic. If they are not insulated now, insulating and sealing them cuts heating costs 20 percent and cooling costs nearly 5 percent in homes with a central air conditioner.
Other Influences: Albuquerque's dry climate helps maintain summer comfort with natural cooling and landscaping for shading. Moderate to high summer humidities in New York and Washington increase cooling costs and make evaporative and natural cooling difficult.

RECOMMENDED MEASURES

		Savings		
Action	*Cost**	*Heating*	*Cooling*	*Water Heating*
1. Water heater at 120°F	$0			14%
2. Automatic 5°F night setback	$120	13%	6%	
3. Water heater blanket	$30			10%
4. Heating system improvements				
Reduce gas orifice	$50	4%		
Electric flue damper	$120	6%		
Seal air ducts	$100	2%		
Electric ignition	$170	3%		
[New furnace]	[$2500]	[20%]		
5. Attic insulation brought up to:				
R-30	$550	7%	7%	
[R-38]	[$625]	[8%]	[8%]	
6. Interior reflective shades	$225	5%	10%	
7. Exterior shading	$350	2%	14%	
8. R-19 floor insulation	$750	15%	2%	
9. Wall insulation (3.5-inch cellulose)	$800	12%	4%	
[2-inch sheathing for masonry]	[$1500]	[12%]	[4%]	
10. Seal cracks and holes in attic; weatherstrip attic hatch	$275	3%		
Totals	$3540	72%	43%	24%
Alternative Measures				
Night window insulation				
R-4	$1125	16%		
R-6	$1550	18%		
R-8	$1750	19%		
Windows				
Storm windows	$1000	10%	1%	
Double glazing	$3500	11%	1%	
Triple glazing	$4500	12%	2%	

* Measures in brackets are alternatives to help you compare savings. Dollar amounts represent average contractor-installed costs.

AVERAGE DOLLAR COST OF ENERGY USE

Before

Total before: $1806

After

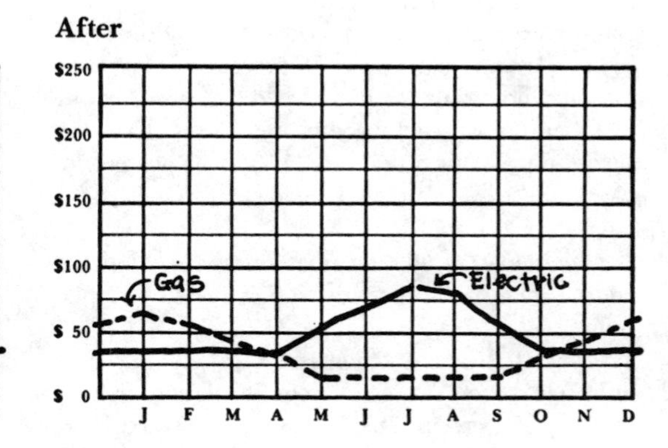

Total after: $985
Savings: 45%

Level I Case Study
San Francisco, Portland, Seattle
Climate Zone 4

HOUSE DESCRIPTION
Single-family, 1225-square-foot, wood frame house with crawl space; no air conditioner; gas furnace and water heater; R-11 attic insulation.

ENERGY PRICES
Natural gas: 60¢/therm; electricity: 7¢/kwh

CLIMATE
Moderate summer and winter temperatures; average daily winter highs in the 40s and 50s; average summer highs in the 70s and low 80s; very few days over 90°F. About 3000 to 5000 heating degree-days; fewer than 1000 cooling degree-days.

LOCATIONS WITH SIMILAR CLIMATE
Coastal N California, W Oregon, W Washington

NOTES

Attic: Case study assumes R-11 insulation; if you have none, bringing your attic up to R-30 will reduce heating costs 35 to 45 percent.

Walls: Case study assumes no insulation; adding R-11 reduces heating costs up to 15 percent. Uninsulated masonry homes use at least 5 percent more heating fuel than uninsulated wood frame houses. Two-inch sheathing cuts heating costs by 5 to 10 percent for block houses and up to 15 percent for solid brick houses.

Windows: Case study assumes no storm windows; adding them reduces your heating costs by 10 percent.

Subfloor: If there's a crawl space (as assumed) or unheated basement, R-19 floor insulation reduces costs by 15 percent. Insulate walls of heated basements to reduce heating costs by about 15 percent. Insulating the edge of slab floors cuts heating costs up to 10 percent.

Thermostat: Lowering winter setting from 68°F (assumed) to 65°F reduces heating costs by 20 percent. A 10°F night setback saves up to 35 percent.

Heating and Cooling: Case study assumes insulated ducts or water/steam pipes. If yours are uninsulated, insulating them will save up to 20 percent. Window shades and a ventilating fan can eliminate cooling needs.

Water Heating: Replace an electric water heater (not gas or oil) with solar or a heat pump to reduce water heating costs by 25 to 40 percent or 40 percent, respectively. Locate heat pumps in a place that doesn't freeze.

Other Influences: San Francisco's heating season is mild but long. For water heaters located in the living space, insulating blankets are a low priority unless the water heater is electric.

RECOMMENDED MEASURES

Action	Cost*	Savings: Heating	Savings: Cooling	Savings: Water Heating
1. Water heater at 120°F	$0			14%
2. Automatic 5°F night setback	$120	15%		
3. Heating system improvements				
Reduce gas orifice	$50	4%		
Electric flue damper	$120	6%		
Electric ignition	$170	3%		
[New furnace]	[$2500]	[20%]		
4. Water heater blanket	$30			10%
5. Attic insulation brought up to:				
R-30	$550	6%		
[R-38]	[$625]	[8%]		
6. R-19 floor insulation	$750	13%		
7. Wall insulation				
3.5-inch cellulose	$800	13%		
[2-inch sheathing for masonry]	[$1500]	[11%]		
8. Seal attic cracks and holes; weatherstrip attic hatch	$275	2%		
Totals	$2865	62%	—	24%
Alternative Measures				
Night window insulation				
R-4	$1125	16%		
R-6	$1550	19%		
R-8	$1750	21%		
Windows				
Storm windows	$1000	10%		
Double glazing	$3500	12%		
Triple glazing	$4500	14%		
Two new insulating doors	$350	2%		

* Measures in brackets are alternatives to help you compare savings. Dollar amounts represent average contractor-installed costs.

AVERAGE DOLLAR COST OF ENERGY USE

Before

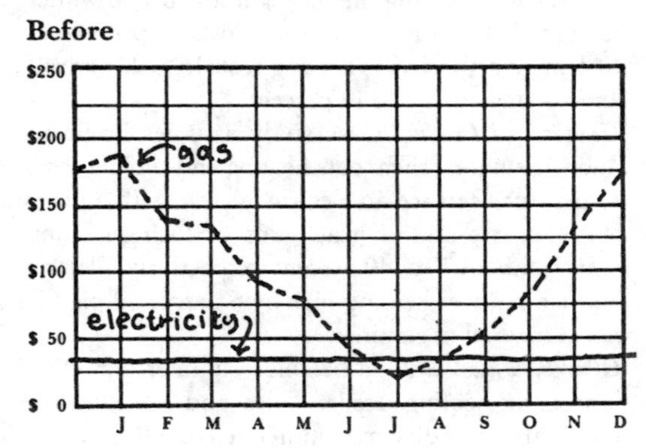

Total before: $1581

After

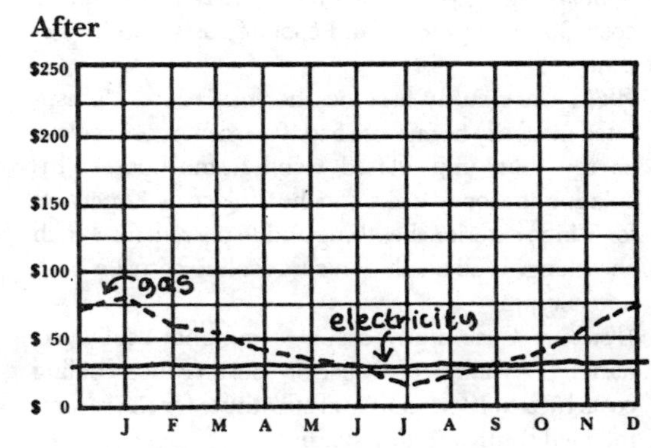

Total after: $906
Savings: 43%

Level I Case Study
Atlanta, Fresno, Tulsa
Climate Zone 5

HOUSE DESCRIPTION

Single-family, 1225-square-foot, wood frame house with crawl space; room air conditioner (2 ton); gas furnace and water heater; R-11 attic insulation.

ENERGY PRICES

Natural gas: 60¢/therm; electricity: 7¢/kwh

CLIMATE

Average daily winter highs in the 50s with fewer than 100 frost days a year; daily summer highs in 90s with 60 or more days over 90°F. About 2000 to 4000 heating degree-days; fewer than 2000 cooling degree-days.

LOCATIONS WITH SIMILAR CLIMATE

SE Virginia, North Carolina, N South Carolina, Tennessee, N Georgia, N Alabama, N central Oklahoma, SE and SW New Mexico, N central Texas, N Arkansas, central and S California excluding coastal areas

---

NOTES

Attic: Case study assumes R-11 insulation; if you have none, bringing your attic up to R-30 reduces heating costs 30 to 45 percent and cooling costs 5 to 10 percent.

Walls: Case study assumes no insulation. Uninsulated masonry homes use 5 to 10 percent more cooling energy than uninsulated wood frame houses. Insulating masonry walls cuts heating costs 12 percent for 2-inch exterior sheathing and 18 percent for 3-inch sheathing. Wall insulation cuts cooling costs for both house types.

Windows: Case study assumes minimal roof overhang. Overhangs of 2 feet or more reduce cooling costs by 5 to 10 percent and substitute for the recommended south window shading.

Subfloor: Case study assumes a crawl space. Houses with basements and slab floors use 10 to 15 more heating fuel; basements can be a source of cool air drawn into the house with a whole-house fan.

Thermostat: Lowering the setting from 68°F in winter (assumed) to 65°F cuts heating costs 15 percent. A 10°F night setback cuts heating costs 15 to 20 percent and cooling costs 5 to 10 percent.

Heating and Cooling: Case study assumes insulated ducts; insulating them cuts heating and cooling costs 15 percent. Replace an electric furnace with a high-efficiency gas unit or heat pump, reducing heating costs by about 70 or 40 percent, respectively. Electric ignition reduces heating bills by 6 percent if pilot is not turned off in summer.

Other Influences: Atlanta has high summer humidity, increasing cooling needs. Tulsa and Fresno have moderate humidity; recommended shading measures and natural and mechanical ventilation can eliminate air conditioning on all but the hottest days.

RECOMMENDED MEASURES

Action	Cost*	Savings: Heating	Savings: Cooling	Savings: Water Heating
1. Water heater at 120°F	$0			14%
2. Automatic 5°F night setback	$120	16%	10%	
3. Water heater blanket	$30			10%
4. Heating and cooling system improvements				
Reduce gas orifice	$50	4%		
Electric flue damper	$120	6%		
Seal air ducts	$100	3%		
Electric ignition	$170	3%		
[New furnace]	[$2500]	[30%]		
[New air conditioner]	[$2500]		[35%]	
5. Exterior shading or landscaping for all windows	$275	5%	8%	
6. Interior reflective shades	$225	4%	5%	
7. Attic insulation brought up to:				
R-30	$550	7%	3%	
[R-38]	[$650]	[8%]	[4%]	
Totals	$1640	48%	26%	24%
Alternative Measures				
Wall insulation		15%	3%	
Cellulose for wood frame walls	$800			
2-inch sheathing for masonry walls	$1500			
R-19 floor insulation	$750	10%	5%	
Windows				
Storm windows	$1000	8%	2%	
Double glazing	$3500	9%	2%	
Seal cracks and holes in attic and weatherstrip attic hatch	$275	3%		

* Measures in brackets are alternatives to help you compare savings. Dollar amounts represent average contractor-installed costs.

AVERAGE DOLLAR COST OF ENERGY USE

Before

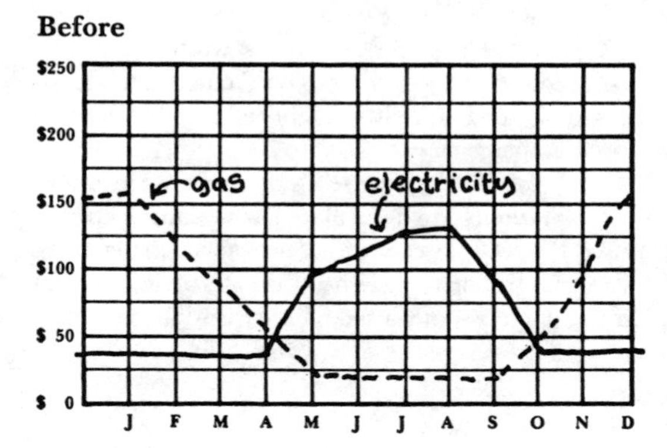

Total before: $1606

After

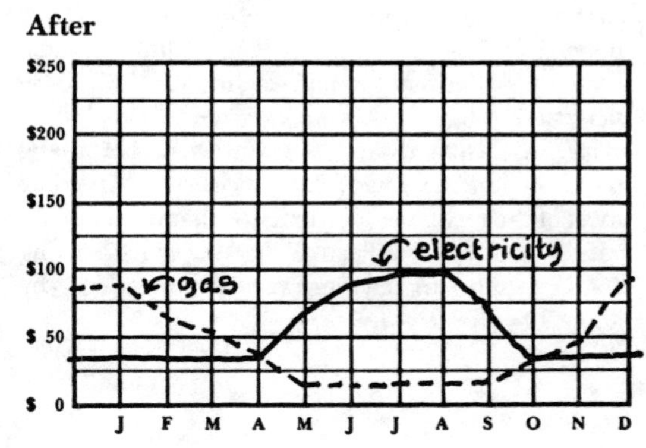

Total after: $1127
Savings: 30%

Level I Case Study
Los Angeles, Santa Ana, San Diego
Climate Zone 6

HOUSE DESCRIPTION
Single-family, 1225-square-foot, wood frame house with crawl space; room air conditioner (0.5 ton); gas furnace and water heater; R-11 attic insulation.

ENERGY PRICES
Natural gas: 60¢/therm; electricity: 7¢/kwh

CLIMATE
Average daily winter highs of 60–65°F with 10 or fewer frost days a year; average daily summer highs of 60–70°F with 30 or fewer days over 90°F. Fewer than 3000 heating degree-days; fewer than 1000 cooling degree-days.

LOCATIONS WITH SIMILAR CLIMATE
Coastal S California

NOTES
Attic: Case study assumes R-11 insulation; if you have none, bringing your attic to R-30 reduces heating costs up to 50 percent and cooling costs 10 to 30 percent.
Windows: Case study assumes minimal roof overhang (6–12 inches). Overhangs of 2 feet or more provide most of the recommended exterior shading for south windows. Interior reflective shades reduce heating costs by approximately 5 percent and cooling costs by about 10 percent.
Subfloor: Slab floors use 5 percent more heating energy but reduce cooling costs in summer.
Thermostat: Case study assumes winter setting of 68°F; lowering the setting to 65°F cuts heating costs up to 30 percent. A 10°F night setback cuts heating costs 25 percent.
Heating and Cooling: Case study assumes insulated ducts. If yours are uninsulated, insulating them will save 15 to 20 percent of heating and cooling costs. Electric ignition reduces heating costs up to 9 percent if pilot light is not turned off after heating season.

RECOMMENDED MEASURES

Action	*Cost**	*Savings* Heating	Cooling	Water Heating
1. Water heater at 120°F	$0			14%
2. Water heater blanket	$30			10%
3. Automatic 5°F night setback	$120	44%		
4. Heating system improvements				
Seal air ducts	$100	3%	7%	
Reduce gas orifice	$50	3%		
Electric flue damper	$120	3%		
5. Exterior shading or landscaping to keep sun from all windows	$350	5%	40%	
Totals	$770	58%	47%	24%
Alternative Measures				
Attic insulation to				
R-19	$550	7%	7%	
R-30	$650	10%	10%	
Wall insulation				
3.5-inch cellulose for wood frame walls	$800			
2-inch sheathing for masonry walls	$1300	10%	5%	
R-19 floor insulation	$750	10%	5%	

* Dollar amounts represent average contractor-installed costs.

AVERAGE DOLLAR COST OF ENERGY USE

Before

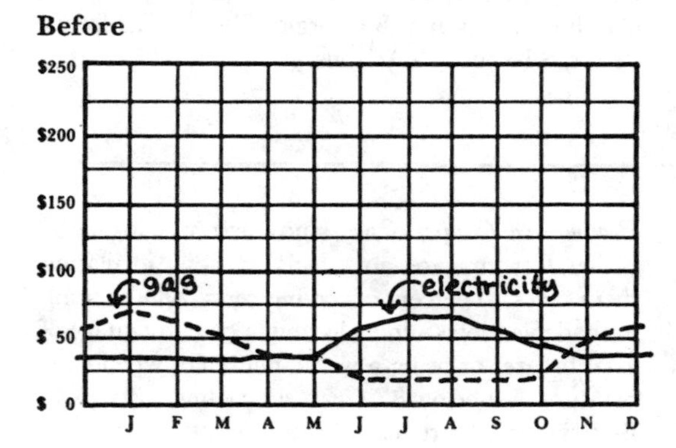

Total before: $1016

After

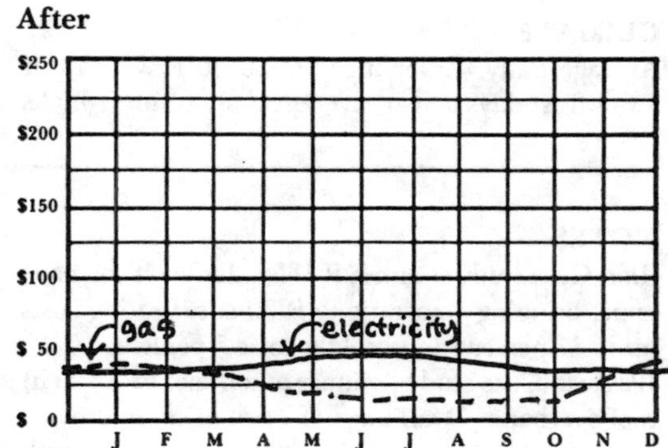

Total after: $722
Savings: 29%

Level I Case Study
Dallas, Miami, Phoenix
Climate Zone 7

HOUSE DESCRIPTION
Single-family, 1225-square-foot, wood frame house with crawl space; central air conditioner (2 ton); gas furnace and water heater; R-11 attic insulation.

ENERGY PRICES
Natural gas: 60¢/therm; electricity: 7¢/kwh

CLIMATE
Average daily winter highs of 50–70°F with 40 or fewer frost days a year; average daily summer highs in high 90s with up to 150 days over 90°F. Fewer than 2000 heating degree-days; more than 2000 cooling degree-days.

LOCATIONS WITH SIMILAR CLIMATE
Texas (except panhandle), SE Oklahoma, central and S Arkansas, Mississippi, S Alabama, S South Carolina, Louisiana, S Georgia, Florida, California desert, S Nevada, S Arizona

---

NOTES
Attic: Case study assumes R-11 insulation; if you have none, bringing your attic to R-30 cuts heating costs up to 37 percent and cooling costs 5 percent.
Windows: Case study assumes a nominal (6–12 inch) roof overhang. Overhangs of 2 feet or more provide most of the recommended exterior shading for south windows.
Subfloor: Case study has a crawl space; house can be cooled in summer by drawing in basement air with a whole-house fan.
Thermostat: Case study assumes winter setting of 68°F and summer setting of 75°F. Lowering winter setting to 65°F cuts heating costs up to 30 percent. Raising thermostat to 78°F in summer reduces cooling costs 15 to 20 percent.
Heating and Cooling: Case study assumes insulated ducts. If yours are not insulated now, insulating them saves 20 percent of cooling costs. Landscaping to shade windows and walls and taking advantage of local breezes or using a whole-house fan when temperatures are below 85°F can cut cooling costs 25%. Electric ignition reduces heating costs 2 percent if pilot is normally shut off in summer and up to 8 percent if pilot is left on through summer.
Water Heating: Insulate hot water pipes to reduce water heating costs 3 percent.
Other Influences: In Miami, almost no heating is required and heating system improvements are not recommended; insulate the ducts of central air conditioning systems.

RECOMMENDED MEASURES

Action	Cost*	Savings		
		Heating	*Cooling*	*Water Heating*
1. Water heater at 120°F	$0			14%
2. Automatic 5°F night setback	$120	22%	13%	
3. Water heater blanket	$30			10%
4. Heating system improvements				
Seal air ducts	$100	4%	2%	
Reduce gas orifice	$50	4%		
Automatic flue damper	$120	3%		
5. Interior reflective shade	$225	4%	5%	
6. Exterior shading or landscaping for all windows	$350	5%	30%	
[New efficient air conditioner]	[$2500]		[35%]	
Totals	$995	42%	50%	24%
Alternative Measures				
Attic insulation to R-30	$550	7%	3%	
Wall insulation		15%	3%	
3.5-inch cellulose for wood frame walls	$800			
2-inch sheathing for masonry walls	$1500			
R-19 floor insulation	$750	10%	3%	

* Measures in brackets are alternatives to help you compare savings. Dollar amounts represent average contractor-installed costs.

AVERAGE DOLLAR COST OF ENERGY USE

Before

$250
$200
$150
$100
$ 50
$ 0
J F M A M J J A S O N D
gas
electricity

Total before: $1536

After

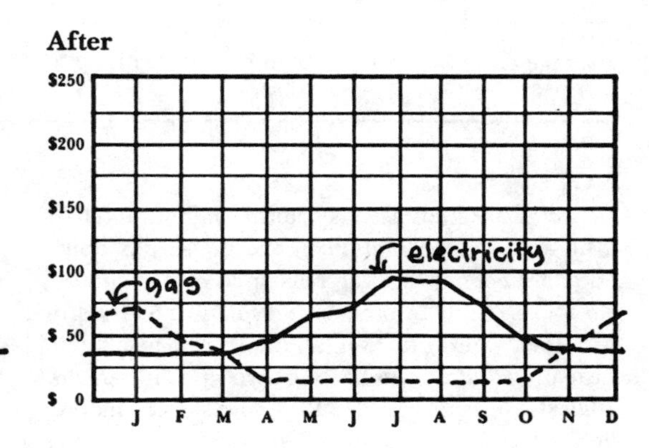

Total after: $1019
Savings: 33%

Level I Case Study
Cold-Weather Row House

HOUSE DESCRIPTION
Single-family, 1225-square-foot, two-story wood frame row house with basement; room air conditioner (0.5 ton); oil furnace and electric water heater; R-11 attic insulation; storm windows; common walls on east and west.

ENERGY PRICES
Oil: 95¢/gallon; electricity: 7¢/kwh

CLIMATE
Average daily winter highs of to 30–40°F with up to 180 frost days a year; average daily summer highs in mid-80s with up to 30 days over 90°F. Up to 7000 heating degree-days; fewer than 1000 cooling degree-days.

LOCATIONS WITH SIMILAR CLIMATE
E Massachusetts, Connecticut, Delaware, upstate New York, N Pennsylvania, Indiana, Illinois

---

NOTES
General: Case study assumes storm windows and R-11 attic and wall insulation; if the house has none, adding them cuts heating bills up to 60 percent.
Attic: Case study assumes R-11 insulation; with storm windows, wall insulation, and R-11 attic insulation, insulating to R-38 cuts heating costs up to 10 percent.
Walls: Case study assumes R-11; with storm windows and attic insulation, adding R-11 to walls cuts heating costs up to 10 percent. Insulating masonry homes with 2-inch exterior sheathing cuts heating costs up to 10 percent.
Windows: Case study assumes storm windows; adding them to houses without cuts heating costs 12 percent. Triple glazing reduces heating costs up to 15 percent.
Subfloor: Insulate floors above crawl spaces or unheated basement or insulate walls of unheated basements to cut heating costs 20 percent.
Thermostat: Lowering winter setting from 68°F (assumed) to 65°F cuts heating costs up to 20 percent. A 10°F night setback cuts heating costs more than 35 percent.
Heating and Cooling: Replace electric furnace with a new oil or gas unit if possible; a heat pump cuts heating costs 30 to 40 percent. Case study assumes insulated ducts or pipes in basement. Insulating them saves 5 to 10 percent (10 to 20 percent if the ducts are located in the attic).
Water Heating: Replace an electric water heater with solar or with a heat pump in a place that doesn't freeze. Do not replace gas or oil units with a heat pump.
Other Influences: Humid climates require more air conditioning. In dry climates, shading and ventilation will eliminate most cooling needs.

RECOMMENDED MEASURES

Action	Cost*	Savings: Heating	Savings: Cooling	Savings: Water Heating
1. Water heater at 120°F	$0			15%
2. Automatic 5°F night setback	$120	7%	10%	
3. Heat pump water heater	$1100			40%
[Active solar water heater]	[$2500]			[30–45%]
[Water heater blanket]	[$30]			[10%]
4. Thoroughly seal cracks and holes in attic, basement, and walls; weatherstrip attic hatch and basement doors	$400	15%		
5. R-19 floor insulation	$375	20%		
6. Heating system improvements				
Replace oil burner nozzle	$70	2%		
Seal air ducts	$100	3%		
Electric flue damper	$120	3%		
[New flame retention burner]	[$350]	[7%]		
[New furnace]	[$2500]	[20%]		[40%]
7. Attic insulation brought up to:				
R-38	$325	6%	2%	
[R-30]	[$275]	[5%]	[2%]	
Totals	$2610	56%	12%	55%
Alternative Measures				
New insulated north door	$175	3%		
Windows				
Interior plastic storm	$500	8%	2%	
Double glazing and present storm windows	$1750	13%	3%	
Triple pane and present storm	$2750	10%	3%	
Night window insulation				
R-4	$575	15%		
R-6	$750	18%		
R-10	$870	20%		
Summer exterior shades	$300		5%	

* Measures in brackets are alternatives to help you compare savings. Dollar amounts represent average contractor-installed costs.

AVERAGE DOLLAR COST OF ENERGY USE

Before

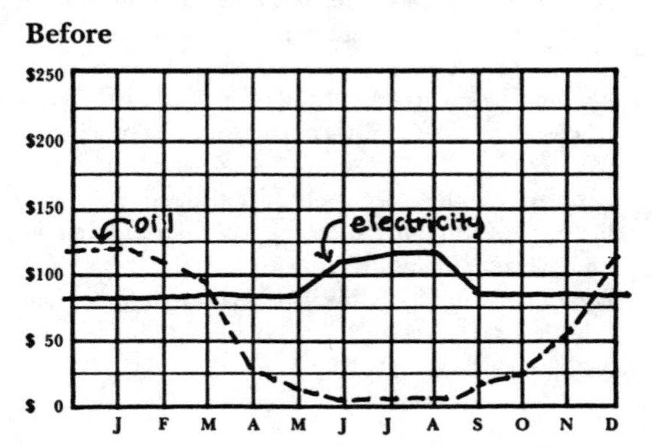

Total before: $1627

After

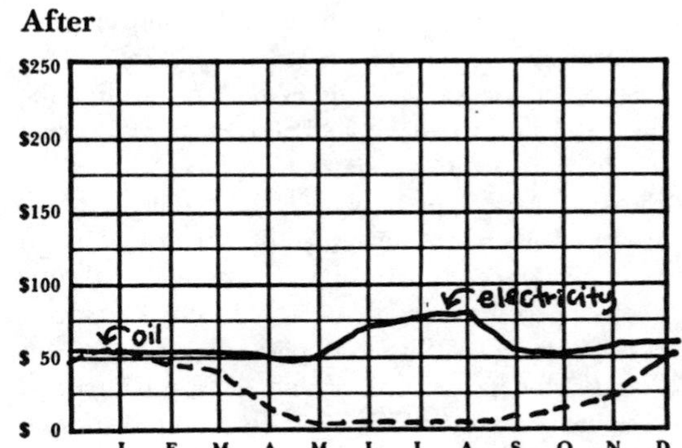

Total after: $939
Savings: 42%

Level I Case Study
Warm-Weather Row House

HOUSE DESCRIPTION
Single-family, 1225-square-foot, two-story wood frame house with basement; central air conditioner (2 ton); gas furnace and water heater; no attic insulation.

ENERGY PRICES
Natural gas: 60¢/therm; electricity: 7¢/kwh

CLIMATE
Average daily winter highs in the 50s with fewer than 100 frost days a year; average daily summer highs in the 90s with around 60 days over 90°F. About 2000 to 4000 heating degree-days; fewer than 2000 cooling degree-days.

LOCATIONS WITH SIMILAR CLIMATE
SE Virginia, North and South Carolina, Tennessee, N Georgia, Alabama

NOTES
Attic: Case study assumes no insulation; if you have R-11, adding to R-30 cuts heating costs 2 percent and cooling costs 1 percent.
Walls: Brick houses use 5 percent more heating fuel than uninsulated frame houses. Adding exterior sheathing cuts heating costs up to 5 percent.
Windows: Case study assumes no storm windows; they cut heating costs up to 8 percent. Remove them in summer in mild climates for ventilation; in hot climates, leave them in place to cut cooling costs.
Subfloor: If there's an unheated basement (assumed) or crawl space, floor insulation cuts heating costs about 5 percent. Insulate walls of heated basements to cut heating costs up to 10 percent.
Thermostat: Change settings from 68°F in winter and 75°F in summer to 65°F and 78°F to cut heating and cooling costs up to 10 percent.
Heating and Cooling: Replace electric furnace with gas or oil unit to cut costs up to 70 percent; a heat pump will cut costs up to 40 percent. Case study assumes insulated ducts or water/steam pipes in attic. Insulating them saves 5 percent in a water/steam system and up to 20 percent in an air system. If they're in basement or crawl space, savings are 3 and 10 percent, respectively. In warm climates, use a whole-house fan to draw cool air from the basement.
Water Heating: Replacing an electric water heater (not gas or oil) with solar or a heat pump reduces water heating costs about 40 percent. Locate heat pump in an area that doesn't freeze.
Other Influences: Use natural ventilation or fans when outside air is below 70°F in moderate-humidity areas such as Tulsa and Dallas.

RECOMMENDED MEASURES

Action	Cost*	Savings: Heating	Savings: Cooling	Savings: Water Heating
1. Water heater at 120°F	$0			14%
2. Automatic 5°F night setback	$120	10%	11%	
2. Furnace improvements				
Reduce gas orifice	$50	3%		
Seal air ducts	$100	6%	2%	
Electric flue damper	$120	6%		
Electric ignition	$170	3%		
[New furnace]	[$2500]	[30%]		
[New air conditioner]	[$2500]		[35%]	
4. Water heater blanket	$30			10%
5. Exterior window shading or landscaping	$350	2%	15%	
6. Attic insulation to:				
R-30	$275	5%	2%	
[R-38]	[$375]	[7%]	[2%]	
7. Seal attic cracks and holes; and weatherstrip attic hatch	$275	5%		
Totals	$1490	40%	30%	24%
Alternative Measures				
Wall insulation		8%		
3.5-inch cellulose for wood frame walls	$225			
2-inch sheathing for masonry walls	$750			
R-19 floor insulation	$675	6%		
Insulate hot water pipes	$100		1%	3%
Windows				
Storm windows	$500	6%	3%	
Double glazing	$1750	7%	2%	

* Measures in brackets are alternatives to help you compare savings. Dollar amounts represent average contractor-installed costs.

AVERAGE DOLLAR COST OF ENERGY USE

Before

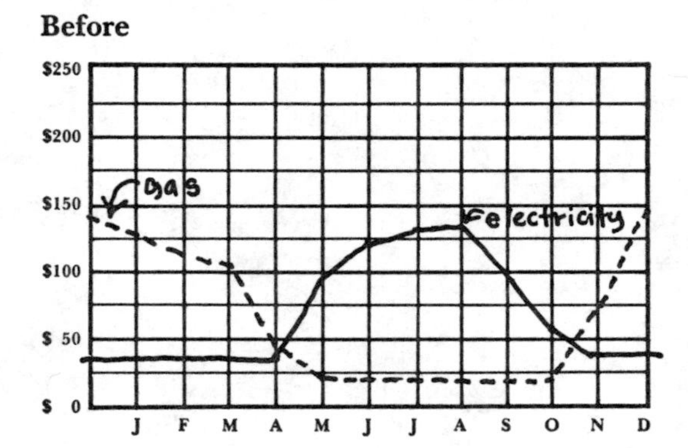

Total before: $1661

After

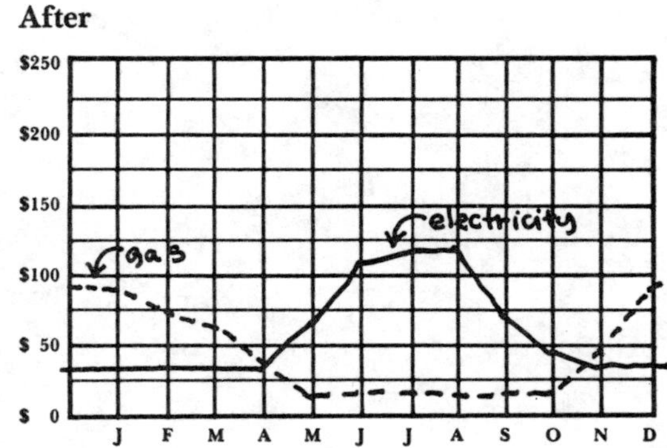

Total after: $1203
Savings: 28%

Chapter Six
Level II: Energy Investments

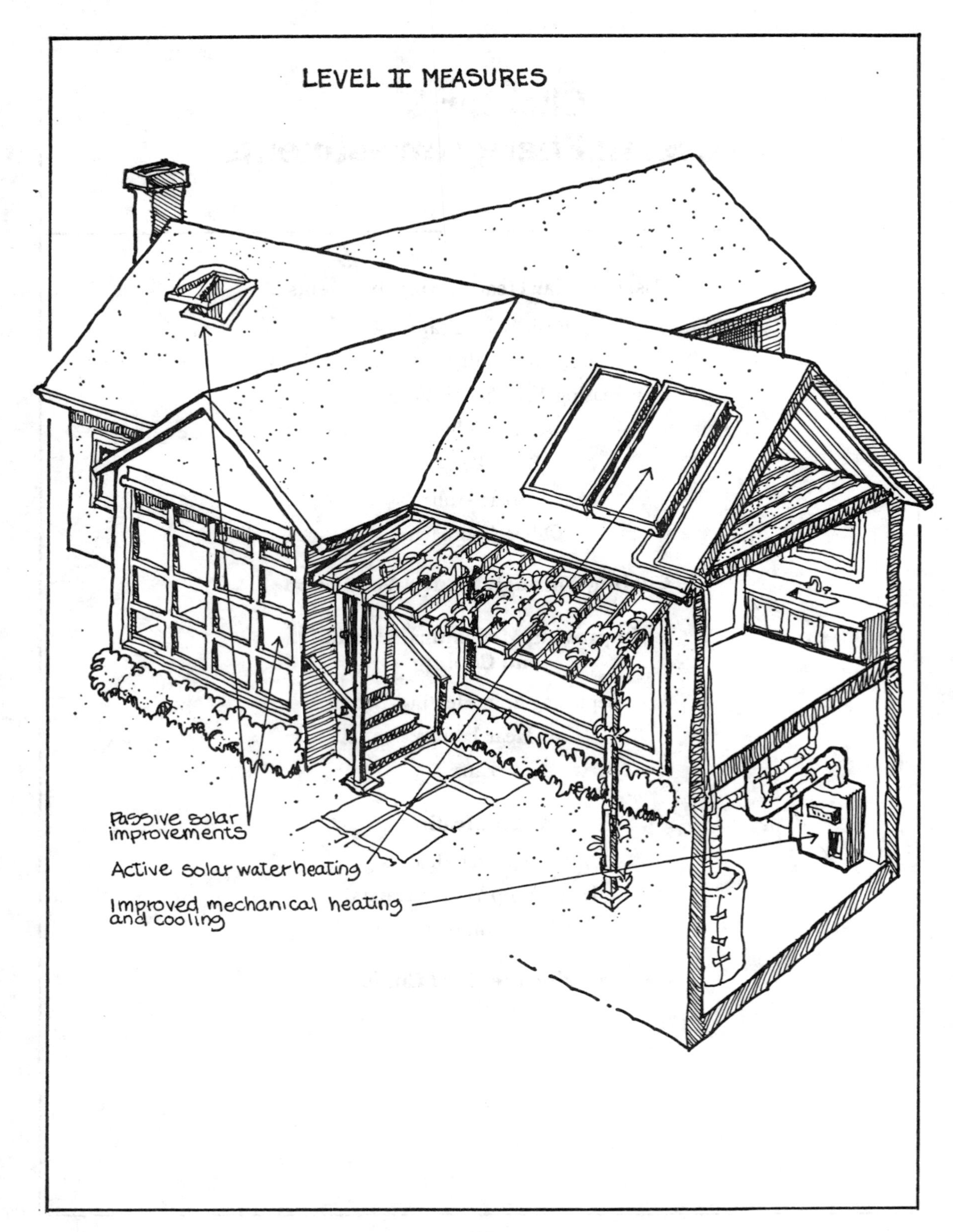
LEVEL II MEASURES
Passive solar improvements
Active solar water heating
Improved mechanical heating and cooling

Level II: Energy Investments

Once your house is more energy conserving as a result of Level I improvements, it's time to think about meeting your remaining energy needs through solar heating, reducing your heating fuel use by installing a high-efficiency furnace or boiler, and cutting your air conditioning needs by cooling with natural ventilation. These measures often require structural alterations to your home—but with careful planning they pay back in fuel cost savings, higher resale value, increased comfort, and greater satisfaction. If you plan to remodel, this chapter helps you recognize opportunities for energy savings.

Depending on your patterns of energy use and how many Level I measures you have completed, your energy-conserving house uses only 30 to 50 percent of the energy it previously used. Level II measures build on these savings; moreover, some actually *supply* energy to your home. Combining measures from Levels I and II can result in a house that uses only one-fifth to one-half the energy of a conventional house.

Level II energy investments are more expensive; most have an initial cost of over $1000. They require more time and planning. And your decisions are harder to make because they depend less on economics and more on personal values.

This chapter reviews solar heating, natural and mechanical ventilation, furnace and air conditioning replacement, and solar and heat pump water heaters. There are two basic types of solar heating methods: active and passive. Active solar energy systems rely on an external source of energy—such as electricity—to operate pumps or fans to move heated air or water from the area in which it is collected to the place it is stored and used. Active solar systems commonly use flat-plate solar collectors. In contrast, passive solar systems rely on natural convection, conduction, and radiation for the movement and storage of heated air or water.

The solar heating systems described in this book are referred to as passive, although in some cases air movement is assisted with a fan. Level II modifi-

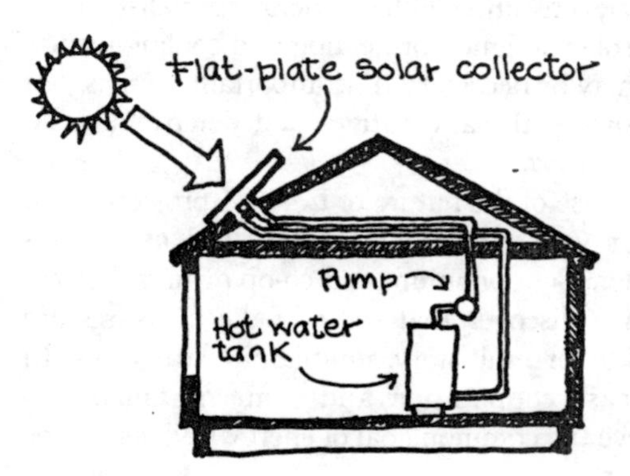

ACTIVE SOLAR WATER HEATING

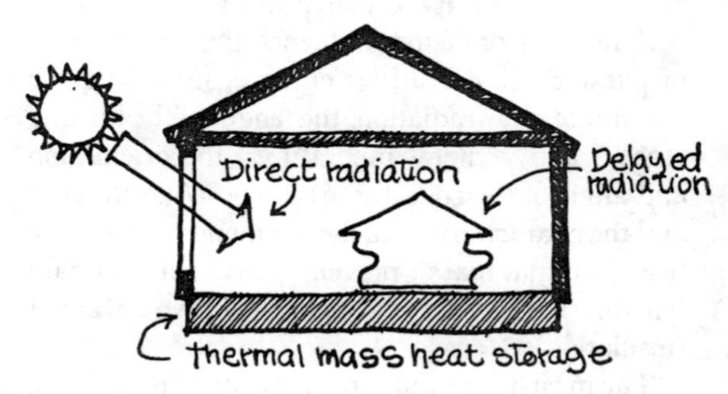

PASSIVE SOLAR SPACE HEATING

cations for passive solar heating include expanding your south window area, installing skylights, glazing in a porch, and adding low-cost, daytime collectors that can be mounted on the side of the house. Not included are active solar heating methods that use flat plates or other collectors. These methods are often hard to adapt to home renovations and are generally more complex and more expensive than passive solar approaches. Breakthroughs in system design, collector and storage efficiency, and collector cost may change the situation in the near future, however. For example, thin plastic film collectors are being developed that may cost only a fraction of many of today's designs. The last section of the chapter reviews both active and passive solar water heating techniques.

This chapter will help you decide which Level II investments are best for you, but this is only a starting point. You then have to determine your budget, calculate the extent of the changes you want to make, and select a contractor. Depending on your skills and time available to work on the project, consulting with an energy specialist, architect, solar designer, or heating and cooling technician may be necessary. The important thing is that you survey the alternatives and determine what works for *you*.

Because of the nature of Level II projects, most renters won't find much of practical use in this chapter. Condominium and co-op owners, however, may discover that some of the measures are suitable for multistory, multifamily structures. In this case cooperation and some organizing to achieve the common goal of energy savings will be necessary.

Passive Solar Heating Improvements

A number of factors influence the performance of passive solar heating: climate, including the amount of solar radiation, the length of the heating season, and winter temperatures; the orientation and angle of the collector area exposed to the sun; and the characteristics of the components that store heat (thermal mass), prevent unwanted heat gain (shading), and keep the heat where you want it (insulation).

The most important aspect of climate is *insolation*, or solar radiation. The amount of insolation your

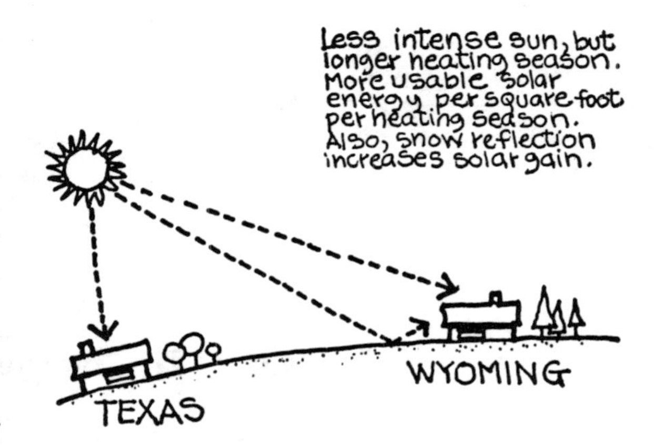

area receives during the heating season is determined by your latitude and by the extent of winter cloud cover. If you live at a high latitude, the sun's rays must travel a long distance through the atmosphere because of the earth's angle in relation to the sun. This distance diffuses the intensity of the solar radiation. If you live near the equator, the earth is more perpendicular to the sun's rays and has less atmosphere through which to travel, so more of the solar radiation strikes the earth's surface.

Less intense sun, but longer heating season. More usable solar energy per square foot per heating season. Also, snow reflection increases solar gain.
WYOMING
TEXAS
Intense sun, but short heating season. Less total solar energy per square foot per heating season.

Although northern latitudes have less total solar radiation than southern latitudes (in the Northern Hemisphere), high latitudes present excellent opportunities for solar heating. For example, the total solar energy received per vertical square foot in Wyoming's heating season is two to three times that received in southern Texas during its much shorter heating season. Even though the Texas sun is more intense, Wyoming's longer heating season offers a longer collection time and attractive solar potential. Moreover, snow on the ground—common in Wyoming and other northern states—increases solar gain by reflecting nearly twice as much sun into windows or collectors than bare ground or grass.

The high heating bills of cold areas definitely improve the economics of solar heating in some cases. Although solar heating systems meet a lesser percentage of total heating needs in these areas, dollar savings can be greater than for solar heating in more moderate climates. Offsetting this advantage, however, is the fact that cold temperatures cause considerable heat losses from windows and other solar collectors. In cold climates, an uninsulated south window can lose more heat at night than it collects during the day.

The insolation map (Table 6-1) gives levels of solar radiation received over the heating season for locations in the continental United States. Insolation maps take into account latitude, cloud cover, and other variables. The case studies in Chapter 7 use insolation levels to characterize the solar heating potential of the different climate zones.

BASIC SOLAR FEATURES

The relationship of a collector surface to the sun's path across the sky—called *orientation*—is important in determining solar heating potential and solar performance. The sun travels in an east-west arc. As the earth moves around the sun, it rotates on its axis, which always points toward the North Star. In winter, the axis points away from the sun, and the sun cuts a lower arc across the sky of the Northern Hemisphere. In summer, the sun is higher in the sky. This seasonal variation determines the orientation and angle of solar collectors.

Because the United States is in the Northern Hemisphere and the sun travels its east-west route in the southern part of the sky, collector surfaces must face south. The further from true south they are, the less energy they collect. A surface facing 45 degrees away from true south, for example, collects only 75 percent of the energy it would gather if it faced directly south.

The collector surface must not be shaded in winter. By observing the shadows on your house in winter you'll get an idea whether you're in the running for a solar heating project. The easiest way to determine how trees or buildings affect your solar heating potential is with a *sun path chart*, a simple device that allows you to identify obstacles in the sun's path during both summer and winter. Several books in the reference section explain how to make

TABLE 6-1
INSOLATION MAP OF THE UNITED STATES

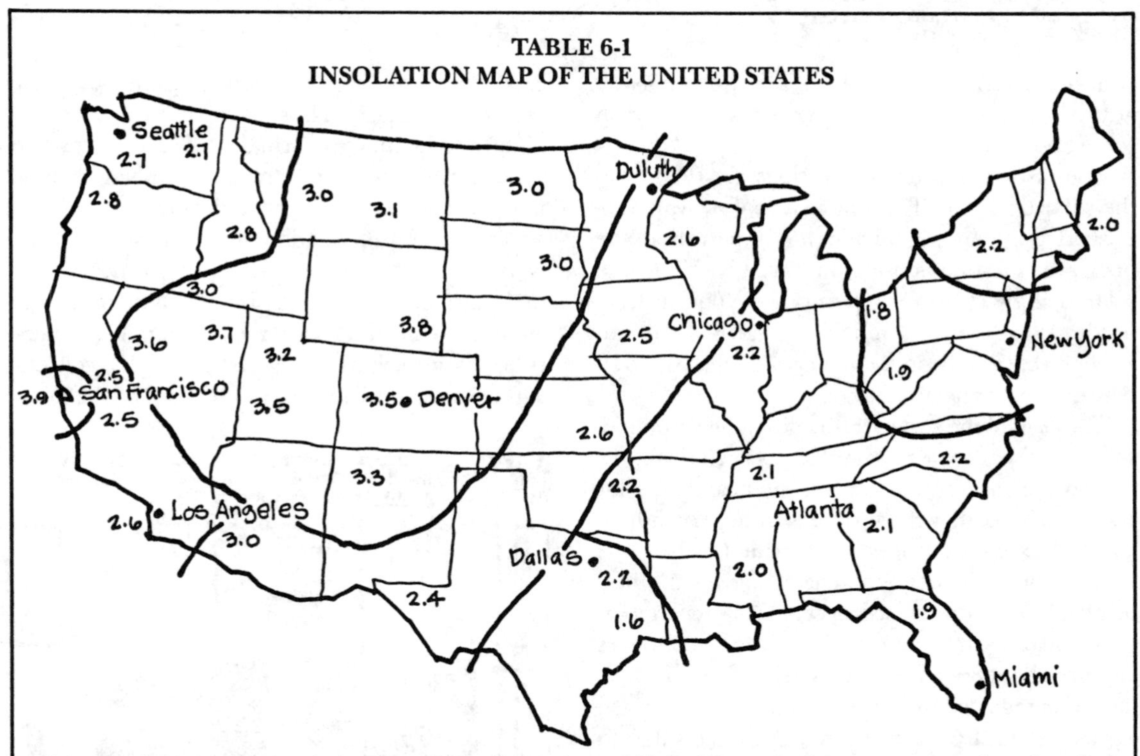

This map shows general insolation patterns for the continental United States, in therms per square foot of vertical surface area over the heating season. Variations in the length of the heating season throughout the country were taken into account. Insolation data are from the *Passive Solar Design Handbook*; heating-season lengths are from the case studies.

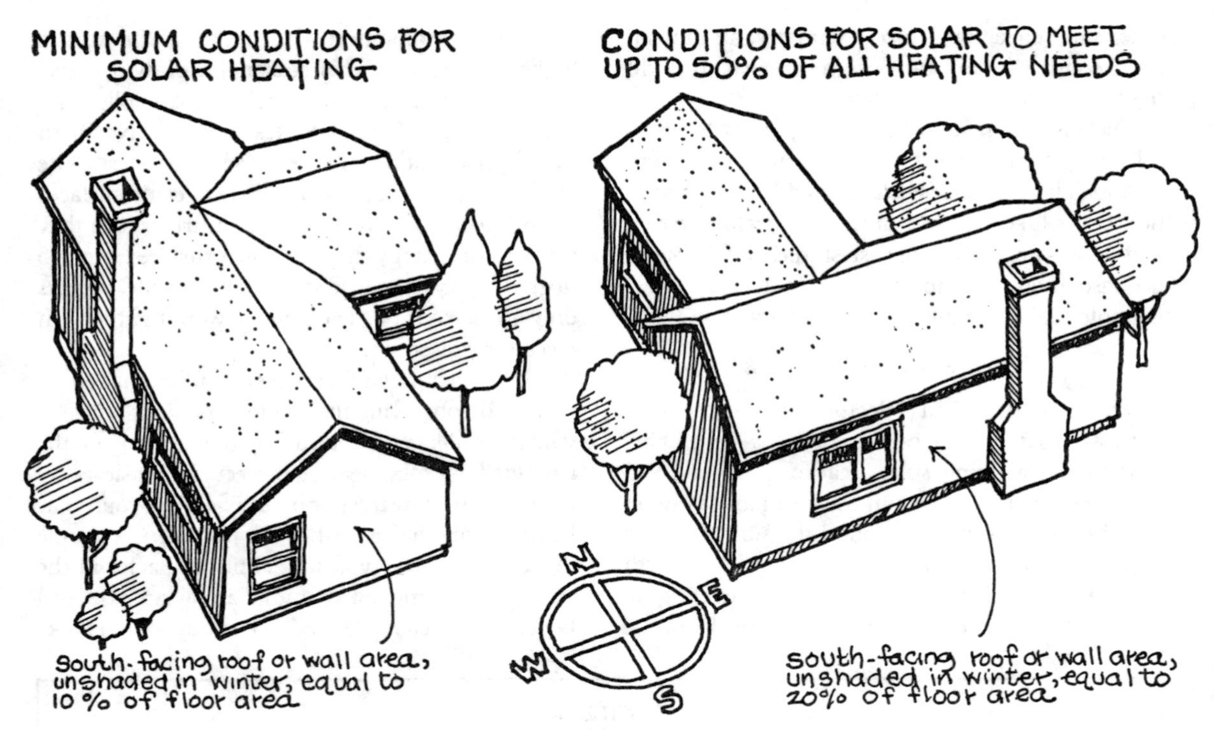

your own chart. Sun path charts are also frequently advertised in solar energy magazines and sold in some bookstores.

The results of your observations are the key to the solar decision. If you have a roof or wall area unshaded in winter equivalent to 10 percent of the floor area of your house, you may be able to use solar energy to meet a portion of your heating needs. With twice as much unshaded area, you may be able to rely on solar energy to meet up to 50 percent of your heating needs.

The *angle* of the surface also affects the amount of solar energy received. A surface perpendicular to the rays of the sun receives all the available solar energy. The further the surface is from perpendicular, the less energy strikes it. For winter heating, an angle of 50 to 65 degrees generally gives the best results, but windows used to catch solar energy for space heating are often vertical. Vertical surfaces capture about 80 percent of the winter sun (including some reflected from the ground) and are much easier to shade from the summer sun and insulate in the winter than angled surfaces.

Thermal mass is an essential part of many passive solar heating systems. The term refers to a material that absorbs heat, holds it, and then radiates it back as the surrounding air temperature drops below that of the mass. Thus it becomes a source of nighttime heating. Thermal mass also helps prevent overheating in solar homes by acting as a *heat sink*—absorbing excess heat during the day and preventing it from building up in a room.

Whether your solar heating system needs thermal mass depends on its size and how much you want it to contribute to home heating. As a general rule, passive solar heating systems with a collector surface area equivalent to 10 percent of the house

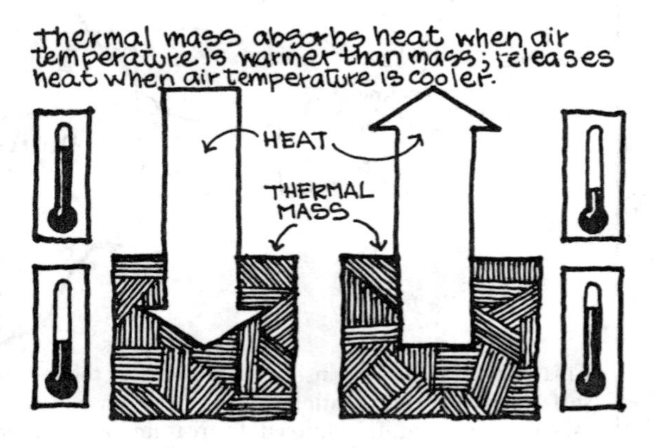

thermal mass absorbs heat when air temperature is warmer than mass; releases heat when air temperature is cooler.
HEAT
THERMAL MASS

HOW THERMAL MASS WORKS

floor area or less do not require thermal mass in excess of that normally present in the floor and walls in an average house. These designs simply do not capture enough solar heat to allow for carryover or to create overheating problems in winter. Systems designed to contribute more than 35 percent to home heating needs, however, should have additional thermal mass. The case studies in Chapter 7 indicate when a modification is likely to achieve a solar contribution of 35 percent and higher.

Thermal mass can be a brick or concrete floor, a wall, or containers filled with water. A recent technical advance is the development of "phase-change" materials that can store more heat per volume than water, rock, or masonry. Phase-change materials weigh less, posing fewer structural problems than traditional materials, but they cost considerably more.

Your choice for thermal mass depends on design, cost, and structural requirements. As a general rule, there should be 3 square feet of thermal mass, 3 to 6 inches thick, for every square foot of south-facing glass. Water is the best form of mass because of its cost, density, and heat capacity. It may be difficult, however, to design containers that can be attractively integrated into a house. Sometimes it is impossible to install thermal mass; shading and insulation then become increasingly important both to prevent heat loss and to protect against excessive heat gain.

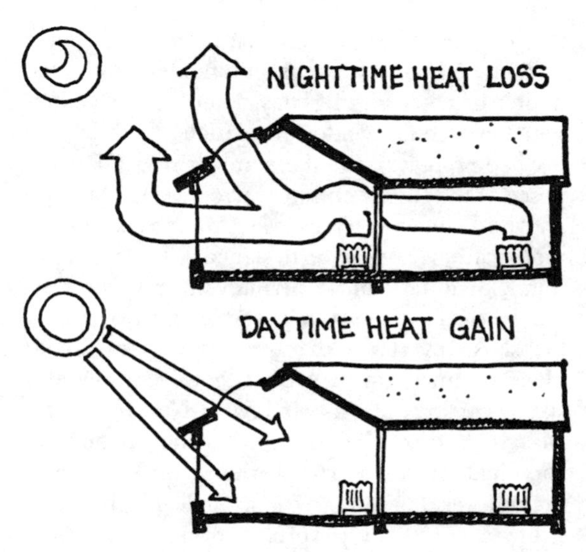

Window insulation is another essential component of a solar heating system. Unless large glass surfaces are insulated, they become avenues for heat loss at night and on cold days, wasting not only the heat gathered by the solar system but also the backup heat produced with conventional fuels.

In most climates an uninsulated or single-pane south-facing window, skylight, or solar wall results in nighttime heat losses equal to 50 to 100 percent or more of daytime heat gains. Most solar projects should include night insulation of at least R-4 in the form of panels, shutters, or thermal curtains, unless the collector area is part of a porch or greenhouse

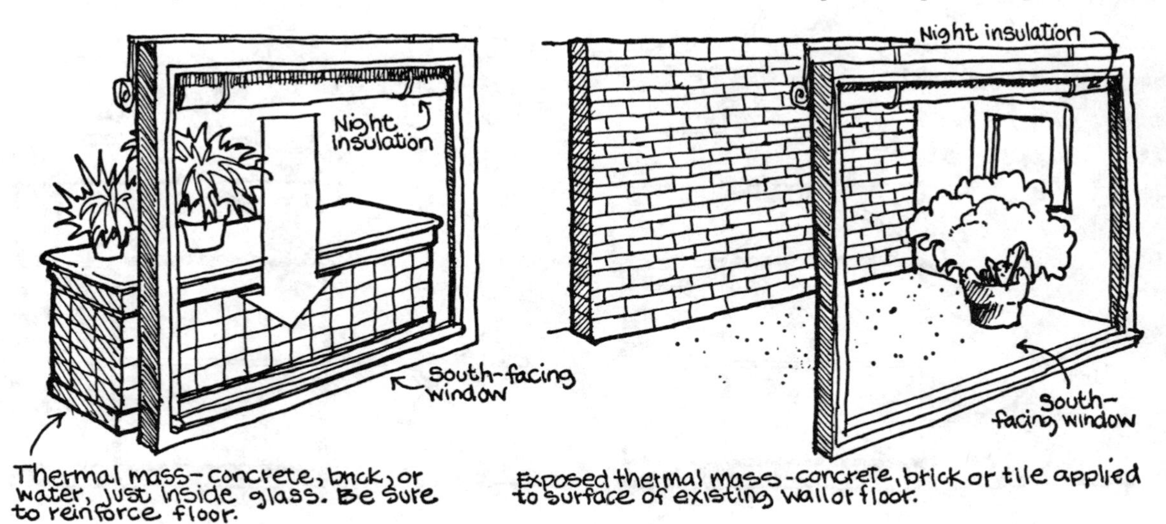

ADDING THERMAL MASS TO A FRAME HOUSE

that can be sealed off from the heated and cooled area of the house. In areas with moderate winters, double or triple glazing may reduce or even eliminate the need for window insulation.

Shading plays a similar summer role. Glass exposed to the sun in summer increases heat buildup and raises your cooling costs. Most passive solar modifications should be designed with shading in mind. Shading can be permanent or removable. For vertical windows, a properly sized overhang helps. An overhang that projects far enough to block summer sun in August, however, may also shade portions of the window in November and March. A removable shade or awning, alone or in combination with a fixed overhang, works better to exclude the hot summer sun while not blocking winter sun. Other types of shading are described in Chapter 4.

Can interior insulating curtains or panels do double duty to block summer sun and keep heat in on winter nights? Insulating curtains help prevent summer heat gain if they have a magnetic tape or track to make a tight seal around the window. Unfortunately, they also block out light at a time when most people want it . . . and they only work if you remember to use them when they are needed.

Don't expect regular drapes to do the job of insulating curtains. Drapes actually increase heating and cooling costs by cycling hot or cold air into the house in a convective loop, much the same way that a Trombe wall cycles heat into the house. Air between the window and drape is heated in the summer and chilled in the winter. In summer this warmer air rises up into the room, drawing cool air in at the bottom to be warmed. In winter the process is reversed.

Balancing solar design factors such as climate, orientation, glazing area, thermal mass, insulation, and shading requires a computer analysis or at least detailed calculations and is usually a job for an experienced professional. Homeowners can perform these calculations to predict the performance of the solar heating system and the resulting energy costs with a fair degree of precision, but extensive research is necessary. Several books listed in the references explain how to estimate the performance of passive solar heating techniques.

DIRECT AND INDIRECT HEATING

Level II includes two types of passive solar heating measures: *direct-gain* solar heating techniques, such as expanding the size of south-facing windows, and *indirect-gain* systems, such as glazed porches or solar walls. Either type of improvement can be incorporated into the building envelope without major structural changes, although solar walls and extensive south window additions require cutting into the south wall. Level III covers

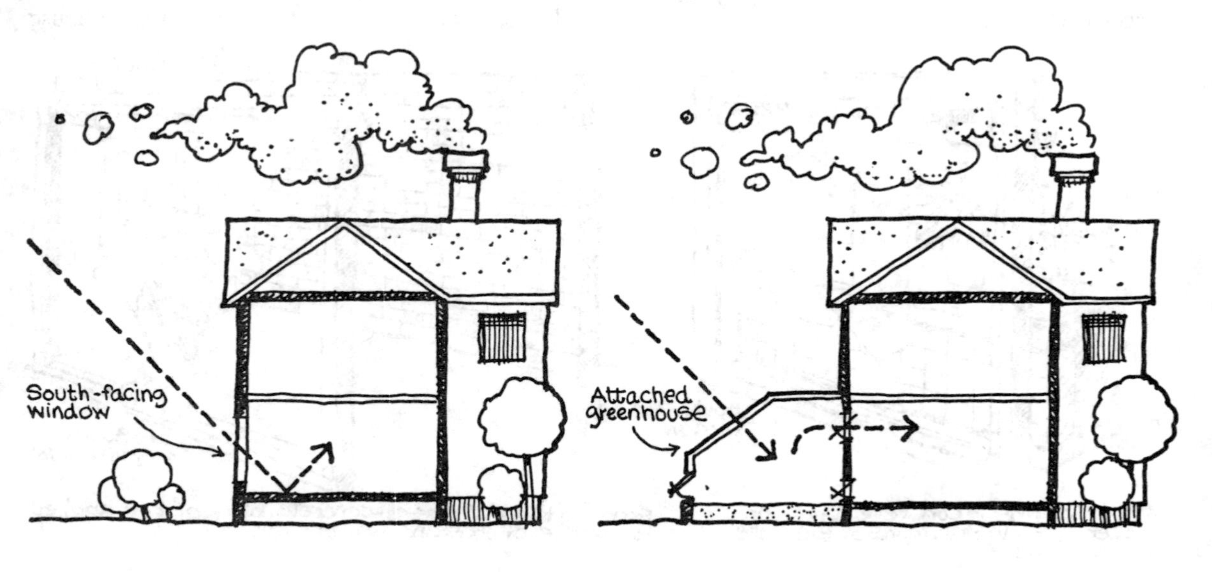

MAKING USE OF EXISTING THERMAL MASS

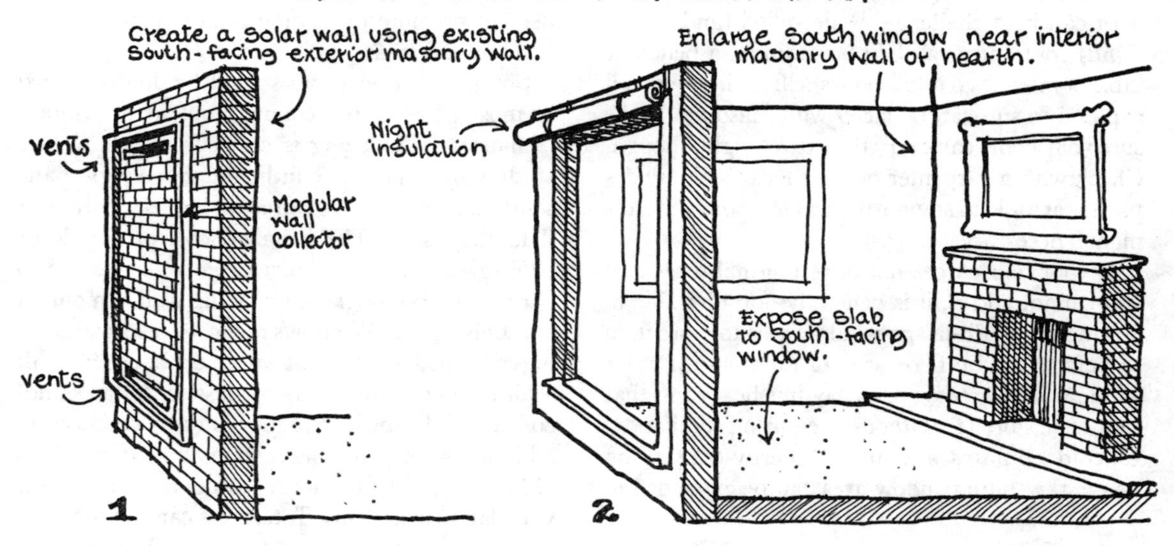

direct and indirect passive solar systems as part of room additions, including greenhouses and solaria; see Chapter 8.

In a direct-gain solar heating system, the sun's energy passes through a window directly into the space to be heated. The heat warms both the living area and whatever thermal mass is present.

In an indirect-gain solar heating system, the sun's energy passes through a collector but does not enter the living space directly. It strikes an absorber plate or thermal mass such as concrete or bricks; then the heat is pulled with fans or transferred by convection to the living area. Some indirect-gain systems can be isolated from the living area on cold and cloudy days and in summer.

The construction of your house limits your choices. Cutting into the walls of most masonry or brick houses is an expensive and difficult proposition. Yet, because of masonry's ability to store heat, it represents an excellent heat storage medium for a solar wall. Slab floors offer another heat storage opportunity.

How are the rooms in your house used? The answer determines whether your house is well suited to using the sun. Which rooms are on the south side of your house? Rooms that are used frequently and centrally located with respect to other rooms are good candidates. A garage or storage room is a poor candidate for passive solar heating but may be ideal for solar water heating collectors. If the rooms you use most in the morning face toward the southeast, the area may be promising even if it doesn't face due south.

INCREASING YOUR SOUTH WINDOW AREA

Expanding your south-facing windows is one way to use windows, normally heat losers, to your advantage. Doing so requires some care. As in any solar measure, you need more than added window area. If you are planning to replace a south-facing window anyway, expanding its size or replacing it with a sliding glass door and designing it as a solar collector may make both energy sense and economic sense.

How can you tell whether your house is a candidate for such a project? The window you plan to expand must be free of shading during winter midday hours, and you need a south wall that can accommodate the expanded window area without major construction problems. A wall that holds extensive plumbing or wiring may present too many problems or too great an expense if they have to be moved to other walls.

What about thermal mass for heat storage? If your house is built on a concrete slab, simply exposing the slab or covering it with a material that does not slow the entry or release of heat appreciably, such as linoleum, brick, or tile, may be the solution. Thick plaster walls and ceilings (preferably 2 inches) provide good thermal mass.

Adding thermal mass to a house with a wooden floor can be a challenge. Water-filled (and watertight!) containers can be placed under a bench or table or integrated into a bookshelf. An interior wall exposed to sun can be faced with masonry. Make sure your floors can carry the extra weight, though. Check with a carpenter or your local building department for load standards, and provide reinforcement if necessary.

If your house does not have thermal mass and you cannot add it, it is generally not advisable to expand the south-facing window area to more than 15 percent of the floor area of the house. Larger window areas create excess daytime heat gains that cannot be stored for later use, requiring ventilation. In cold climates and in an energy-conserving house, the south window area can be expanded to 25 to 40 percent of the floor area and will provide 30 percent or more of heating requirements—if you add thermal mass.

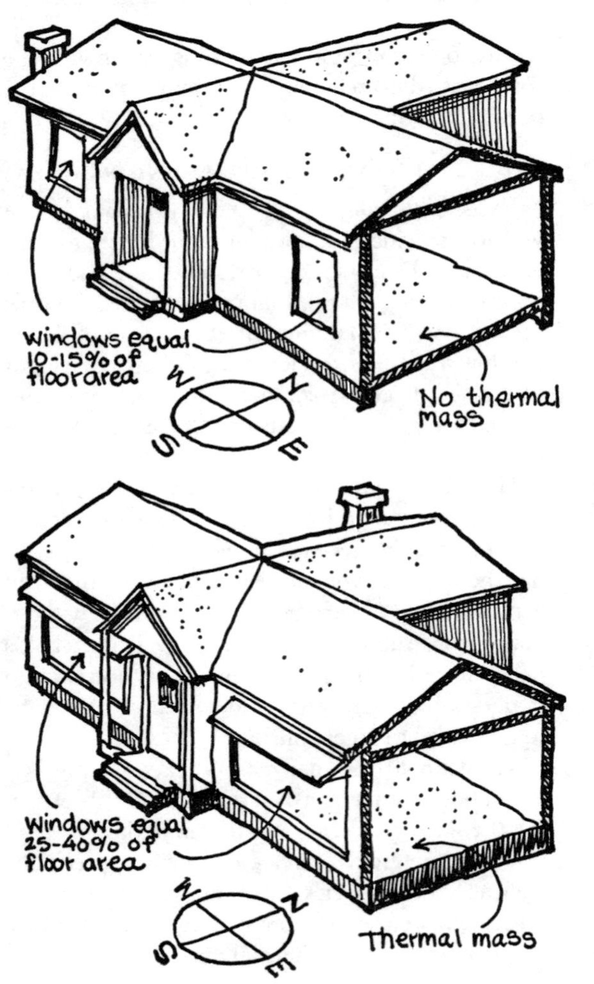

South-facing windows should be double glazed in most parts of the country, but in the coldest climates triple glazing is cost effective. The case studies in Chapter 7 indicate that single-pane south-facing windows can actually lose more heat than they gain. The installed cost of double or triple-glazed windows ranges from about $20 to $40 per square foot of glass, including wall demolition and finish work. Windows made with special coatings designed to trap heat within the house (or with a film between the layers of glass to do the same) cost more. To the cost of the windows you need to add the cost of insulating curtains or shutters ($2 to $13 per square foot) and the cost of thermal mass if you plan to install any. Total costs can run to $30 to $55 per square foot of window area. Adding shading, if you do not already have it, increases this cost.

Structurally, most frame houses can support significant increases in window area, but posts and headers in the wall are required—along with a certain tolerance for mess and disruption during construction. A contractor can usually make the change in a week or two.

Increasing the south-facing window area is a popular method for providing solar heating because it offers added benefits: increased natural lighting, improved quality of the living area, and views to the outside. The discussion and case studies in Chapter 7 will help you judge the overall performance of south-facing windows in your climate zone.

SKYLIGHTS

Skylights are generally a good choice for natural lighting but a poor choice for solar heating. Although they are usually installed for aesthetic reasons, care should be taken to assure that they are not energy losers.

Small skylights can reduce your electricity bills if their placement allows you to cut down on the use of electric lights. A skylight designed for daylighting need not be large. On sunny days, a clear 2 × 2 foot skylight transmits as much light as that produced by ten to fifteen 100-watt light bulbs. If it eliminates the need for two 100-watt bulbs that would otherwise burn for five hours a day, the skylight

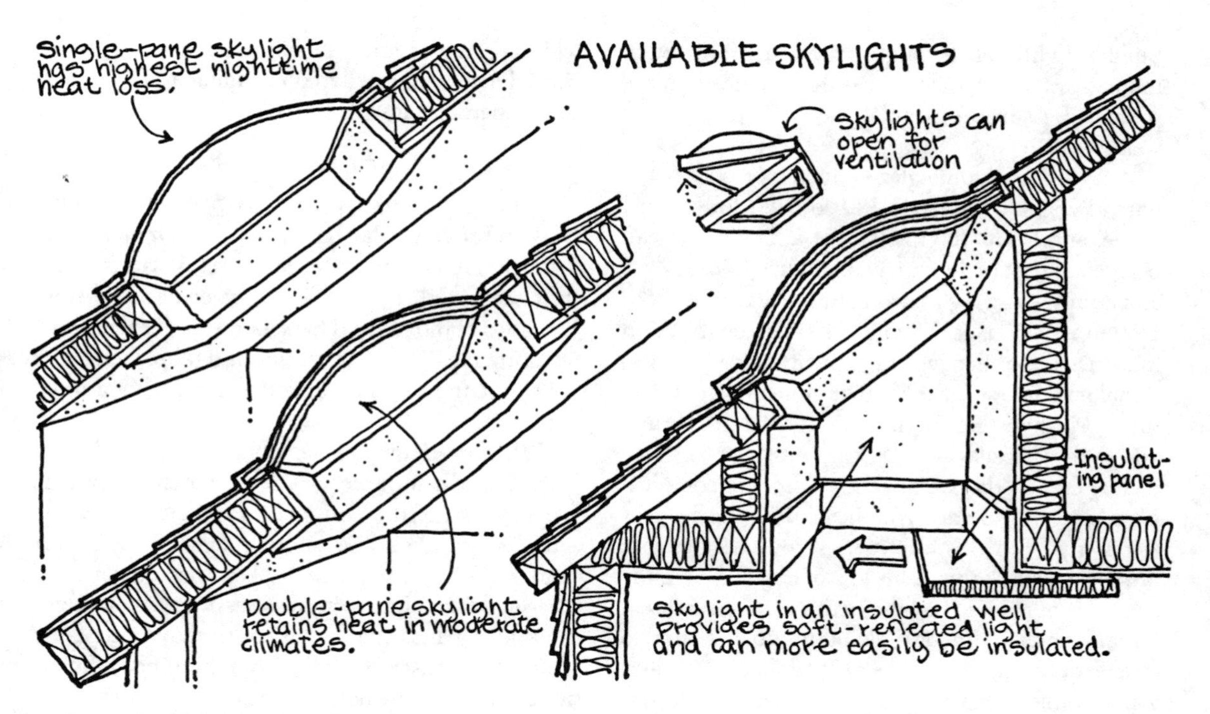
AVAILABLE SKYLIGHTS
Single-pane skylight has highest nighttime heat loss.
Skylights can open for ventilation
Double-pane skylight retains heat in moderate climates.
Skylight in an insulated well provides soft-reflected light and can more easily be insulated.
Insulating panel

reduces electricity bills by about $25 a year (at 7¢/kwh).

Larger south-facing skylights can be used for solar heating, but they are usually not the best alternative. Because skylights are located in roofs and are usually difficult to reach, you may find it hard to provide night insulation and shading, essential features for avoiding heat loss and overheating. Heat rises and collects near ceilings, speeding heat loss through uninsulated skylights. Single-glazed skylights actually increase heating costs by 1 to 5 percent in moderate and cold climates. Heat loss can be reduced by using skylights with multiple panes, weatherstripping them well, and adding movable insulation. In all but very warm climates, skylights should always be double or triple glazed. In cold climates, triple glazing with night insulation is a necessity to avoid costly heat loss.

There are a number of commercially available skylights that come with shading and insulation. Skylights made with a layer of clear, heat-reflective film between layers of glass provide an R-value of 4, twice that of a double layer of clear glass. Skylights used as a light source in warm climates should be located on north or east-facing roofs to prevent overheating. In warm climates, skylights that can be opened to vent hot air and provide natural air movement can save on cooling costs (see the section on cooling through natural ventilation), but only if they are shaded in summer.

Skylights come in three common materials: glass, acrylic, and polycarbonate. Glass is more expensive but less susceptible to scratching than the other materials. Acrylic has been widely used for twenty-five years, and its durability has been proved. Acrylic scratches easily, and it loses some of its transparency with time, but not its ability to collect heat. If the view through your skylight is important, steer clear of acrylic. Polycarbonate materials have not been used for skylights as long as acrylics, and their long-term durability is not as well established.

If daylighting is your objective, a clear skylight transmits more light but does not distribute it well; shadows and glare may be a problem, as well as fading in fabrics. Use a clear skylight with louvers or a deep light well to diffuse the light. Translucent white acrylic domes distribute the light better, providing uniform illumination. Tinted glazing reduces glare and solar heat gain, but it provides poor light distribution.

Installing a skylight is rarely complicated if you have a cathedral ceiling or flat roof. If you don't, you must cut through your present ceiling and build a light well through your attic. This work increases the cost, hassle, and time involved in the project. Be sure to insulate the walls of the light well.

A 2×2 foot double-glazed acrylic or polycarbonate skylight costs from $80 to $120 for a fixed model and from $160 to $250 for a model that can be opened (not including installation costs). A 2×2 foot double-glazed glass skylight ranges in cost from $150 to $200 if fixed, $300 to $400 if openable, and more if a heat-reflective film is incorporated. Professional installation costs $500 or more depending on the work involved. Night insulation and shading add to these costs.

The energy dynamics of skylights are complex. Because they provide light, they reduce the need for electricity—but this also means you lose the heat produced from lights. This loss of heat is fine in the summer, of course, but the heat must be made up for in winter. Although skylights do not always represent a clear energy benefit, the aesthetic and visual comfort they provide make them worth considering. By keeping in mind some of the issues raised here, you can avoid installing a skylight that is an energy drain.

SOLAR PORCHES

Adding glass to a south-facing porch is another way to provide solar heating without major structural modifications to your house. This approach has been used successfully on balconies, two-story porches, and front and back porches. A solar porch can provide both solar heating and more living area or a greenhouse at a fraction of the cost of a room addition.

When designing a solar porch, consider the advantages of being able to close the porch off from the heated area of the house. This feature allows you greater latitude in the amount of glazing and thermal mass installed and makes the daily use of shading and night window less important. Temperature swings may be broader than acceptable inside the house but well within the range of tolerance during many hours of the day.

If the porch does not already have thermal mass (in a slab floor or masonry wall), you will need to add mass if the glazing exceeds 20 percent of house floor space—an unlikely situation. For thermal mass, use planting beds or dark containers filled with water or rocks. Window fans can be used to move warm air from the porch into your home; windows or vents high and low in the wall allow cool air to flow from the house to the porch. Vents should be approximately 6 percent of the area of the south glazing. If your porch is open to the house at all times, night insulation (and daytime shading, if your summers are especially hot) is necessary to avoid energy losses.

A solar porch has benefits beyond the solar heat you capture. Even when the sun is not shining, the porch is a buffer that insulates the living area from cold weather, helps keep cold air out of your house as you come and go, and reduces the level of noise that penetrates your home.

SOLAR WALLS

One method of indirect passive solar heating is the solar wall. The thermal mass in a solar wall is directly behind the glass; the mass catches the sun before it reaches the room. The system consists of one to three layers of glazing and a wall of brick, concrete, adobe, or containers filled with water.

In a Trombe wall, a type of thermal wall named after its French designer, air between the glazing and the wall is heated by the sun and rises up and out vents, into the living space. This flow draws cooler air in from the living space through the lower vents. This *convective loop* heats the room throughout the day. At night, the vents are closed and heat absorbed by the wall during the day continues to heat the room. Water walls, made of water-filled containers, work in a similar fashion.

Not all thermal storage walls have vents. A brick or masonry wall can simply have an outside covering of glass. During the day, heat is collected in the mass of the wall. At night, or when indoor temperatures are lower than the temperature of the mass, heat is radiated into the room.

The thickness of the thermal mass, whether masonry or water, affects its performance. The optimal thickness for thermal mass ranges from 6 to 24 inches, depending on the material, unless you are using phase-change materials. The amount of liv-

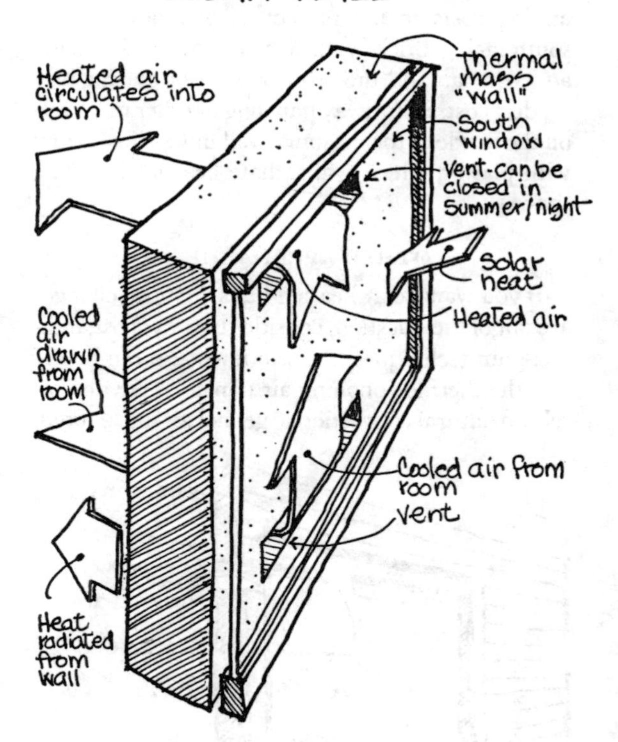

ing area you can heat depends on the expanse of glazing and wall and the wall's thickness.

You need not entirely give up sunlight through your south wall when you convert it to a solar wall. A window in the mass or above it allows some light into the room.

Because of its mass, a thermal storage wall reduces the temperature fluctuations that often occur in direct-gain systems.

Moreover, it can provide solar heating without letting direct sunlight into a room, eliminating the need to consider possibe sun damage to floors and furniture. On days when insufficient sunshine or excess heat is a problem, the thermal storage wall can be isolated from the living area by closing the vents and covering the wall with insulating panels or with curtains that form a seal at the edges.

In hot summer areas, solar walls can be designed to help with cooling if vents to the outside are provided above and below the glazing. (See the next section: Cooling Through Natural Ventilation.)

Replacing an existing wood frame wall with a solar wall can be difficult. Because of its weight, the solar wall may require extra foundation support, adding costs to the project. If you now have a south-facing brick wall, it can provide the mass, and you can add the layer of exterior glazing at a modest cost. Strip away paneling or other materials on the inside of the masonry wall unless it is coated with plaster, which will radiate heat to the living space.

OTHER APPROACHES

If you want solar heating but structural changes are out of the question, consider two low-cost, indirect-gain techniques: the windowbox room heater and the thermosiphoning air panel. These devices rely on natural convection to get hot air into a room, and they require little or no structural alteration to your house. Neither makes a major solar contribution, and neither has a way of storing heat, but both are good candidates for parts of the country characterized by cold and clear winter days where additional heating is needed during the day.

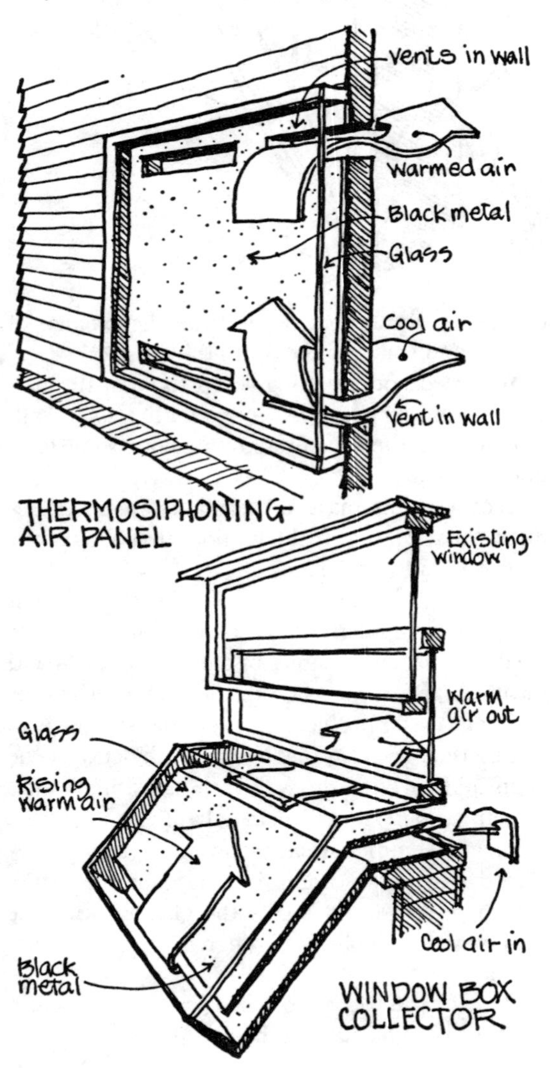

A windowbox collector requires a south-facing window. It must have an outlet to the room at the top of the collector; normally one end of the collector box rests on the ground or other support and the other fits into the bottom of a window. I must be carefully constructed to be airtight. The materials to build a 3×6 foot collector cost $100 or less; see the references for books that include plans. Complete units are available for $500 to $800. Because windowbox collectors are easily moved, they are options of interest to renters.

A thermosiphoning air panel works on the same passive principles as a windowbox collector, but it is larger and designed to be mounted on a vertical wall. An air panel requires vents in the wall to allow for circulation of household air through the collector. With its low cost it may be your best bet if you want more heat than a windowbox collector can deliver and you have south-facing unshaded walls adjacent to rooms that are used frequently. A thermosiphoning air panel can be built for less than $200. Several books listed in the references contain plans.

Cooling Through Natural Ventilation

Cutting the cost of cooling can be just as important as cutting the cost of heating—particularly as electricity bills soar throughout the country. These cuts can be made by reducing unwanted heat gain and increasing natural ventilation.

The biggest causes of heat gain in a house are unshaded windows, uninsulated walls and attics, and heat from appliances and people. The basic conservation investments of Level I are the best defense against overheating. Shading and landscaping can go a long way toward cooling both the house and its surroundings. Further cooling requires attention to natural airflow.

In winter, winds drain away energy and comfort from a house, but winds are usually welcome in summer. To manage the wind to your advantage you must know the directions it blows at different

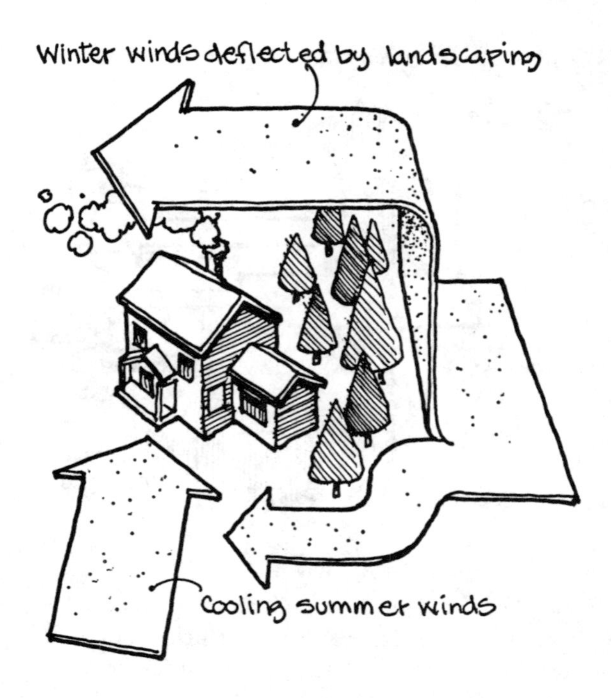

times of the year. Make some personal observations, or consult with the local office of the National Weather Service. Consider local geographical features—hills or a valley—that tend to force the wind into a certain pattern. A dense stand of trees has the same effect. Knowing these patterns will help you to take advantage of them. Determine the windward side of your house (where the wind strikes) and the leeward (sheltered) side for both summer and winter.

Natural ventilation strategies work best where there are evening breezes you can count on to cool the house. Position your air entry vents or openable windows toward incoming evening breezes. You can combine some of these strategies with landscaping to funnel breezes toward your house. Ideally, exit vents (such as an open skylight) should be on the leeward side of the house, and there should be a relatively unobstructed pathway for airflow within the house.

Natural ventilation can also be achieved by taking advantage of the tendency of hot air to rise. Giving warm air an escape route and cool air a way in creates a natural convective flow throughout the house. Vents high in a wall or in a ceiling—paired with floor or lower wall vents on the cooler north or east side of the house—facilitate this exchange. Vents can also be placed to draw air into the house from a cool crawl space or basement. An open skylight is a natural escape point for warm air.

For effective natural ventilation, the incoming air must not be warmer than the air in the house; otherwise the warming of the house offsets the cooling benefit of air movement. Where regular winds cannot be counted on to cool the house, consider adding a fan to draw cool air through your home at night. For more information, see the following section.

Some solar techniques can be used in summer to provide cooling. A Trombe wall, discussed earlier in this chapter, contributes to natural cooling and ventilation if vents are provided to the outside at the top of the glazing. On a warm day when temperatures outside are cooler than temperatures inside, these vents are opened, as are the vents into the house at the bottom of the Trombe wall. This arrangement creates a thermal chimney—as heated air rises out the vents, it draws air through the house, increasing air movement. The Trombe wall can also be used for cooling if both upper and lower vents to the outside are added. By opening both sets of outer vents at night, you allow the masonry to give off heat to the night air. The vents should be closed in the morning. The cooled masonry helps the house remain cool through the day.

Where summers are hot and the climate does not favor natural cooling, houses need some form of mechanical cooling. A whole-house fan or evaporative cooler provides comfort for the least cost, but an efficient, well-maintained air conditioner can provide moderate-cost cooling.

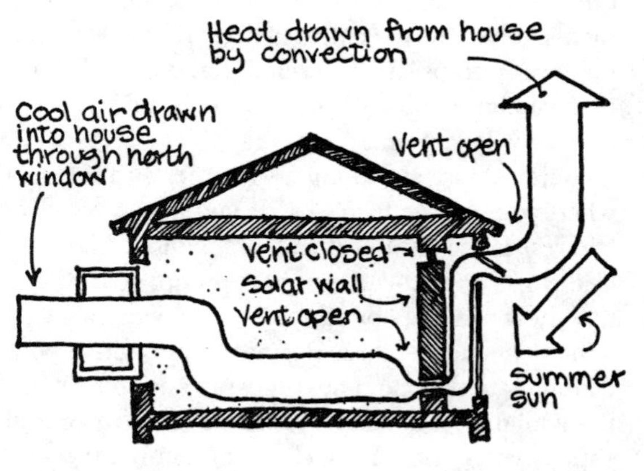

VENTILATING WITH A SOLAR WALL

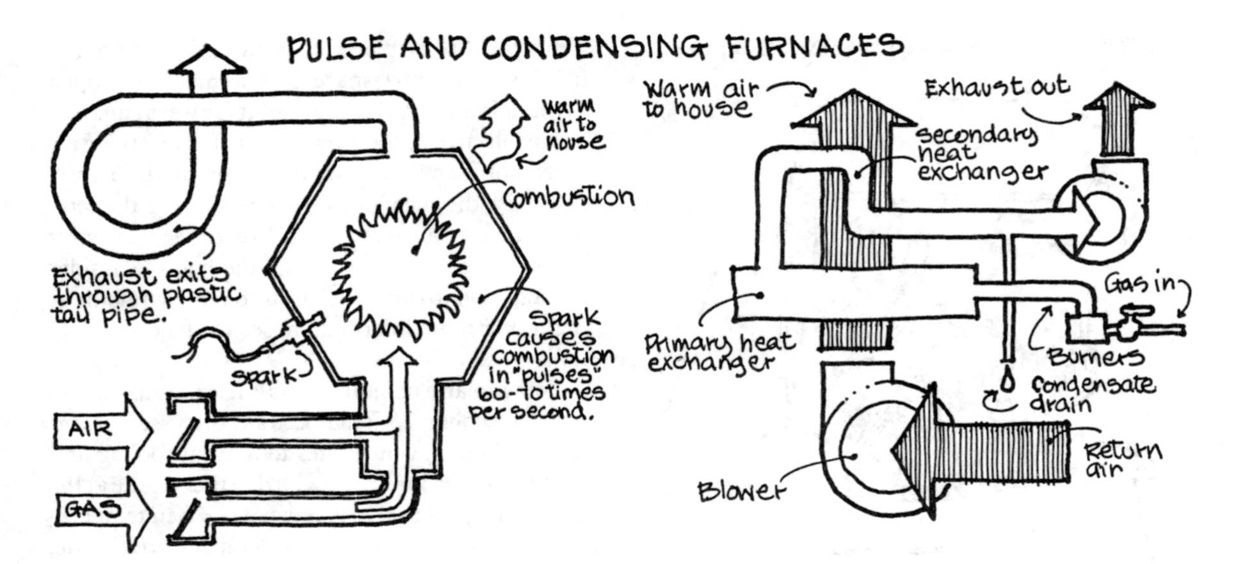

Improving Mechanical Heating and Cooling

Chapter 4 described different efficiency measures and modifications for your furnace or boiler. Complete these measures first unless your heating bills are more than $700 a year. If your bills are high, have your furnace or boiler efficiency tested; if it's old and inefficient, a new superefficient heating system—perhaps one that combines water and space heating—may be an excellent energy investment. You do more than save energy and money: A new furnace or boiler can be an asset should you decide to sell your home.There's a new generation of high-efficiency gas and oil furnaces and boilers on the market, and you should be able to find a new unit that matches your fuel and heating requirements. If you have central electric resistance heating, heat pumps can be a reliable and cost-effective replacement, reducing heating bills in some climates by 35 to 45 percent.

What about switching to another heating fuel when you change furnaces? If you now have electric resistance heat and can change to a high-efficiency gas or oil furnace or heat pump, do it. If you now heat with gas or oil, there is no clear answer. When one fuel is scarce it is natural to think about changing to the one that is cheaper and more readily available. The only problem is that price and supply variations are likely to be temporary, and the experts have been notoriously inaccurate in predicting long-term supplies and costs. The best long-term solution is an energy-efficient house. By reducing overall fuel use, you lessen the impact of rising energy prices and the importance of price differences between one fuel and another.

If you're thinking of changing your heating fuel, remember to factor in the cost of extending gas lines or installing an oil tank.

REPLACING YOUR HEATING SYSTEM

Furnaces and boilers are like automobiles. They need tune-ups and eventually they need replacing. With today's high fuel costs, it may be cheaper to replace an old, inefficient furnace rather than to keep operating it. Just as miles per gallon has become an important factor in selecting a new car, fuel efficiency should be a major consideration when you select a new furnace or boiler.

Have your furnace or boiler's efficiency tested and arrange for a tune-up. If its steady-state efficiency cannot be brought higher than 70 percent, consider replacing it. To narrow down the economics of the decision, see Table 7-I in Chapter 7 on the economics of buying a new furnace or boiler.

There are many greatly improved new furnaces and boilers available on the market, but the types with the greatest efficiency improvements fall into two categories: *condensing* or *recuperative* models and *pulse combustion* models. These new designs achieve efficiencies of 85 to 96 percent.

Condensing furnaces achieve high efficiency by

BOX 6-1
WHERE TO FIND A HIGH-EFFICIENCY FURNACE OR BOILER

Furnace and boiler efficiencies continue to rise. The following list includes the high-efficiency models available at the time of publication. Write to the manufacturer for current information. For an up-to-date listing of gas and oil furnace efficiencies, write to the Gas Appliance Manufacturers Association, P.O. Box 9245, Arlington, VA 22209. Ask for the Directory of Certified Furnace and Boiler Efficiency Ratings.

Manufacturer	*Model*	*AFUE**
Amana Refrigeration Amana, IO 52204	Energy Command (condensing gas furnace with water heater option)	95%
Arkla Industries, Inc. Box 534 Evansville, IN 47704	Arkla Recuperative Heating System (condensing gas furnace)	85–87%
BDP Company Box 70 City of Industry Indianapolis, IN 46206	Day and Night (condensing gas furnace)	82%
Clare Brothers, Ltd. 223 King Street Cambridge, Ontario Canada N3H 4t5	The Megasave I (condensing gas furnace)	93%
Energy Kinetics, Inc. P.O. Box 407 Bernardsville, NJ 07924	System 2000 (oil-fired boiler)	86%
Heil Quaker Corporation 635 Thompson Lane Nashville, TN 37204	Energy Marshal (condensing gas furnace)	90%
HydroTherm, Inc. Rockland Avenue Northvale, NY 07647	Hydro-Pulse (gas or propane pulse combustion boiler)	90–91%
Lennox Industries, Inc. P.O. Box 400450 Department SA Dallas, TX 75240	Lennox Pulse (gas pulse combustion furnace)	96%
Magic Chef 851 W. Third Avenue Columbus, OH 43212	Ultra Series (condensing gas furnace)	86–87%
Weil-McLain Blaine Street Michigan City, IN 46360	The VHE (condensing gas boiler)	87%

*AFUE (average fuel use efficiency) is the average heating efficiency over a heating season.

extracting most of the heat from the exhaust gases after combustion. When the furnace is turned on, the burner is lit by electric ignition. After combustion, exhaust gases flow through a primary heat exchanger, heating household air, and then through a secondary heat exchanger where water vapor condenses and additional heat is transferred to household air. The gases and condensed water, at 100 to 200°F, flow out through a plastic pipe. Some models use three heat exchangers, and one uses the gases to heat an alcohol fluid that then heats household air.

Pulse combustion furnaces and boilers achieve high efficiency by burning fuel completely and extracting as much heat as possible from exhaust gases. Valves feed a measured quantity of air and natural gas into a sealed combustion chamber and then close. The fuel mixture is ignited with a spark, and combustion continues at a pulsing rate of about 60 cycles per minute until the gas is burned completely. At this point, more fuel enters the chamber and the exhaust gases are fed through a heat exchanger, where they transfer heat to air in a furnace (or to water in a boiler). Exhaust gases, cooled to just over 100°F, exit through a plastic pipe.

Most furnaces and boilers are sold on the basis of installed cost, and installation costs vary widely. Total costs range from $1100 to $3500, depending on the model. Replacing the furnace or boiler is simply a matter of contacting a reputable installer in your community. It pays to research the alternatives first, however. The companies listed in Box 6-I will send you information about the equipment and a list of local dealers.

When you buy a new furnace or boiler, make sure that its size reflects the energy-efficient modifications you have made to your house. The American Society of Heating, Refrigeration, and Air Conditioning Engineers estimates that this type of equipment has traditionally been oversized by 50 to 200 percent—with a corresponding increase in cost and energy waste. A furnace or boiler too large for the space it is heating cycles on and off frequently. This cycling increases heat losses while the unit is not operating (standby losses), lowers seasonal performance, and makes the unit more costly to operate. An oversized heating system also costs more to begin with, of course.

The issue of whether or not to replace electric baseboard heating presents a more difficult decision. Electricity costs keep climbing, but the cost of replacing your baseboard heaters with another system, whether a heat pump or new gas furnace, is high because you must install ducts to deliver heated air to the rooms. And the duct work can cost more than the new furnace. Moreover, baseboard heaters have the advantage of zone heating: You need only heat the rooms you actually use. This feature is not always present in a warm-air system.

Condensing and pulse furnaces do not require chimneys—they have no flue because the exhaust gases are not hot enough to need them. Thus the total replacement costs are reduced somewhat. Because you do not need to build a flue chimney, a high-efficiency gas furnace is generally a better buy than a heat pump as a replacement for electric baseboard heating if your house already has gas service.

HEAT PUMPS

Consider installing a heat pump if your current heating source is an electric furnace or electric baseboard heaters. Heat pumps combine heating and cooling in one unit and, in the appropriate climates, can yield significant savings. They are also becoming increasingly efficient, so it pays to shop carefully.

A heat pump, using electricity, transfers heat from one body of air or water to another, and it can deliver more energy (in the form of heat) than it uses (as electricity) in the process. Because it can "move" heat to or from a house, a heat pump can be used for both heating and cooling. Refrigerators and air conditioners are heat pumps. Just as a refrigerator gives off heat to the room while it is cooling your macaroni salad, a heat pump heats outside air during its cooling cycle and indoor air during its heating cycle.

Heat pumps work well in mild and warm climates. When temperatures fall below 35°F, though, frost tends to form on the outer coils of the unit and their ability to absorb heat from the air declines rapidly. To counteract this effect, many units rely on supplemental electric heating to deliver a heat boost and protect the unit from damage when outdoor temperatures are low. Thus the heat pump has no economic advantage where average winter temperatures are below 35°F.

Because of their built-in electric heaters, most heat pumps can't be placed on a standard setback thermostat. When called on to heat or cool a house quickly, most heat pumps supplement their heating ability with the resistance heater, offsetting the savings from a night setback. Some new thermostats solve this problem by raising thermostat settings step by step.

Heat pump efficiences are measured in different ways for heating and cooling. Cooling is measured by using the *seasonal energy efficiency ratio* (SEER), a measure of the electricity it takes to remove heat from the air, taking into account seasonal fluctuations in efficiency. This number is listed on heat pumps. An SEER of 8 is good, but shop for the best combination of price and performance; models are available with an SEER of 11 and higher. A heat pump with an SEER of 11 uses 27 percent less electricity for cooling than a model with an SEER of 8.

There are two indicators for measuring the heating efficiency of a heat pump: the *coefficient of performance* (COP) and the *heating seasonal performance factor* (HSPF). The COP measures the energy output against the energy input of the equipment at any point in time. Many heat pumps now available have a COP of over 3.0 compared to an average COP of 1.7 in older units. Don't buy a heat pump with a COP under 2.5, and look for one that is better. The added cost of a more efficient heat pump is likely to quickly pay off its initial cost in electricity saved.

The HSPF is the rating found on most heat pumps. It measures the unit's performance based on an actual season of operation, taking into account the effects of cycling on and off, frosting, defrosting, and the need for supplemental heat. HSPF represents the total annual heating output divided by electrical input over a season. Although HSPFs of 6 are common, models are now available with HSPFs of 8 and above. Look for a heat pump with an HSPF of at least 7.

Heating and cooling efficiencies are not equivalent from model to model; some are efficient heaters but poor coolers and vice versa. When weighing heating and cooling efficiencies, consider your *primary* use. If cooling is your major need, look for a high SEER. If your need is more for heating, look for the best HSPF and compromise on SEER.

Heat pumps bear watching as new technical developments make them increasingly efficient. New heat pumps are available, for example, that draw heat from water rather than the surrounding air. These models can perform more efficiently than air-source heat pumps, attaining COPs of 3.5 and higher. Because of the relatively constant temperature of the heat source, climate is less of a factor. For this type of heat pump, you must have a water source such as a well or a lake. For the unit to work efficiently, the water source's temperature should be between 50 and 60° F.

A solar-assisted heat pump is another option. These units use solar collectors to raise the temperature of air or water, providing a heat source for the heat pump to use. A heat pump works best at moderate temperatures, where solar collector efficiencies are highest. Thus a heat pump plus solar is a good combination in cold climates. Costs are very high, though, and special design expertise is needed.

FANS

If you live in a climate with high summer temperatures, considerable humidity, or both, a fan may provide part of your cooling solution. Even if air conditioning is still necessary, a fan can reduce the amount of time the air conditioner needs to be on. There are two types of fans: ventilating and circulating. Ventilating fans exhaust warm air from the house and draw in outside air. Circulating fans increase comfort by creating movements of air within the house.

Ventilating fans draw outside air in through the house and send it out a window or through the attic. When outdoor temperatures are lower than indoor temperatures in the morning or evening, a ventilating fan can be used to cool the house. When indoor and outdoor temperatures are roughly the same, the air movement created by a ventilating fan improves indoor comfort. When the outdoor air is significantly warmer than indoor air, a ventilating fan does not help.

Large ventilating fans built to draw air through the ceiling of a room to the attic or directly to the outside are called *whole-house fans*. Whole-house fans draw air through a house at the rate of twenty or more air changes per hour, compared to about three air changes per hour in a house without a fan. A whole-house fan can be used after outdoor temperatures fall in the evening to draw cool air into the house. Keeping windows and doors shut in the morning helps maintain the coolness into midmorning or after.

Large whole-house fans have some drawbacks. Where both day and night temperatures stay high, they have little or no cooling effect, and they may be too noisy or too powerful to be used solely to create air movement. And if you don't have an attic, a whole-house fan is difficult to install. It can be installed on a flat roof, but the job is tricky and requires the help of a professional.

To protect against heat loss through the fan grate

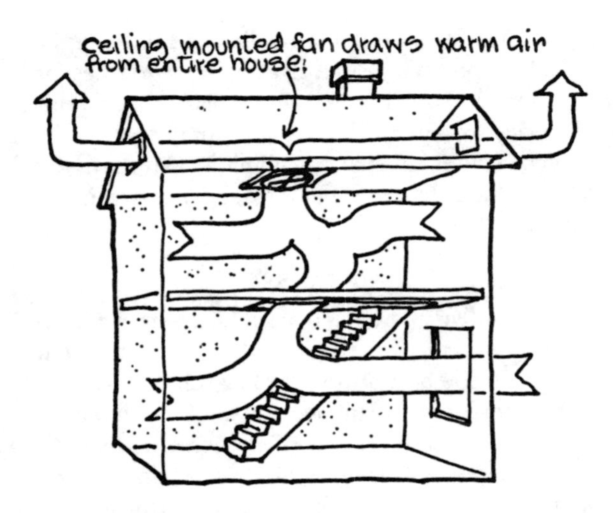
Ceiling mounted fan draws warm air from entire house.

when the fan isn't operating, whole-house fans have louvers that can be shut. These louvers are usually not sufficient to protect against infiltration and winter heat losses, though, and must be covered with an insulated panel during the heating season.

In many climates, whole-house fans provide energy and dollar savings if you use air conditioning and increased comfort if you don't. Whole-house fans are rated according to the cubic feet per minute (cfm) of air they can exhaust. For a house with 1200 square feet of floor area, the fan should be capable of at least 3500 cfm. For a 2000-square-foot home, select a 6000-cfm model. Two-speed models are available that allow you to ventilate at a slower rate.

Retail prices for whole-house fans range from $150 to $250; installed costs are $400 or more, depending on the size of fan and details of installation. A whole-house fan is usually installed by a professional, but a homeowner with carpentry and electrical experience can do the job.

Smaller ventilating fans are designed to be placed in a window or permanently mounted to exhaust air through a wall or the attic. These models move air at a rate of 1500 cfm or less. Since they are well suited to providing adequate air movement for long periods, they may be a good choice where indoor and outdoor temperatures are similar much of the time or where circumstances prevent the installation of a whole-house fan. A window fan may be a good choice for the renter or apartment dweller because it can be moved and adjusted to various window sizes.

Many fans designed for window or wall installation are reversible—that is, they allow you to exhaust air or bring outside air in. Variable-speed fans cost slightly more, but they may be more convenient in some applications. A variable-speed fan can be run at a high setting to exhaust warm air and then switched to a lower setting to provide air movement. Window fans cost from $50 to $150 and are quickly and easily installed. To avoid heat losses through the fan, it should be removed before the heating season begins.

A permanently installed wall fan costs more because of the installation. Expect to spend up to $500 —more if special problems are involved. The wall fan, like the whole-house fan, should be covered during the heating season to eliminate the loss of heated air.

Water Heating

As you carry out structural modifications and heating and cooling improvements your water heating costs become a proportionally larger part of your total energy bill. The low-cost measures of Chapter 4 reduce your water heating costs, but only so far. Level II includes measures to cut your dependence on conventional fuels even further: by using solar energy or by replacing your present system with an electric heat pump water heater.

Also consider installing a new high-efficiency water heater of conventional design, particularly if you need to replace your present one. Gas and oil water heaters are increasing in efficiency as manufacturers improve flue design, and some manufacturers are considering models with flue dampers and electronic ignition, improvements that would further increase efficiency. Although new water heaters have more jacket insulation than older models, they still benefit from an insulating blanket. Apart from these three alternatives, there is a fourth to explore if you plan to replace your furnace. Some of the new high-efficiency furnaces include a water heating option. Incorporating water heating at the time you replace your furnace can save up to 40 percent in water heating bills.

SOLAR WATER HEATERS

The basic principles of climate and solar design for passive solar heating apply in many respects to solar water heating. Solar collectors for water heating need to face south (or near-south) and must be free of shading in winter and summer. Some solar water heating systems (called *batch* systems) need to be insulated at night, but most types function well without night insulation.

Because solar water heaters gather the sun's energy all year, collectors must be angled accurately to collect the maximum amount of solar radiation year round. In most areas, the best angle for solar water-heating collectors is the degree of latitude.

Most solar water heaters have these basic features: collectors, a storage tank, a pump to circulate water from the tank through the collectors, and an electronic controller that turns the pump on and off.

Solar water heaters ciculate either water or a working fluid through the collectors. In cold areas, working fluid systems have an advantage. Since working fluids have an alcohol or petroleum base, they have very low freezing points—preventing freezing during the winter—and high heat retention properties. A working fluid system requires a storage tank with a heat exchanger to transfer heat without contaminating the potable water in the tank.

Other types of solar water heaters circulate water through the collectors but need a way of protecting the water in the collectors against freezing. Some systems employ a drain-down mechanism: As temperatures drop below 38°F, automatic valves isolate the collectors from the tank and allow them to empty. Other water circulating systems rely on the electronic controller to recirculate warm water from the tank to the collectors as temperatures approach freezing.

Some solar water heaters dispense with the pump and controller by locating the tanks above the collectors. These are called *thermosiphon systems*. As water is heated it rises into a storage tank. This movement of heated water creates a natural convective current drawing cold water into the bottom

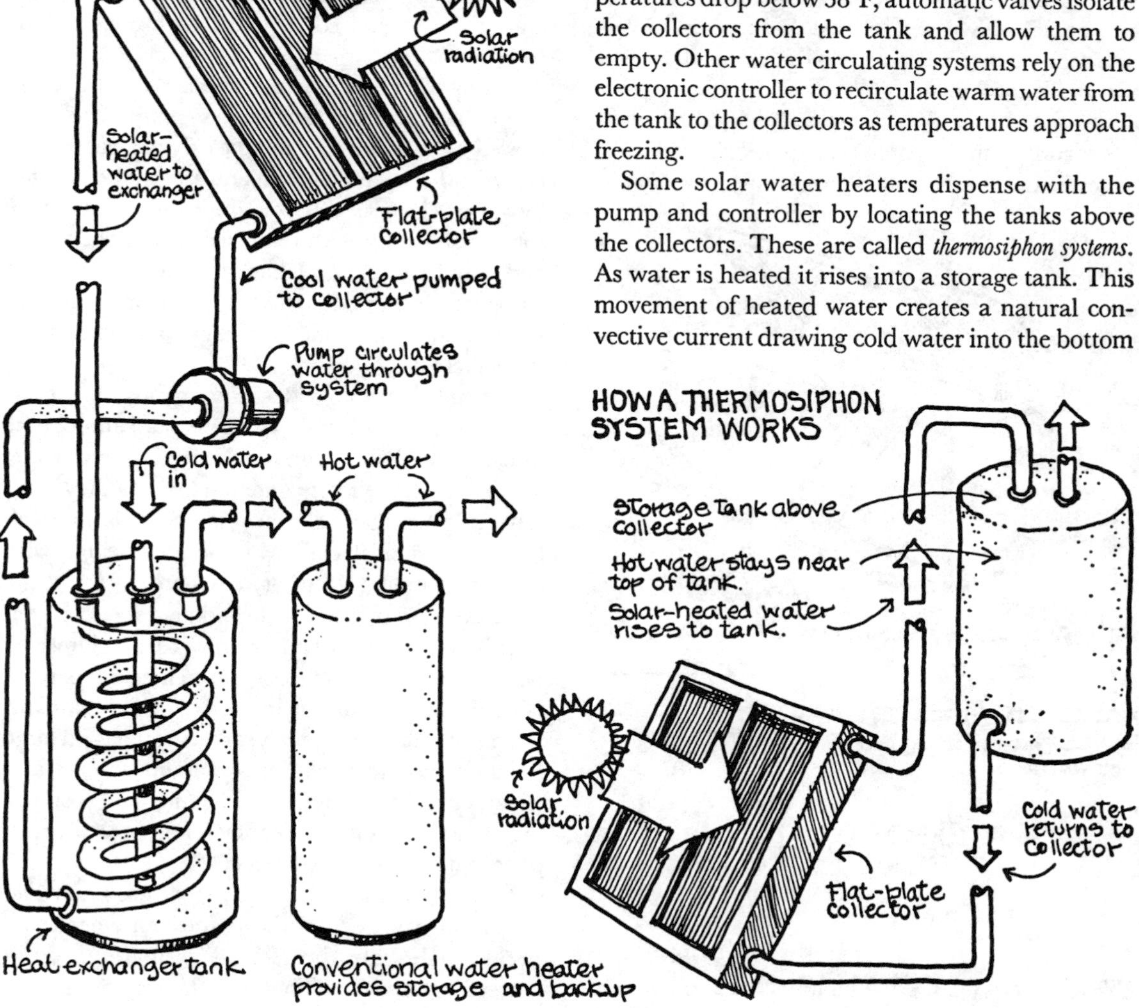

of the collector to be heated. Water for domestic use is then drawn off the top of the storage tank.

Tanks for thermosiphon water heaters can be part of the collector array, or they can be placed in an attic or on a roof where they are at least 2 feet above the collectors. Heated water can then run from the storage tank above the collectors to your old water heater. The old water heater can then function as a backup when solar heating is not sufficient.

The simplest solar water heater is a batch water heater. By combining collector and storage tank, this type eliminates the need for separate collectors, pump, and controller. A tank is placed in an insulated, glass-covered box that can be opened and exposed to the sun. The sun heats the batch of water in the tank; water circulates through the tank only as it is drawn off and used. Because the tank is in a box, a batch heater is often referred to as a *breadbox* water heater.

As in a thermosiphon system, the solar-heated water runs from the batch tank to the gas or electric water heater. Preheating water in this way can cut

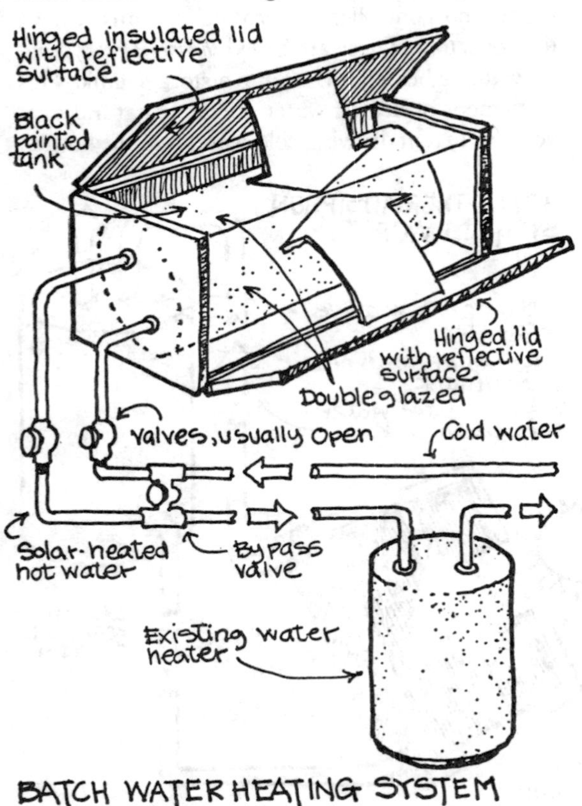

BATCH WATER HEATING SYSTEM

water heating costs by a third or more. Because it is simple and uses common materials, you can build a breadbox water heater for less than $500. In cold climates, batch water heaters require an insulated cover that must be closed every night. In milder climates, this manual task is less important. If you live in a climate where nighttime heat losses are significant and you're not really likely to keep up this routine, consider investing in a more elaborate system with an automatic draining feature or other freeze protection mechanism.

Solar water heating systems require a conventional backup water heater since they meet generally only 40 to 60 percent of hot water needs in most areas. Producing a higher percentage of hot water is technically feasible, but it may require a prohibitively high investment in the large collector area and storage required to make it through cloudy weather.

Your present water heater can serve as the backup for batch and thermosiphon systems. The solar-heated water is fed through the existing water heater; when necessary its temperature can be boosted by gas or electricity. If you are installing an active solar system, keep your present water heater for additional storage and backup heat or replace it with a larger tank designed for solar water heating systems and containing its own gas or electric backup heater.

For most people, a decision on buying a solar water heater depends on what they can afford, how much manual operation they're willing to provide, how much of their conventional fuel use they want it to replace, and where they live. Solar is an excellent investment if your water is now heated with electricity, unless electricity costs are exceptionally low in your area. Federal and some state tax incentives have helped lower the initial cost of solar water heaters, and a system designed to meet 60 percent of your hot water needs in a moderate climate can pay for itself in five to ten years. If you have a large family or use an exceptional amount of hot water for other reasons, your water heating fuel costs are higher and a solar water heater may be correspondingly more cost effective.

Because of their simplicity, thermosiphon and batch water heaters are the least expensive alternatives. Batch water heaters are primarily a do-it-yourself alternative. Thermosiphon systems have some physical constraints. The tank must be located above the collectors for it to work properly—and not all roofs or attics can accommodate this weight. Your climate dictates the type of freeze protection you'll need for the system. Systems that rely on warm water circulation (including thermosiphon systems) lose a large amount of heat in cold climates unless you consistently close the valves to the collector and drain it when frost is imminent.

You also need to consider where the collector panels can be placed. They need a south-facing house, garage, or patio roof or a safe location on the ground. Most roofs can support the weight of collector panels, but plan to consult a carpenter or your local building department if you have any questions about the ability of your roof or attic joists to support a heavy thermosiphon or batch system. Locating a batch system on the ground provides easy access for opening and closing the insulated cover. Whether you are planning to design and install your system yourself or to rely on a contractor, you should shop carefully. Box 6-2 offers guidelines for buying a solar water heater; these will help you avoid problems.

You can save money by designing your system and doing some or all of the plumbing and installation yourself. The books listed in the references (see "Solar How-To") provide guidance and plans. They'll help you determine whether your roof can support the added weight of collectors (and tank, if you are considering a thermosiphon or batch system), help you decide how many collectors and how big a storage tank you'll need, and help you choose the right system and freeze protection for your area.

Plan to have someone familiar with solar collector installation review your work. Most problems that arise are a result of faulty installation. Many states have a solar industries association that can refer you to a local solar expert.

BOX 6-2
BUYING A SOLAR WATER HEATER

As you shop for a solar water heater, keep in mind these principles:

1. Seek out reputable local dealers who will stand behind their product. Always talk to more than one dealer.
2. Read the warranty. It should cover collectors and other components for at least five years, and it should be transferable to a future owner.
3. Specify a system and collectors that have been certified by the Solar Rating and Certification Corporation (SRCC) or the Air Conditioning and Refrigeration Institute (ARI). The ARI tests collectors and the SRCC tests both collectors and systems and certifies those that meet minimum standards of efficiency and reliability. The certifications may not always be displayed, so be sure to ask.
4. Be sure you are buying a collector system that has a proven reputation for quality. Don't be pressured into buying something you don't know anything about or are unsure of. Ask for names of people who have purchased the type of solar water heater you're considering and ask them if they have been satisfied.
5. Don't insist on too much collector area in order to make the solar setup meet all your hot water needs. In most areas, a solar water heater will meet 40 to 60 percent of annual household needs; pushing for more isn't worth it.
6. If you have a choice between systems that are equivalent in performance and price, go for the simpler system. There will be less to go wrong.

HEAT PUMP WATER HEATERS

Heat pump water heaters work by drawing warmth from the surrounding air to heat water in a tank. Although they use electricity, they can be two or three times more efficient than electric water heaters. Some models are designed to be installed next to an existing water heater. The old heating unit is disconnected and the tank is retained for storage.

Sound like a simple and lower-cost alternative to a solar water heater? It may be. Heat pump water heaters are efficient and only moderately expensive, but they do have some disadvantages. Heat pump water heaters don't work well below 45°F, and they are damaged by freezing temperatures. The best location for a heat pump water heater is in a garage, crawl space, or unheated utility room that stays above the freezing point.

In most climates, the heat pump water heater should not be installed in a living area. Since a heat pump *extracts* heat from the air around it, it acts like a small air conditioner. Whatever your heating fuel, you will be paying twice for water heating during the winter: once to run the heat pump and once to heat its cold exhaust air. If the heat pump water is indoors and you have electric heat, the efficiency and cost advantages of the heat pump disappear.

There may be some exceptions to this rule. In Hawaii, for example, a heat pump water heater indoors helps reduce cooling costs, and it dehumidifies indoor air as well. The heat pump is also somehwat noisy, equivalent to a room air conditioner. Some thought needs to be given to its location in relation to sleeping and other living areas.

A heat pump water heater costs from $1000 to $1300. Compared to an electric water heater, it can reduce your water heating fuel costs by 30 to 50 percent (excluding its effect on space heating if it is located in the living area). Although it is not eligible for the federal tax credits you may gain for solar energy systems, some utilities offer rebates to customers who purchase a heat pump water heater.

SOLAR, HEAT PUMP, OR NEITHER?

If you've decided to reduce the fuel use of your water heating system or your present water heater is worn out, consider three alternatives: a new efficient gas or oil water heater of conventional design; a solar water heater; and a heat pump water heater. The new gas or oil water heater is the least expensive option. It costs less to purchase and it's easy to install if you alrady have gas or oil service. In most parts of the country, at 1983 gas prices, a new, highly efficient gas water heater has a lower life cycle cost than a heat pump water heater or an active solar water heater.

If you've decided to make a greater investment to gain more savings, how do you decide whether to install a solar water heater or a heat pump water heater? Each saves roughly the same amount of fossil fuel, depending on your location. Solar water heaters (unless they include a pump and controller) give you a measure of independence in the event of an electric power failure.

Whatever your decision, you won't be noticeably affecting the quality of the end product: hot water. Therefore economics may be your best guide in areas where heat pump water heaters and solar units perform equally well.

If you now have a natural gas water heater in good condition, it will not be worth your while to shift to solar water heating or a heat pump. If dollar savings are your only motive, your best course—at least until natural gas prices rise—is to stick with your present gas system with the efficiency improvements outlined in Chapter 4.

If, on the other hand, you want to supplement your natural gas water heater with a solar water heater, do so in good conscience. You will be replacing a fossil fuel with a renewable energy source, and, over the long term, your investment will be a good one, particularly if federal and state tax credits are available to offset the initial cost.

Consider a heat pump water heater only if you now heat water with a conventional electric water heater. Whether a heat pump water heater is actually cost effective depends on the fuel you now use for space heating, its cost, and your climate. If your climate is mild and you can install the heat pump water heater in a crawl space or garage that only rarely falls below 45°F and never freezes, the conversion makes sense. If winters are harsh and you must place the heat pump in a heated area, conversion is cost effective if you heat with oil or gas but your savings will be less than if you had installed a new efficient gas or oil water heater. Do not put a heat pump water heater indoors if you heat your house with electricity.

Solar water heating is a logical first choice in several situations. Federal tax credits—and state credits in some areas—reduce its cost relative to other options. If you are currently heating water with electricity, solar is a good investment. In southern states where sunshine is abundant all year, a solar water system may be able to meet all your water heating needs. And cold, clear areas where a heat pump is impractical may be favorable for solar water heating.

Making the Hard Choices

Because there are often several ways of achieving the effect you want, you are likely to be faced with choosing between different Level II measures. The trade-offs you make depend on economics and the goals you've set for yourself. Chapter 7 indicates the range of economic benefits of passive solar heating options and water heating strategies and shows how to calculate the benefits of buying a new furnace.

Are you primarily interested in saving money? If you live in a cold climate where gas and oil are available, the new high-efficiency furnaces are extremely cost effective; they are a more predictable investment than solar space or water heating, because their performance is guaranteed in most instances and they require little maintenance or involvement on your part. A solar space heating investment entails a higher risk because performance depends on the weather, your habits, and the effectiveness of your design and installation. If you have electric space heating or an electric water heater, look closely at the information in this book and other references before you reject either solar energy or a heat pump to meet either need.

Are you concerned with your home's resale value? New furnaces and properly integrated solar energy measures can return their initial investment in increased resale value, particularly in areas where heating costs are high and tax credits are available. A poorly designed solar installation, on the other hand, may detract from resale value.

An energy-efficient house may also be easier for a buyer to finance. Many financial institutions are beginning to recognize the importance of lower monthly utility bills in helping people meet mortgage payments. Banks, however, are usually concerned only with basic conservation measures. Keep track of your utility bills to document your savings to a prospective homebuyer or a loan officer.

Is increased comfort your objective? New furnaces do not alter comfort; they simply provide the same comfort at a considerably reduced cost. Solar modifications and natural cooling can dramatically increase your physical comfort while improving the aesthetic quality of your living space, but they require maintenance and operation to ensure that comfort.

Are you concerned about environmental quality? If your goal is to reduce your dependence on a nonrenewable fuel or to lessen the adverse environmental effects of fossil fuel use, weigh your options carefully. A new highly efficient furnace reduces your fossil fuel use by 20 or 30 percent which is more than the savings from a typical passive solar heating system added to an existing home in a cold climate. In some areas, wood heating reduces or even eliminates conventional fuel use for heating, but in the city the cost of firewood along with air pollution problems may make wood a less favorable choice.

Solar heating investments can increase your security and independence. An energy-conserving passive solar home may never fall below 60°F if fuel is cut off, even in the coldest climates. Yet an efficient conventionally heated house can drop well below 45°F without a heating source in cold climates.

Whichever combination of goals guides your decision making, economics is an important consideration. The case studies in Chapter 7 indicate the costs and benefits of investing in Level II home energy improvements.

Chapter Seven
The Economics of Level II: Case Studies

The Economics of Level II: Case Studies

How much money will you save with Level II measures? In contrast to Level I measures, your decision to undertake these investments rests more on your personal idea of comfort, environmental concerns, or interest in using a renewable resource than on economic considerations.

Many solar improvements have immediate economic returns if you live in an area with high energy costs or you qualify for federal and state tax benefits. Without high energy costs or tax benefits, these measures still have an economic advantage, but the payback won't come till later. The measures increase your personal comfort, security, and home resale value, and they serve as a hedge against escalating fuel costs. If you contribute your own labor or use recycled materials you can cut the cost of installation in half; this saving increases your economic returns, depending on how you value your time. A poorly planned or carelessly installed Level II project, however, may well detract from your home's resale value and add to your energy costs.

Except for furnace or boiler replacement, you are likely to have more than simply economic reasons for completing a Level II measure. Furnace replacement is not included in these case studies. To help determine the costs and benefits of replacing your furnace, complete Table 7-1 and see also the Chapter 5 case studies.

About the Case Studies

In the case studies solar space heating modifications have been divided into three categories: expanded south-facing window area, a solar wall, and glazed-in south porch. Other types of solar heating systems, such as clerestory windows, windowbox air heaters, and thermosiphoning air panels, are not included. The case studies also look at water heating measures: active solar water heating and heat pump water heating.

Expanding your south-facing window area, the first category, is a straightforward way to increase solar heating. More south glass—such as sliding glass doors—can be easily included in a home renovation project. The case studies cover three approaches to expanding your south window area: single glazing, double glazing plus an overhang to block summer heat, and a strategy that combines these techniques with thermal mass and night insulation.

Single glazing is the least expensive way to go, but it yields the smallest savings. And in most locations a single-glazed south wall loses more heat at night than it collects during the day. You can compare the costs and savings of this low-cost approach with the other solar options.

The daytime solar heating approach incorporates double glazing (except in the Minneapolis and Chicago case studies, which assume triple glazing) and an overhang to block summer heat gain. This approach provides the home with heat during the day but not enough to store for heating at night, and so it has no thermal mass. Because it does not incorporate night insulation, this approach requires minimal daily operation. Both costs and savings are higher compared to single-glazing. In some areas, daytime solar heating provides significant savings, particularly if the home is normally heated during the day.

The day-and-night strategy is more expensive

TABLE 7-1
BUYING A NEW FURNACE OR BOILER

The following calculations will help you decide whether a new oil or gas furnace makes economic sense. Be sure that you are basing your calculations on the cost of a new furnace that is sized appropriately for your newly energy-efficient house and take into account a home addition if you plan one. The chances are excellent that you can meet your comfort requirements with a smaller furnace than the one you had before.

A. Identify your last year's heating fuel costs (use the figure you have on the Home Energy Survey and Checklist in Table 3-2):

$________

B. Estimated seasonal efficiency of your present furnace or boiler (you can figure that your seasonal efficiency will be 5 to 10% less than the tested steady-state efficiency—the average is 60%):

________%

C. Efficiency of the new furnace (85 to 96%):

________%

D. Fuel costs of the new furnace: Divide your present furnace's efficiency (B) by the new furnace's efficiency (C) and multiply by your heating bill (A): ($A \times B \div C$; for example, $1200 × 60% ÷ 85% = 847):

$________

E. Fuel saved by the new furnace ($A - D$; for example, $1200 − $847 = $353):

$________

F. Cost of the new furnace including installation ($2500):

$________

G. Return on your investment ($F \div G$; for example, $353 ÷ $2500 = 14%):

________%

and generally more effective than the daytime approach. It incorporates all the solar components discussed above, as well as thermal mass and night insulation. The mass allows the system to store heat during the day and release it into the house at night, and the window insulation slows the loss of this heat through the glass at night.

The second type of solar modification considered in the case studies is a solar wall. Two types of solar walls are covered: a wall designed for daytime heating and a wall designed to provide heat both day and night. Daytime solar walls make use of thin or low-mass masonry walls incapable of storing significant amounts of heat for later use. An example of a daytime strategy is converting an existing brick wall into a Trombe wall by providing vents and exterior glazing. Such a wall would normally not have sufficient mass to provide heat at night. The day-and-night solar wall strategy requires a greater investment in a thicker wall able to store more heat, and night insulation to slow heat loss.

The third type of solar space heating system considered in the case studies is a glazed south porch. As we have seen, several different types of systems, reflecting different costs and levels of effectiveness, are considered. The single-glazed approach is least expensive, but it provides substantial overall benefits if the porch can be sealed off from the house at night. The daytime solar heating approach uses double glazing and window insulation to reduce heat losses; this strategy makes sense if the porch is to be used as a living or work area during the day. The day-and-night heating strategy, by adding thermal mass, night insulation, and double glazing, results in a system capable of storing heat for use at night.

Water heating measures include active solar water heaters and heat pump water heaters. The case studies assume 60 square feet of single-glazed collector area and a 110-gallon storage tank.

The performance estimates for these measures are based on the Lawrence Berkeley Laboratory's Computerized Instrumented Residential Audit program, the Los Alamos National Laboratory's load collector ratio method (*Passive Solar Design Handbook, vol. 3*), and various design papers. The designs used in the case studies are realistic but not optimal. They are not the ideal combination of mass, collector area, and materials, but they do reflect what an experienced designer, working within the constraints of an existing house, might come up with.

One word of caution: A poor design can increase your heating bills, your cooling bills, or both. In

POTENTIAL SOLAR MODIFICATIONS

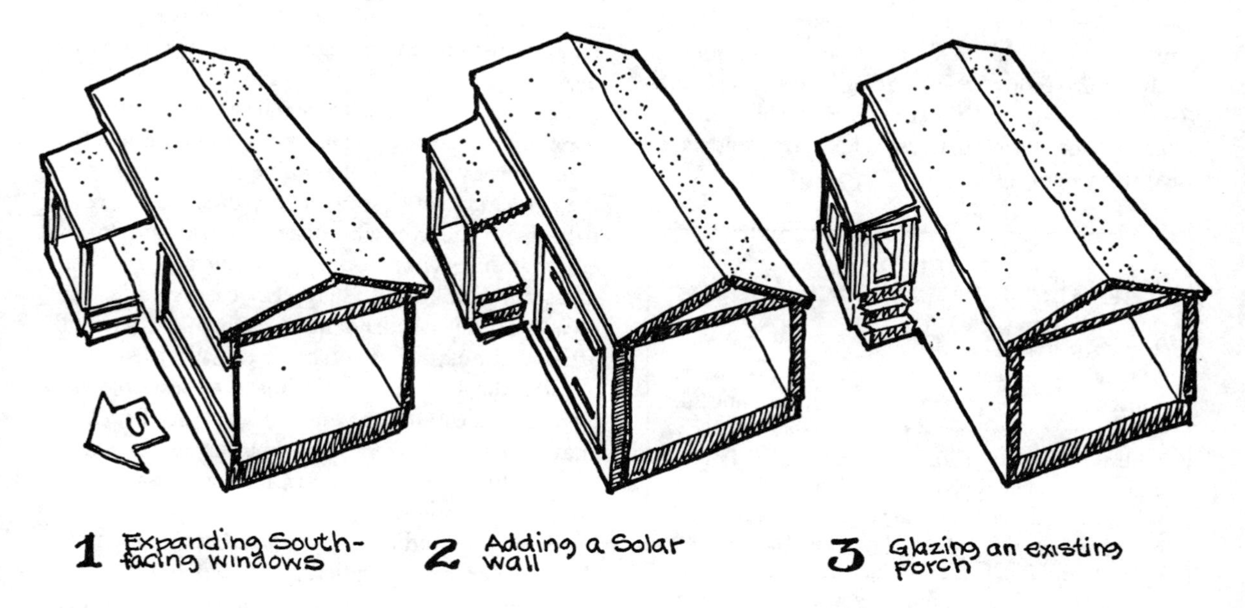

the Minneapolis case study, for example, an indirect passive solar approach, such as a Trombe wall without night insulation, can increase the heating requirements of the house because the wall cannot gain enough solar energy to compensate for the heat it loses at night. In this situation, a well-insulated conventional wall provides lower heating costs.

We have not included the ongoing operating and maintenance costs of these measures. Exterior night insulation—to cover a solar wall, for example—may only last a few years if it isn't periodically weatherproofed. Inside night insulation, however, such as thermal drapes, may last ten to fifteen years before being replaced or recovered. Operating costs are assumed to be negligible for passive heating measures.

The potential for cooling in warm climates is not indicated in these case studies. For one thing, the dynamics of cooling are not as well understood; far more work has gone into quantifying solar heating performance than cooling performance. In climates where cooling costs are higher than heating costs, energy efficiency measures are generally a better investment than solar heating.

The cost of adapting an existing home for passive solar heating can be high. Installing passive solar heating measures in existing homes ranges from $10 to $50 per square foot of glazed area—depending on the measure, the amount of thermal mass, and whether night insulation is provided. More complex renovations, such as replacing a south-facing wood frame wall with a masonry Trombe wall, may cost even more.

Tax credits for passive solar measures are available from the federal government and many states; however, the eligibility of many passive solar retrofit costs are in question. Investigate this issue carefully if you're counting on the federal tax credit to help pay for the project.

The economic value of a passive solar heating system depends on your present heating system, the price you pay for fuel, and the performance of the measures during the times you heat. An average gas furnace (like the one assumed in the Chapter 5 case studies) delivers about 1 therm (100,000 Btu's) of useful heat to the house for every 1.5 therms of fuel it burns. The solar energy received during the heating season on a vertical surface ranges from 1.5 to 4 therms for the continental United States (see Table 6-1).

Passive solar heating systems, with efficiencies ranging from 25 to 75 percent, deliver from 0.4 to 3 therms per square foot over the heating season.

With a natural gas price of 60¢ per therm and the heating system efficiencies assumed in the Level I case studies, the value of this collected solar energy ranges from 35¢ to $2.70 each heating season for each square foot of south-facing glass. Use Table 7-2 to estimate the dollar value of solar energy collected for your area, your fuel cost, and your heating system.

TABLE 7-2
THE VALUE OF SOLAR SPACE HEATING

The economic value of the energy provided by a passive solar heating system is determined by the efficiency of your present heating system and the price you pay for fuel. The case studies assume a central gas furnace with an efficiency of 70 percent and distribution system losses of about 8 percent. Getting an estimate of the average value of the solar energy provided for your fuel type and cost requires three steps. First, find the dollar savings estimate in the case studies for the project you are considering. Second, multiply this percentage by the price per unit of your heating fuel (see Table 3-2). Third, multiply the resulting number by the factor corresponding to the heating system you use:

For electrical furnaces: 32
For heat pumps: 16
For oil furnaces/boilers: 0.77
For coal furnaces (assuming coal with a heat value of 13,000 Btu/lb): 12
For wood stoves: 0.13
For propane: 1.07

Suppose, for example, the savings from the solar heating system (from the case study) is estimated to be $100, you have an electric furnace, and you pay 7¢/kwh for electricity. In this case the computation of your savings is

$100 × 7¢ × 32 = $224

Making the Case Studies Work for You

The case studies in this chapter look at the costs and savings of improving the energy performance of your home. They show you how the effectiveness of the measures varies with climate and the amount of solar radiation received during the heating season. They also show the relative savings of the measures and their typical cost when installed by a contractor. Finally, they indicate the value of the energy saved in an average house after the investment.

Each case study has three parts: a description of the climate, the house, and the energy prices; a list of measures with the dollar value of the savings and the percentage of heating energy the measure contributes to an average efficient house and to an energy-conserving house; and the cost of each measure. Unlike the Chapter 5 case studies, the measures are independent of each other; savings are not cumulative as you move down the list.

Find the location and climate closest to your own, as you did in the Chapter 5 case studies. The characteristics of your house matter less for these case studies than they did in Chapter 5, so we have not included notes.

These case studies use the same climate zones as the Chapter 5 case studies, so the heating requirements are the same. Within each climate zone, however, the amount of solar energy received during the heating season varies. Use the insolation map (Table 6-1) to see how much solar energy is received in a general area. This will help you judge how well the solar measure can meet your heating demands.

In the Climate 1 case study, for example, Albany and Cheyenne have similar heating requirements. Cheyenne, however, receives almost twice as much solar energy per vertical square foot during the heating season as Albany does, presenting excellent solar opportunities. The performance of solar measures in Cheyenne will be at the high end of the range given in the case study, and Albany will be at or near the bottom. Albany residents may be better off looking to additional conservation measures, such as furnace replacement, to save energy.

The houses in these cases have the same general characteristics as the homes in Chapter 5. In this chapter, two versions of the basic house are used: Savings percentages are given for an average house (the Chapter 5 house before conservation) and an efficient house (the Chapter 5 house with recommended efficiency measures).

Each case study includes an estimated range of savings for each type of investment. This range represents performance at the low end and the high end of the amount of solar energy received during the heating season. The Climate 1 case study, for example, shows the difference between the performance of the solar project in Albany, which receives only 2.2 therms of solar energy per vertical square foot during the heating season, and Cheyenne, which receives more than 4.0 therms per vertical square foot. Minneapolis receives about 2.3 therms per square foot of solar energy during the heating season.

To apply the case studies to your location, find the case with a similar climate and insolation (see Table 6-1). Use the percentage savings estimates with your current heating cost (see Table 3-2) to get an estimate of your potential dollar savings for each measure. If your heating costs are higher than those assumed in the case studies, the contribution from low-mass daytime heating systems will generally be higher than those listed and the contribution for an indirect-gain system with thermal mass will be lower.

The costs listed are approximate averages for contractor installations; actual costs vary widely according to local prices, the characteristics of your house, and the specifics of your project. The costs can help you determine whether it's worth your time to do further research on the potential benefits of the solar improvement. Remember, these costs are total costs and do not take into account tax benefits or the cost reductions possible if you are adding passive solar heating measures in the course of a remodeling project.

After looking at the case studies, you should begin to see some trends. Note that the solar heating contribution increases with the installation of energy conservation measures and with the expansion of collector area. Conservation measures almost always cost less and are more cost effective than solar measures. For the best results, then, plan the solar contribution after you've completed the conservation projects.

In locations where the savings are below 35 percent, the solar heating systems provide mostly daytime heating. Thermal mass becomes less important and the amount of glazing and night insulation becomes critical. As a result, low-cost daytime strategies become increasingly desirable.

In southern locations or places where solar can contribute a higher share of heating, thermal mass is very important and indirect solar heating sys-

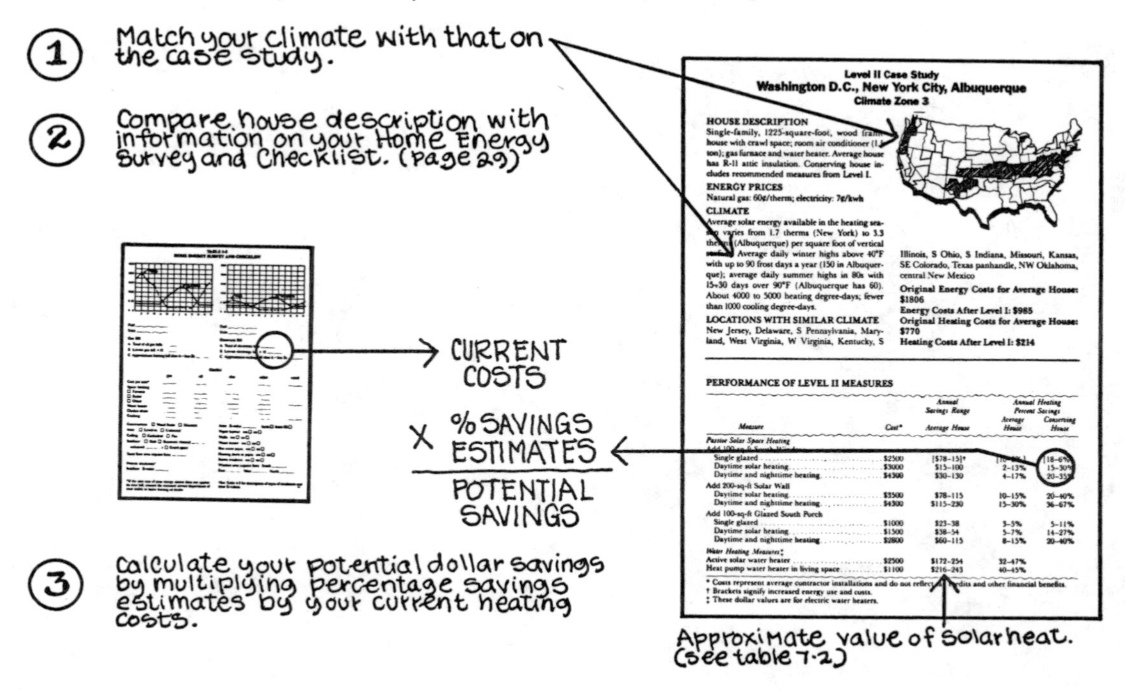

tems have advantages. In these locations, there is less heating demand and a small system can provide significant savings. Because of the higher solar heat gained by the system, more mass allows it to contribute to nighttime heating. Moreover, increased mass helps reduce potential problems of overheating.

In northern climates such as Minneapolis, Cheyenne, and Chicago, adding south windows generally results in nighttime heat losses that exceed daytime heat gains. To prevent this loss, use triple glazing and night insulation. In a direct-gain system, night insulation increases the contribution of solar energy by 20 percent in places like Albuquerque and Santa Maria, California; by 30 to 50 percent in Boston and Portland, Oregon; and by as much as 100 percent in Madison, Wisconsin. For energy-conserving homes in the case studies, any type of thermal mass—such as plaster walls or tiles—can significantly improve performance (as much as twofold) if it's not a light color or isn't covered. In locations such as Washington, D.C., Albuquerque, and Seattle, houses with night insulation gain little from multiple glazing.

For solar walls, proper sizing becomes critical because of their higher cost. The optimal thickness increases with night insulation. Vents are important for the average home, requiring about 6 percent of the solar wall's area to be open to the house (half high in the wall and half low). For energy-conserving homes in locations where the solar contribution is high (more than 50 percent), less vent area is required.

Trombe walls are sensitive to orientation. If the wall is more than 30 degrees from true south to the east, or 40 degrees to the west, savings are reduced by 10 to 50 percent.

In mild and warm climates, porches can be single glazed if they provide daytime heating only. Multiple glazing is best in climates similar to Chicago, Minneapolis, and New York. In these climates, porches should be single glazed only if they can be completely sealed off from the house at night.

Orientation is important if the sides of the porch are solid, not glazed. Solar collection is reduced by as much as 15 percent if the porch faces 35 degrees east or west of true south.

Level II Case Study
Minneapolis, Albany, Cheyenne
Climate Zone 1

HOUSE DESCRIPTION
Single-family, 1225-square-foot, wood frame house with basement; oil boiler with water distribution; electric water heater; no air conditioning. Average house has R-19 attic insulation, R-11 wall insulation; storm windows. Conserving house includes recommended measures from Level I.

ENERGY PRICES
Oil: 95¢/gallon; electricity: 7¢/kwh

CLIMATE
Average solar energy available in the heating season varies from 2.2 therms (Albany) to 4.1 therms (Cheyenne) per square foot of vertical surface. Average daily winter highs up to 30°F with up to 180 frost days a year; average daily summer highs in low 80s with 15 fewer days over 90°F. Over 7000 heating degree-days; fewer than 1000 cooling degree days.

LOCATIONS WITH SIMILAR CLIMATE
Upstate New York, Maine, New Hampshire, Vermont, W Massachusetts, N Michigan, N Iowa, Wisconsin, Minnesota, North Dakota, South Dakota, NW Nebraska, Montana, Wyoming, W Colorado, NW Nevada, N and E Idaho, N central Washington

Original Energy Costs for Average House: $2152

Energy Costs After Level I: $1097

Original Heating Costs for Average House: $1180

Heating Costs After Level I: $505

PERFORMANCE OF LEVEL II MEASURES

Measure	*Cost**	*Annual Savings Range Average House*	*Annual Heating Percent Savings Average House*	*Annual Heating Percent Savings Conserving House*
Passive Solar Space Heating				
Add 100-sq-ft South Window				
Single glazed	$2500	[$35–20]†	[3–2%]	[7–3%]
Daytime solar heating	$3500	$120–180	10–15%	15–20%
Daytime and nighttime heating	$4300	$120–200	10–17%	20–27%
Add 200-sq-ft Solar Wall				
Daytime solar heating	$3500	$60–180	5–15%	10–30%
Daytime and nighttime heating	$4300	$120–240	10–20%	20–40%
Add 100-sq-ft Glazed South Porch				
Single glazed	$1000	$20–120	2–10%	3–17%
Daytime solar heating	$2000	$60–180	5–15%	10–15%
Daytime and nighttime heating	$2800	$80–240	7–20%	15–25%
Water Heating Measures‡				
Active solar water heater	$2500	$230–290	43–53%	
Heat pump water heater in living space	$1100	$216–240	40–45%	

* Costs represent average contractor installations and do not reflect tax credits and other financial benefits.
† Brackets signify increased energy use and costs. ‡ These dollar values are for electric water heaters.

Level II Case Study
Chicago, Boston, Colorado Springs
Climate Zone 2

HOUSE DESCRIPTION
Single-family, 1225-square-foot, wood frame house; room air conditioner (1 ton); gas furnace and water heater. Average house has R-19 attic insulation, R-11 wall insulation, storm windows. Conserving house includes recommended measures from Level I.

ENERGY PRICES
Natural gas: 60¢/therm; electricity: 7¢/kwh

CLIMATE
Average solar energy available in the heating season varies from 2 therms (Boston) to 3.5 therms (Colorado Springs) per square foot of vertical surface. Average daily winter highs of 30–40°F with up to 180 frost days a year; average daily summer highs in mid-80s with up to 30 days over 90°F. About 5500 to 7000 heating degree-days; fewer than 1000 cooling degree-days.

LOCATIONS WITH SIMILAR CLIMATE
E Massachusetts, Connecticut, Rhode Island, S and W New York, N Pennsylvania, N Indiana, N Illinois, S Iowa, S Michigan, N Ohio, Nebraska, NW Kansas, NE Colorado, N New Mexico, N Arizona, NW and central Nevada, NE California and high Sierra, E Oregon, Utah, E Washington, central and W Idaho

Original Energy Costs for Average House: $1626
Energy Costs After Level I: $980
Original Heating Costs for Average House: $775
Heating Costs After Level I: $269

PERFORMANCE OF LEVEL II MEASURES

Measure	*Cost**	*Annual Savings Range* *Average House*	*Annual Heating Percent Savings* *Average House*	*Conserving House*
Passive Solar Space Heating				
Add 100-sq-ft South Window				
Single glazed	$2500	[$90–40]†	[12–5%]	[25–23%]
Daytime solar heating	$3500	$40–100	5–13%	15–20%
Daytime and nighttime heating	$4300	$40–115	5–15%	13–35%
Add 200-sq-ft Solar Wall				
Daytime solar heating	$3500	$8–30	1–4%	5–20%
Daytime and nighttime heating	$4300	$115–155	15–20%	30–45%
Add 100-sq-ft Glazed South Porch				
Single glazed	$1000	$15–40	2–5%	5–10%
Daytime solar heating	$2000	$23–60	3–8%	8–15%
Daytime and nighttime heating	$2800	$40–80	5–10%	20–35%
Water Heating Measures‡				
Active solar water heater	$2500	$162–243	30–45%	
Heat pump water heater in living space	$1100	$216–234	40–45%	

* Costs represent average contractor installations and do not reflect tax credits and other financial benefits.
† Brackets signify increased energy use and costs. ‡ These dollar values are for electric water heaters.

Level II Case Study
Washington D.C., New York City, Albuquerque
Climate Zone 3

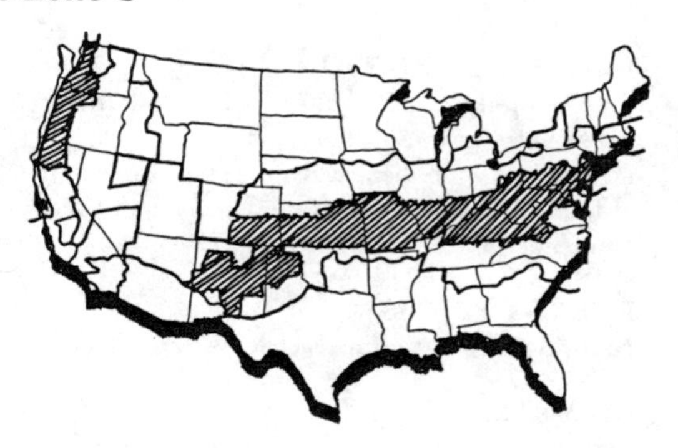

HOUSE DESCRIPTION

Single-family, 1225-square-foot, wood frame house with crawl space; room air conditioner (1.5 ton); gas furnace and water heater. Average house has R-11 attic insulation. Conserving house includes recommended measures from Level I.

ENERGY PRICES

Natural gas: 60¢/therm; electricity: 7¢/kwh

CLIMATE

Average solar energy available in the heating season varies from 1.7 therms (New York) to 3.3 therms (Albuquerque) per square foot of vertical surface. Average daily winter highs above 40°F with up to 90 frost days a year (150 in Albuquerque); average daily summer highs in 80s with 15–30 days over 90°F (Albuquerque has 60). About 4000 to 5500 heating degree-days; fewer than 1000 cooling degree-days.

LOCATIONS WITH SIMILAR CLIMATE

New Jersey, Delaware, S Pennsylvania, Maryland, West Virginia, W Virginia, Kentucky, S Illinois, S Ohio, S Indiana, Missouri, Kansas, SE Colorado, Texas panhandle, NW Oklahoma, central New Mexico

Original Energy Costs for Average House: $1806

Energy Costs After Level I: $985

Original Heating Costs for Average House: $770

Heating Costs After Level I: $214

PERFORMANCE OF LEVEL II MEASURES

Measure	*Cost**	*Annual Savings Range Average House*	*Annual Heating Percent Savings Average House*	*Annual Heating Percent Savings Conserving House*
Passive Solar Space Heating				
Add 100-sq-ft South Window				
Single glazed	$2500	[$78–15]†	[10–2%]	[18–6%]
Daytime solar heating	$3000	$15–100	2–13%	15–30%
Daytime and nighttime heating	$4300	$30–130	4–17%	20–35%
Add 200-sq-ft Solar Wall				
Daytime solar heating	$3500	$78–115	10–15%	20–40%
Daytime and nighttime heating	$4300	$115–230	15–30%	36–67%
Add 100-sq-ft Glazed South Porch				
Single glazed	$1000	$23–38	3–5%	5–11%
Daytime solar heating	$1500	$38–54	5–7%	14–27%
Daytime and nighttime heating	$2800	$60–115	8–15%	20–40%
Water Heating Measures‡				
Active solar water heater	$2500	$172–254	32–47%	
Heat pump water heater in living space	$1100	$216–243	40–45%	

* Costs represent average contractor installations and do not reflect tax credits and other financial benefits.
† Brackets signify increased energy use and costs. ‡ These dollar values are for electric water heaters.

Level II Case Study
San Francisco, Portland, Seattle
Climate Zone 4

HOUSE DESCRIPTION
Single-family, 1225-square-foot, wood frame house with crawl space; no air conditioner; gas furnace and water heater. Average house has R-11 attic insulation. Conserving house includes recommended measures from Level I.

ENERGY PRICES
Natural gas: 60¢/therm; electricity: 7¢/kwh

CLIMATE
Average solar energy available in the heating season varies from 2.7 therms (Portland) to 3.9 therms (San Francisco) per square foot of vertical surface. Moderate summer and winter temperatures; average daily winter highs in 40s and 50s; average summer highs in 70s and low 80s; very few days over 90°F. From 3000 to 5000 heating degree-days; fewer than 1000 cooling degree-days.

LOCATIONS WITH SIMILAR CLIMATE
Coastal N California, W Oregon, W Washington

Original Energy Costs for Average House: $1581
Energy Costs After Level I: $906
Original Heating Costs for Average House: $885
Heating Costs After Level I: $330

PERFORMANCE OF LEVEL II MEASURES

Measure	*Cost**	*Annual Savings Range* *Average House*	*Annual Heating Percent Savings* *Average House*	*Conserving House*
Passive Solar Space Heating				
Add 100-sq-ft South Window				
Single glazed	$2500	[$80–53]†	[9–6%]	[10%]
Daytime solar heating	$3000	$18–62	2–7%	10–30%
Daytime and nighttime heating	$4300	$18–80	2–9%	10–30%
Add 200-sq-ft Solar Wall				
Daytime solar heating	$3500	$62–124	7–14%	20–40%
Daytime and nighttime heating	$4300	$141–292	16–33%	30–65%
Add 100-sq-ft Glazed South Porch				
Single glazed	$1000	$124–212	14–24%	16–30%
Daytime solar heating	$1500	$133–221	15–25%	18–35%
Daytime and nighttime heating	$2800	$133–266	15–30%	18–45%
Water Heating Measures‡				
Active solar water heater	$2500	$119–205	22–38%	
Heat pump water heater in living space	$1100	$216–243	40–45%	

* Costs represent average contractor installations and do not reflect tax credits and other financial benefits.
† Brackets signify increased energy use and costs. ‡ These dollar values are for electric water heaters.

Level II Case Study
Atlanta, Fresno, Tulsa
Climate Zone 5

HOUSE DESCRIPTION
Single-family, 1225-square-foot, wood frame house with crawl space; room air conditioner (2 ton); gas furnace and water heater. Average house has R-11 attic insulation. Conserving house includes recommended measures from Level I.

ENERGY PRICES
Natural gas: 60¢/therm; electricity: 7¢/kwh

CLIMATE
Average solar energy available in the heating season varies from 2.5 therms (Fresno) to 2.2 therms (Tulsa) per square foot of vertical surface. Average daily winter highs in the 50s with fewer than 100 frost days a year; average daily summer highs in 90s with 60 or more days over 90°F. From 2000 to 4000 heating degree-days; fewer than 2000 cooling degree-days.

LOCATIONS WITH SIMILAR CLIMATE
SE Virginia, North Carolina, N South Carolina, Tennessee, N Georgia, N Alabama, N Arkansas, N central Oklahoma, N central Texas, SE and SW New Mexico, central and S California excluding coastal areas

Original Energy Costs for Average House: $1606
Energy Costs After Level I: $1127
Original Heating Costs for Average House: $550
Heating Costs After Level I: $285

PERFORMANCE OF LEVEL II MEASURES

Measure	Cost*	*Annual Savings Range* Average House	*Annual Heating Percent Savings* Average House	Conserving House
Passive Solar Space Heating				
Add 100-sq-ft South Window				
Single glazed	$2500	[$45–16]†	[8–3%]	[10–5%]
Daytime solar heating	$3000	$66	12%	15–17%
Daytime and nighttime heating	$4300	$16–94	3–17%	17–25%
Add 200-sq-ft Solar Wall				
Daytime solar heating	$3500	$55–82	10–15%	30–35%
Daytime and nighttime heating	$4300	$82–138	15–25%	40–45%
Add 100-sq-ft Glazed South Porch				
Single glazed	$1000	$38–55	7–10%	10–15%
Daytime solar heating	$1500	$55–72	10–13%	18–25%
Daytime and nighttime heating	$2800	$66–82	12–15%	20–40%
Water Heating Measures‡				
Active solar water heater	$2500	$184–232	34–43%	
Heat pump water heater in living space	$1100	$216–243	40–45%	

* Costs represent average contractor installations and do not reflect tax credits and other financial benefits.
† Brackets signify increased energy use and costs. ‡ These dollar values are for electric water heaters.

Level II Case Study
Los Angeles, Santa Ana, San Diego
Climate Zone 6

HOUSE DESCRIPTION
Single-family, 1225-square-foot, wood frame house with crawl space; room air conditioner (0.5 ton); gas furnace and water heater. Average house has R-11 attic insulation. Conserving house includes recommended measures from Level I.

ENERGY PRICES
Natural gas: 60¢/therm; electricity: 7¢/kwh

CLIMATE
Average solar energy available in the heating season is about 2.6 therms per square foot of vertical surface. Average daily winter highs of 60–65°F with 10 or fewer frost days a year; average daily summer highs of 60–70°F with 30 or fewer days over 90°F. Fewer than 3000 heating degree-days; fewer than 1000 cooling degree-days. Because of San Diego's mild climate, these measures perform better there.

LOCATIONS WITH SIMILAR CLIMATE
Coastal S California

Original Energy Costs for Average House: $1016
Energy Costs After Level I: $722
Original Heating Costs for Average House: $210
Heating Costs After Level I: $88

PERFORMANCE OF LEVEL II MEASURES

Measure	Cost*	Annual Savings Range Average House	Annual Heating Percent Savings Average House	Annual Heating Percent Savings Conserving House
Passive Solar Space Heating				
Add 100-sq-ft South Window				
Single glazed	$2500	[$6–8]†	[3–4%]	[15–20%]
Daytime solar heating	$3000	$29–32	14–15%	51–55%
Daytime and nighttime heating	$4300	$57–78	27–37%	65–70%
Add 200-sq-ft Solar Wall				
Daytime solar heating	$3500	$50–63	24–30%	65–70%
Daytime and nighttime heating	$4300	$122–137	58–65%	95%
Add 100-sq-ft Glazed South Porch				
Single glazed	$1000	$59–74	28–35%	40–45%
Daytime solar heating	$1500	$59–74	28–35%	40–45%
Daytime and nighttime heating	$2800	$80–95	38–45%	73–74%
Water Heating Measures‡				
Active solar water heater	$2500	$210–216	39–40%	
Heat pump water heater in living space	$1100	$216–243	40–45%	

* Costs represent average contractor installations and do not reflect tax credits and other financial benefits.
† Brackets signify increased energy use and costs.
‡ These dollar values are for electric water heaters.

Level II Case Study
Dallas and Phoenix
Climate Zone 7

HOUSE DESCRIPTION

Single-family, 1225-square-foot, wood frame house with crawl space; room air conditioner (2 ton); gas furnace and water heater. Average house has R-11 attic insulation. Conserving house includes recommended measures from Level I.

ENERGY PRICES

Natural gas: 60¢/therm; electricity: 7¢/kwh

CLIMATE

Average solar energy available in the heating season varies from 1.6 therms (Dallas) to 2.3 therms (Phoenix) per square foot of vertical surface. Average daily winter highs of 50–70°F with 40 or fewer frost days a year; average daily summer highs in high 90s with up to 150 days over 90°F. Fewer than 2000 heating degree-days; more than 2000 cooling degree-days. Exclude Miami and similar climates, which rarely require space heating. In these areas, solar water heating will save 40 percent of water heating bills (over $100 annually).

LOCATIONS WITH SIMILAR CLIMATE

Texas (except panhandle), SE Oklahoma, central and S Arkansas, Mississippi, S Alabama, S South Carolina, Louisiana, S Georgia, Florida, California desert, S Nevada, S Arizona

Original Energy Costs for Average House: $1536

Energy Costs After Level I: $1019

Original Heating Costs for Average House: $295

Heating Costs After Level I: $171

PERFORMANCE OF LEVEL II MEASURES

Measure	*Cost**	*Annual Savings Range*	*Annual Heating Percent Savings*	
		Average House	*Average House*	*Conserving House*
Passive Solar Space Heating				
Add 100-sq-ft South Window				
Single glazed	$2500	[$15–35]†	[5–12%]	[9–20%]
Daytime solar heating	$3000	$18–30	6–10%	15–25%
Daytime and nighttime heating	$4300	$45–60	15–20%	25–50%
Add 200-sq-ft Solar Wall				
Daytime solar heating	$3500	$35–75	12–25%	20–35%
Daytime and nighttime heating	$4300	$90–135	30–45%	40–60%
Add 100-sq-ft Glazed South Porch				
Single glazed	$1000	$50–60	17–20%	20–22%
Daytime solar heating	$1500	$50–60	17–20%	22–25%
Daytime and nighttime heating	$2800	$53–88	18–30%	25–35%
Water Heating Measures‡				
Active solar water heater	$2500	$194–265	36–49%	
Heat pump water heater in living space	$1100	$216–243	40–45%	

* Costs represent average contractor installations and do not reflect tax credits and other financial benefits.
† Brackets signify increased energy use and costs. ‡ These dollar values are for electric water heaters.

Chapter Eight
Level III: Energy-Conscious Home Additions

LEVEL III MEASURES
An energy-efficient solar addition

Level III: Energy-Conscious Home Additions

Since the dramatic increase in both housing costs and mortgage rates began in the mid-1970s, more and more families are considering enlarging their present home instead of purchasing a new one. Other trends have reinforced this pattern. An aversion to long commute times and the rising price of gasoline have led many families to locate in older, closer-in neighborhoods where the houses may be small, in need of repair, or costly to heat and cool. As families and their incomes grow, many decide to enlarge or renovate their present home rather than leave the neighborhood.

For these reasons, adding on has become an activity rivaling and in many areas outpacing new home construction. In some cities, contractors have shifted the focus of their business to remodeling. Lumber stores cater to those who want to do-it-themselves. Community organizations and local governments offer guidelines and classes for those who want to repair or add to their homes.

The remodeler does not have the design flexibility of the new home builder, but the possibilities are extensive nonetheless. They range from a single room addition, such as a new bedroom or family room, to the addition of a second story. Whatever your plans, home expansion opens up a number of energy opportunities. As in any home energy project, the starting point is energy efficiency. The first part of this chapter reviews Level I and II measures you can integrate into your room addition and your present structure. Later we'll look at the appropriateness of these measures for different types of home additions.

If you are planning a new house, the principles outlined in this chapter apply equally well. Whether you are considering a solar home or one that is simply energy efficient, you can integrate energy efficiency into the planning and construction process, getting more for every dollar you invest. For a new home in an area with very cold winters such as Minneapolis or Cheyenne, explore the concept of *superinsulation*. Superinsulated houses require little or no conventional energy for heating or cooling. For more on this option, see Box 8-1 later in the chapter.

The fourth section of this chapter looks at economics and trade-offs. By extending a few of the case studies from Chapters 5-7, this section shows the range of savings you can expect from adding solar features and conservation measures in several types of home additions. The chapter concludes with information on selecting a contractor or architect to help you with an addition.

In this chapter we assume that economy is important, but in a different way. The savings that will accrue from energy efficiency or solar measures may be only one element in a decision to invest in an addition. Your primary need is for more space or an extensive renovation of your home. The challenge will be to keep from regarding the energy measures as "extras." As the project progresses, budget constraints may force you to make some trade-offs, and it will be tempting to drop certain energy features, sacrificing future savings. In the context of a home addition, energy "extras" can provide important long-term benefits at a modest additional cost.

An Energy-Efficient Home Addition

Aiming for a high level of efficiency in your room addition makes sense for several reasons. Since you are starting from scratch, you can incorporate more insulation, an effective vapor barrier, and thermal windows at a fraction of the expense and bother involved in retrofitting these items to an existing house.

Second, by making your addition highly efficient and adding conservation measures to your present structure at the same time, you can keep your heating needs steady or even reduce them, making it possible to heat and cool the entire house comfortably without expanding your current heating and air conditioning system.

Third, you will be investing for the future. As energy prices rise, you (or a future owner) are likely to find yourself wishing you had made the efficiency impovements at a time when it was less complicated and less costly to do so. By opting for a high level of efficiency now, you reduce your energy bills and avoid the added expense and headache of doing it later. And, of course, you'll be improving your household's comfort and adding to the resale value of your home.

What types of energy efficiency measures should you incorporate in your addition? Most Level I and some Level II actions are appropriate, depending on your climate, heating fuel, and the configuration of your house. Many of the decisions you face are the same as those outlined in Chapters 4 and 6.

Insulate the new walls to R-19 (6 inches of fiberglass) unless you live in an area with a climate similar to Los Angeles, Phoenix, Dallas, or Miami; these areas require only R-11. Using 2×6 studs allows you to insulate to this level, and 2×6 walls may actually save you money. Most local building codes allow 2×6 studs to be spaced 24 inches apart (compared to 16 inches for 2×4 studs)—and fewer studs means the walls go together with less labor, saving on construction costs.

Insulate the roof or attic of your addition to R-38 in most areas. In moderate climate areas (such as San Francisco, Portland, Seattle, Atlanta, and Fresno), R-30 should be installed. Warm southern areas (Miami, San Diego, Los Angeles, Dallas) require only R-19. Provide a vapor barrier with both wall and attic insulation.

Use single-glazed windows in climates like those of Los Angeles, San Diego, Dallas, and Miami. Triple glazing is required in colder climates such as Chicago, Minneapolis, Washington, D.C., and

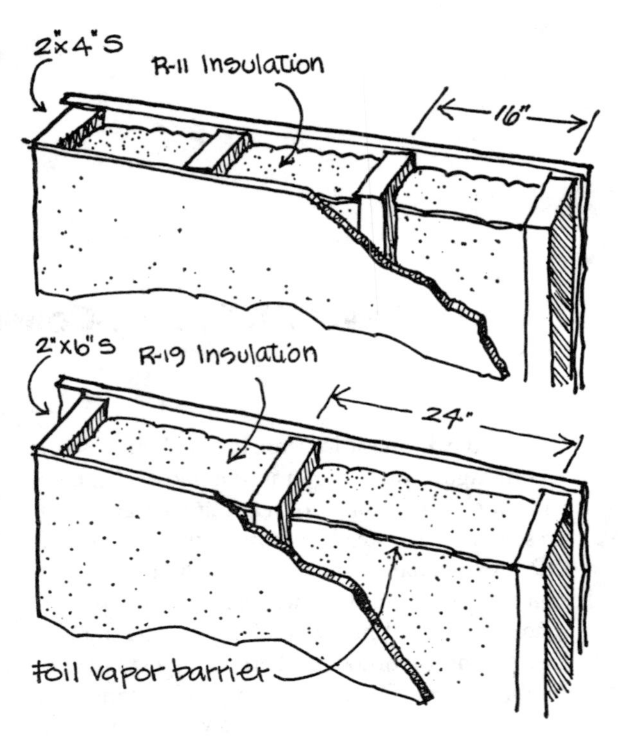

Boston. Other areas require double glazing. If summers are exceptionally hot in your area, locate east and west windows where they can be shaded. If your climate is appropriate for a whole-house fan (hot days, mild nights), installation will cost less if you can locate the fan in your addition rather than in an existing portion of your house.

Floors should be insulated to R-19 except in warm areas like Los Angeles, Phoenix, and Miami, where no floor insulation is necessary. And unless you live in these warm climates, slab floors should be insulated around the perimeter with weatherproofed polystyrene or a similar material to a depth of 24 inches.

Remember that the cost of incorporating these measures in your addition is less than the expense of retrofit items, so more measures will be cost effective than if they were retrofit items. If you're replacing a single-glazed window in your present house with a thermal window, for example, the cost of the replacement includes the labor to remove the old window, the expense of the new window, and the labor to install it. In a new addition, you have to pay for the cost and the installation of a window anyway, so you can base your decision to install a double or triple-glazed window simply on the difference in cost between an energy-efficient window and its single-pane alternative. Double-pane windows may add $5 to $10 per square foot of window to your costs but pay for themselves in five to ten years.

While You're at It . . .

Not only can you strive for optimum efficiency in your addition, but the construction process may provide you with specific opportunities to carry out Level I and II improvements on the existing structure. Doing so while you expand will mean a more efficient and comfortable home at considerably less expense than approaching these projects piecemeal.

If your alterations require extensive work on—or replacement of—the heating and air conditioning system, for example, estimate the cost of installing a new high-efficiency unit. If you're working with a contractor anyway, he or she may be able to do the improvements or replacement at a lower cost now than if you wait a few years to replace the furnace.

If you are financing the addition with a loan, adding such a major item to your project may increase your loan payments only modestly, but the new furnace may deliver savings that more than cover the increase. If you take out a $10,000, fifteen-year loan at 12 percent interest, your monthly payment will be just over $120, or $1470 annually. Adding $2500 for the purchase and installation of a new furnace increases your monthly payment by only $30, or $360 annually. In colder areas like Chicago, the new furnace can reduce monthly bills by as much as 30 to 40 percent, roughly $600 a year, easily paying for the increased loan payments. Chapter 7 includes a step-by-step formula (Table 7-1) for calculating the savings for furnace or boiler replacement. Use Table 7-1 to get a better estimate of your energy and cost savings. At a minimum, plan to seal and insulate ducts that are usually hard to get at but will be accessible while your home is undergoing construction.

A home expansion also provides opportunities to upgrade the insulation of your present house at less cost. If your remodeling involves cutting into a portion of the existing roof, think about upgrading your attic insulation while you're at it. If your expansion requires new sheetrock, plaster, or paneling on some interior walls, insulate the walls with fiberglass batts and install an effective vapor barrier while they're open. This operation costs less than blowing in insulation at a later date.

If you plan to repaint your house after the addition is complete, this is a good opportunity to have insulation blown into the remaining uninsulated walls. Since this technique involves drilling holes in exterior stucco or siding and then patching, it is wise to have the work done before you repaint.

If you're planning to install thermal windows in your addition, have your contractor estimate the cost of replacing some or all of the windows in your present structure with the same window type. Buying in volume may cut your costs—and with a work crew already on site, labor costs will be lower than if you approach window replacement as a separate job.

While you're adding on, also consider installing solar water heating. If your house or addition includes a good location for solar water heating panels, installing the panels and the plumbing will be easier and cheaper in the course of construction. If you decide not to put in a solar water heater at the time of your construction, consider having the necessary plumbing completed anway. By running pipes and wires (for the temperature sensors required in some solar systems) to the roof at the time of construction, you eliminate much added expense should you (or a future owner) decide to install a solar water heater later. Run the pipes and wires from the likely site for a storage and backup tank to the best south-facing roof surface. The pipes should go through the roof and be capped at both ends.

Weighing Solar Opportunities

Adding onto your home will open up opportunities to use the sun to heat your house and enhance the quality of your living space. A properly designed and operated solar addition can collect solar heat when it is available and store it for later use. Because of the large window area of some solar additions, you may also be creating new habitats within the house for people and plants. You will thus have a home that is brighter, warmer, and in effect more spacious—in tune with the seasons, not at the mercy of the weather. The decision to pursue extensive solar heating modifications should be weighed carefully, however. It is not an energy source that is suited to every type of addition, house, or lifestyle.

The major features of solar heating—orientation, glazing, window insulation, thermal mass, heat storage and distribution, shading, and lifestyle—were described in Chapter 6. These features apply equally to a home addition, with one important distinction: Combining solar design with new construction lifts many of the constraints imposed by the present building, allowing you to design the addition to make the most effective use of the sun's energy.

There is a second, equally important, distinction. Adding onto a house is expensive. Including passive solar heating or natural ventilation in a new addition has a number of benefits, all of which result from conscientious and accurate design. Consult with an experienced designer, architect, contractor, or engineer to ensure your project's success. If you want to understand more about what goes into the design and performance of a solar home, there are several excellent guides listed in the reference section at the end of the book.

Common passive solar heating additions include adding a direct-gain solar room, incorporating a solar wall into a new room, or adding a greenhouse or solarium. Adding a room that employs direct-gain solar heating requires many of the elements of successful solar heating explored in Chapter 6: exposed thermal mass in floor and walls, an unobstructed southern exposure, shading, insulation, and a means of distributing heat (if wanted) to other rooms in the house.

If you are adding a direct-gain solar room to an existing masonry wall, you can use the wall as a "thermal link" between the solar room and the adjoining spaces as long as the wall doesn't contain exterior insulation or other materials that are poor conductors. If it does, use existing windows to get the solar heat to the adjoining rooms or cut high and low vents in the wall. If you plan to use this masonry as a direct-gain surface, the room should be sized so that the sun strikes the masonry surface.

What if your southern exposure is poor or you don't want the heat fluctuations and bright light associated with most direct-gain passive solar designs? If your primary interest is daylighting or what the experts call *light awareness* (being able to see or sense the outdoors), skylights and clerestory

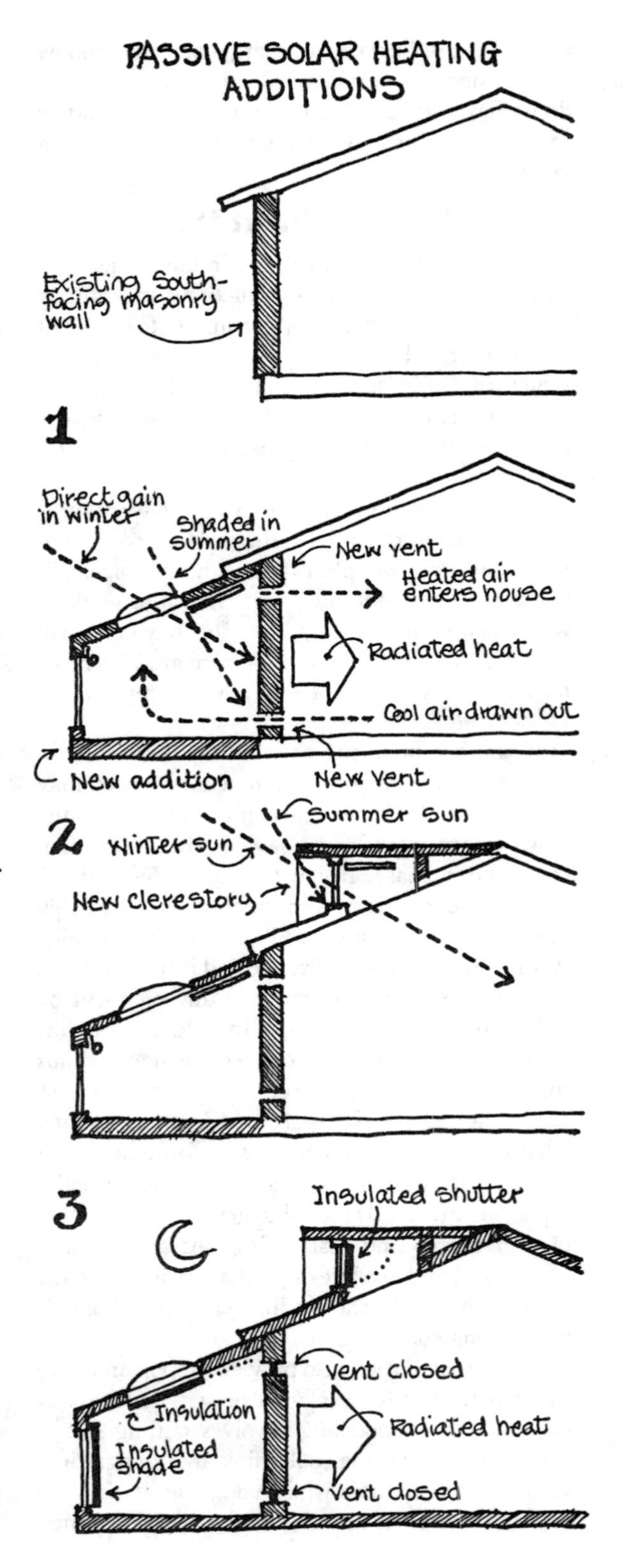

windows offer an attractive alternative. Clerestories are vertical windows set into a roof. Their advantages are that they do not need a perfect southern exposure to gather sufficient light for most general room lighting and, if designed to be opened, they can be used for natural ventilation. But there are disadvantages too. They can lose significant amounts of heat if not multiple glazed, insulated at night, and well weatherstripped, and they can create glare and heat gain during summer if not properly shaded.

Clerestories can supply daytime heating, but if they are to contribute to nighttime heating, thermal mass must be located in the direct path of the sun. In a good energy-efficient design, clerestories can provide a modest portion of your heating needs.

Clerestory windows can be expensive because they involve modifying the roofline of the house. If your goal is to increase daylighting and you do not already plan to modify your roofline, skylights can be incorporated into a conventional roof at lower cost and provide similar daylighting benefits. For more on skylights, see Chapter 6.

Solar walls can also be incorporated into room additions, particularly ones that are occupied at night or where nighttime heating is needed. They are a good alternative when the view is not important. Water walls that use clear acrylic containers allow diffuse lighting but will block a direct view. Thin (low-mass) solar walls require larger vents and contribute primarily to daytime heating needs. In an energy-conserving home addition, thick solar walls, if properly designed, will store sufficient heat for nighttime needs. These walls can also incorporate windows to achieve a mix of daylighting and heating needs.

One of the most popular solar room additions incorporates both direct and indirect-gain features in a greenhouse or solarium. Many of the principles are the same as those governing all solar additions. Heat is collected in a glazed greenhouse where it can be circulated immediately to other rooms in the house or stored for nighttime use. The thermal storage medium can be an exposed slab floor, a masonry wall between the greenhouse and existing house, water-filled containers or planter beds in the

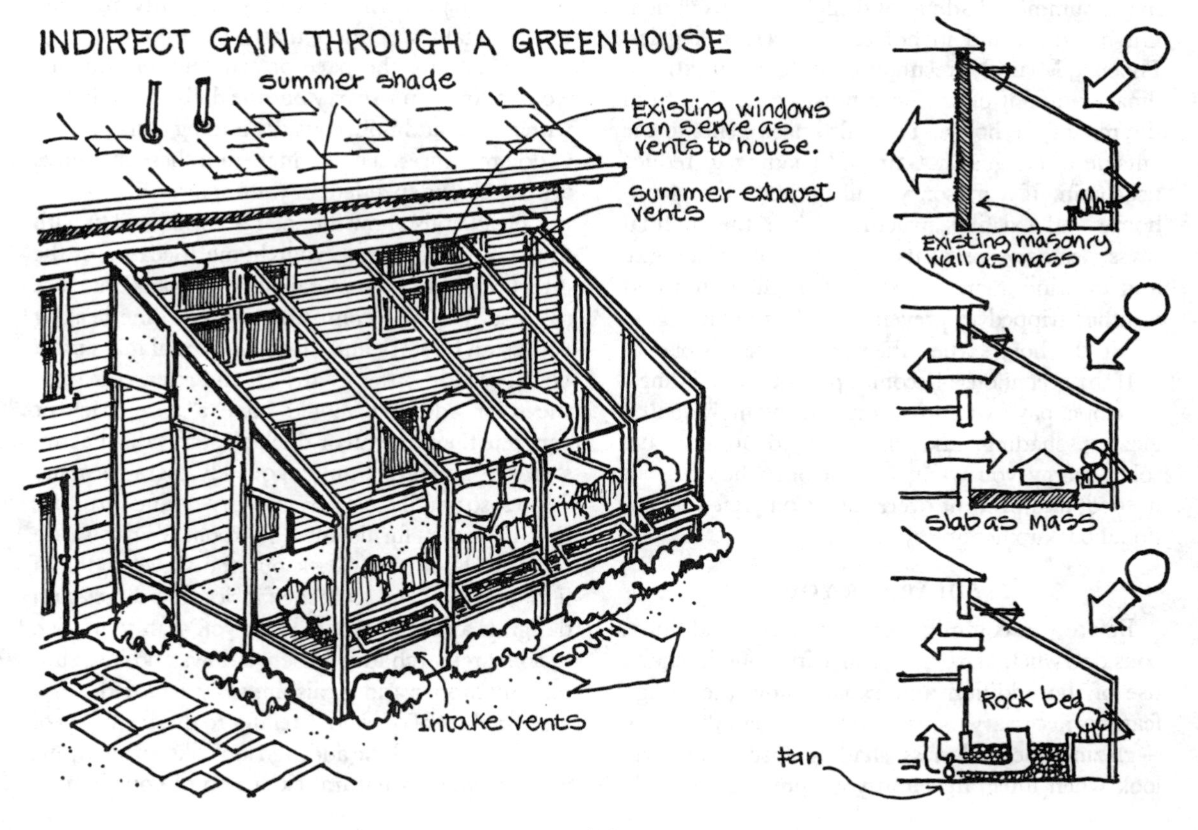

greenhouse itself, or—in a more elaborate design—a bed of rocks located beneath the floor of the greenhouse.

To some extent, the type of thermal mass will determine the best means of distributing heat. Heat rises to the top of the greenhouse and flows through vents cut into the wall between the greenhouse and existing rooms, pulling cooler air in from the adjoining room through vents located at the base of the connecting wall. Existing windows or doors between the house and the greenhouse addition can also provide entryways for heat, but the area of the vents should be about 6 percent of the total south-facing glazed area with vents evenly distributed high and low on the connecting wall. A rockbed heat storage system requires a way of drawing air through the rockbed and distributing it where it's needed. Thermostatically controlled fans can assist in the distribution of heat.

As with any space that receives direct sunlight through glazing, there will be wide fluctuations in temperature inside the greenhouse. These variations can be modified somewhat by using thermal mass, summer shading, and nighttime insulation. On hot days and in hot climates (Los Angeles, Phoenix, Miami), greenhouses can gain an extraordinary amount of heat and must be isolated from the rest of the house. They also need vents to the outside to exhaust hot air and shading to reduce heat gain. If a masonry wall between the greenhouse and existing structure is not the thermal mass, windows or vents between the greenhouse and existing structure should be insulated and weatherstripped to prevent heat loss or heat gain inside the house when the greenhouse is isolated.

If the greenhouse becomes part of the building's envelope, pay extra attention to using high-quality glazing, shading, and insulation to preserve the solar energy you want, keep it out when it's not needed, and prevent overreliance on your conventional backup heating system.

IS SOLAR FOR YOU?

Before you commit yourself to a solar addition, consider whether solar fits in with your intended use of the addition and explore how the design features necessary to make a solar system work well—glazing, thermal mass, shading, insulation—will look when integrated into your present house. Is your lifestyle suited to a solar home? In most cases, if you expect your solar addition to supply a large percentage of your heating needs, you need to perform daily tasks. In the winter, shutters, blinds, and vents should be closed in the evening and opened in the morning. In the summer, shading may need to be adjusted. Daytime heating approaches using double or triple glazing require little operation, but they also contribute less to your heating needs.

These daily rituals can make the difference between energy savings and energy losses. The difference in energy bills between a carefully tended and an untended solar addition are significant. These tasks are particularly important if your solar addition is heated when necessary by your furnace. If you add an unheated solarium or greenhouse, window insulation is less important, but you'll need to open and close the vents that allow transfer of heat from these spaces to your dwelling during the day when needed and then close them off at night. Failure to do this reduces your energy gains and increases your energy bills. These tasks can easily become a pleasant part of your daily routine, through, taking no more than a few minutes.

If you think the pace or schedule of your life won't allow you to carry out the daily tasks that go with a solar addition, consider adding extra conservation measures. The savings from these measures are largely independent of your behavior.

Consider also how the solar addition will fit with the way you decorate your home. Because of the direct sunlight, direct-gain solar rooms that are sized so they also contribute to nighttime heating needs can be stark and bright. Thermal mass must be exposed in order to absorb and release heat, so the solar addition should have a bare brick or concrete floor or wall or thick plaster walls that are struck by sunlight. Sunlight quickly degrades many fabrics, so you'll have to select carpets and furniture carefully when furnishing a sunroom. Windows are now available that block out the wavelengths of light that damage and fade fabrics. If a direct-gain design is appealing to you and you plan to furnish it, some research into these windows and into sun-tolerant fabrics and furnishings is warranted.

A final set of questions relates to the aesthetics of an addition. Will the addition look like an awkward appendage or a natural extension of your home's character? Will it add or detract from resale value? Passive solar designs can be successfully integrated into nearly any style of house, from old row houses to suburban ranch-style homes. Research the alternatives on your own or with an architect or designer to find the approach best suited to your existing structure and needs.

Most people add on because they need a larger kitchen, new family room, or new bedroom and bath. Passive solar heating techniques should be an integral part of the design of a house, providing comfort, beauty and energy benefits in each of these situations. How these rooms will be used dictates the best solar solution . . . or rules it out altogether. The following sections look at passive solar heating trade-offs for some typical additions.

THE BEDROOM/BATH ADDITION

When families need more room, they usually add another bedroom (or bedrooms) and bath to accommodate their needs. Bedrooms can be suitable for solar heating, but incorporating solar features requires careful planning.

At the outset, consider whether your new bedroom needs a heating source of any kind. In some homes, bedrooms remain unheated day and night. If this is the case, an additional investment in solar heating will improve your comfort but it won't save money. If your bedroom is normally heated during the day, a direct-gain system can provide much of its heat during daytime hours. If your bedroom is used and heated only at night, both direct-gain and indirect-gain approaches require thermal mass and window insulation to keep collected heat in at night.

If daytime heating of the bedroom is your goal, it can be achieved with a south-facing glazed collector area of 5 to 10 percent of the floor space of the addition. Larger collector areas can provide surplus heat for other parts of the house, but you'll need fans to help move the heated air. If nighttime heating is wanted, additional window insulation is necessary and thermal mass is needed to store heat for evening use and prevent overheating during the day.

Is it realistic to expect a solar bedroom to be a heat source for the rest of the house? In most cases, no. Most bedroom additions add no more than 10 percent to the total square footage of the house. An

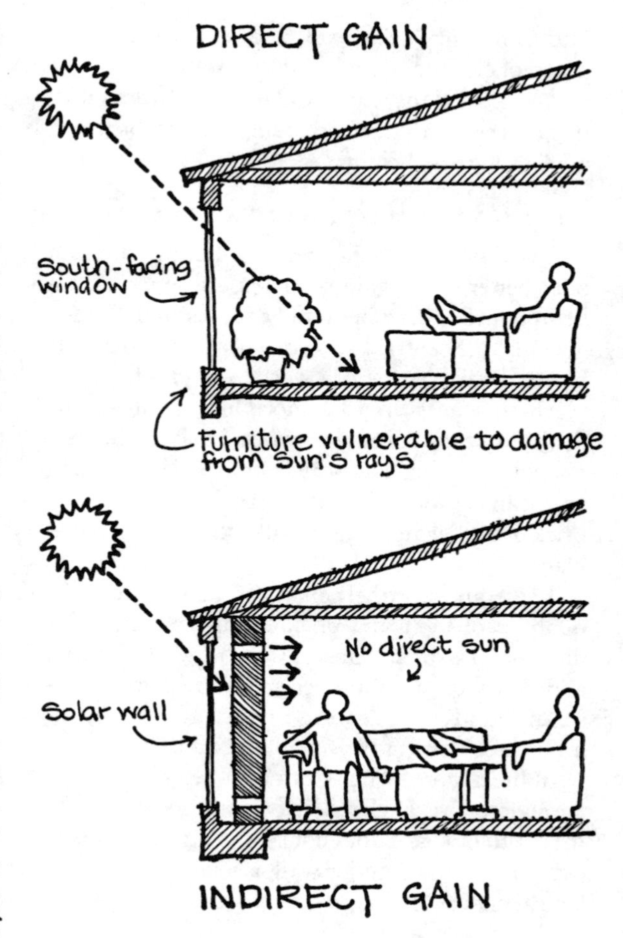

addition of this size has at best a south wall surface area equal to about 6 percent of total floor space, an amount insufficient to heat an entire house. Except in very warm areas (such as Los Angeles, Phoenix, or Miami), meeting 30 percent or more of home heating needs requires a collector area equivalent to 15 percent or more of total floor area in a home that includes Level I conservation measures. Moreover, unless your addition is close to the major living areas of the home, it can be difficult to move solar-heated air to where it is needed.

If direct-gain solar heating isn't appropriate, consider indirect solar heating. A solar wall gives you flexibility in the use and furnishing of the bedroom and releases heat during the evening hours. The bedroom can be carpeted and glare will not be a problem. A middle approach is a solar wall with windows. Windows that are intended primarily for daylighting and not solar heating can be integrated into a masonry solar wall, and water walls composed of clear containers reflect a soft, diffuse light into a room. If the water wall is carefully designed, it can result in a good compromise between daylighting and heating.

FAMILY ROOM OR KITCHEN EXPANSION

A new kitchen, dining room, or family room can offer better direct-gain solar opportunities than a bedroom. Because the family rooms and kitchen are often the central living area of a home, the solar heat is available where it is needed most often.

These spaces are also more likely to have the flexibility to incorporate properly sized thermal mass. An exposed masonry floor in a play or dining area can be located next to the windows, and a brick or aggregate floor or wall will not seem out of place.

These areas of the home also benefit from the qualities of light and openness that characterize direct-gain solar systems. A window wall makes an addition seem bright, cheerful, and spacious. Insulating and shading are as important to maintaining comfort here as in any other solar design.

Indirect-gain systems can also be adapted to a family room or kitchen. If your best view is not to the south or space does not permit an open area of exposed floor or interior wall, a solar wall makes a logical choice.

GREENHOUSES AND SOLARIA

If you plan to add on a greenhouse or solarium, there is every reason to make it contribute energy to your house. Solar greenhouse design is compatible with the traditional function of a greenhouse—growing plants—and also with the need for more space, daylight, or a pleasant sitting area.

Solar greenhouses and solaria, described earlier in this chapter, can be added directly to a south-facing wall or incorporated into the design of a bedroom or kitchen addition. This strategy allows for some design flexibility: minimizing direct-gain where you do not want it while maximizing the heating potential of the greenhouse.

The greenhouse or solarium must be able to be closed off from the rest of the house so that it won't drain heat from your home during prolonged cloudy and cold periods or add to air conditioning costs during the summer.

A solar greenhouse addition can meet a greater portion of home heating needs than other passive solar modifications because of the larger collector area and your ability to select an optimal glazing angle. Moreover, greenhouses can be allowed to reach temperatures higher than those desirable within a living space—thus providing more heat for transfer to the house or storage in mass for later use. This feature is particularly efficient if the greenhouse design is combined with a rockbed heat storage system.

Most people who have solar homes believe that the solar elements contribute to the value of their homes and to the quality of their life as well as to a more affordable utility bill. Visit a few solar homes to make sure you agree with them before you embark on your project.

Weighing Your Choices

Solar homes have advantages and they have limitations. Two important limitations bear repeating here. First, they work well only if the occupants are conscientious about operating them to gain maximum heat in the winter and exclude it in the summer. Second, there are many locations in cities or wooded areas where the dwelling gets too little sun to be a candidate for a serious solar remodeling. If your house is not suitable for a solar addition, consider investing extra money in increased efficiency. Or even consider a "superinsulated" house if you live in a very cold climate (see Box 8-1).

If you have elected to build a passive solar addition, don't be lured into thinking of energy efficiency investments and solar investments as alternatives. They go together. An inefficient solar home is uncomfortable, expensive to operate, and perhaps hard to sell. A mix of conservation and solar yields the greatest savings for your investment.

BALANCING SOLAR AND CONSERVATION

There is no simple way to determine an optimum mix of solar and conservation improvements. You should begin by spending money where it produces the greatest energy savings for each dollar: on simple insulation, weatherstripping, and other Level I measures if you haven't already done them.

If you're adding on and seriously considering incorporating passive solar heating, it pays to research the area thoroughly or contact a professional architect, designer, or engineer to define the most cost-effective mix of solar and conservation investments for your home. An experienced professional can design the solar elements of the addition to provide the maximum amount of heating when you need it and help you avoid design flaws that could lead to overheating and wide temperature swings.

If you want to research the technical issues before you contact a professional or wish to learn more about solar design yourself, there are several books listed in the reference section that can help. The most comprehensive and technical of these is *The Passive Solar Design Handbook* vols. 2 and 3, published by the American Solar Energy Society. An excellent starting point is the less technical *Passive Solar Energy Book*. Although this book was written for new home construction, there is much that is relevant to the solar retrofit. Several of the works in the reference section provide detailed worksheets for calculating glass area and mass requirements.

SOLAR SAVINGS

We can't give you a precise estimate tailored to your situation and climate, but we have developed some examples using our basic house as a starting point. The basic house has 1225 square feet of floor space and, at this point, the full range of Level I efficiency measures. It is a wood frame house with a gas furnace. The furnace provides enough auxiliarly heat to keep the addition at 68°F except in the case of the greenhouse, which is allowed to cool to 40°F. In winter the new addition is free of shading and in summer it is well shaded.

We've computed the benefits of three solar additions to the basic house: a bedroom and bath with an indirect Trombe wall system; a kitchen/family

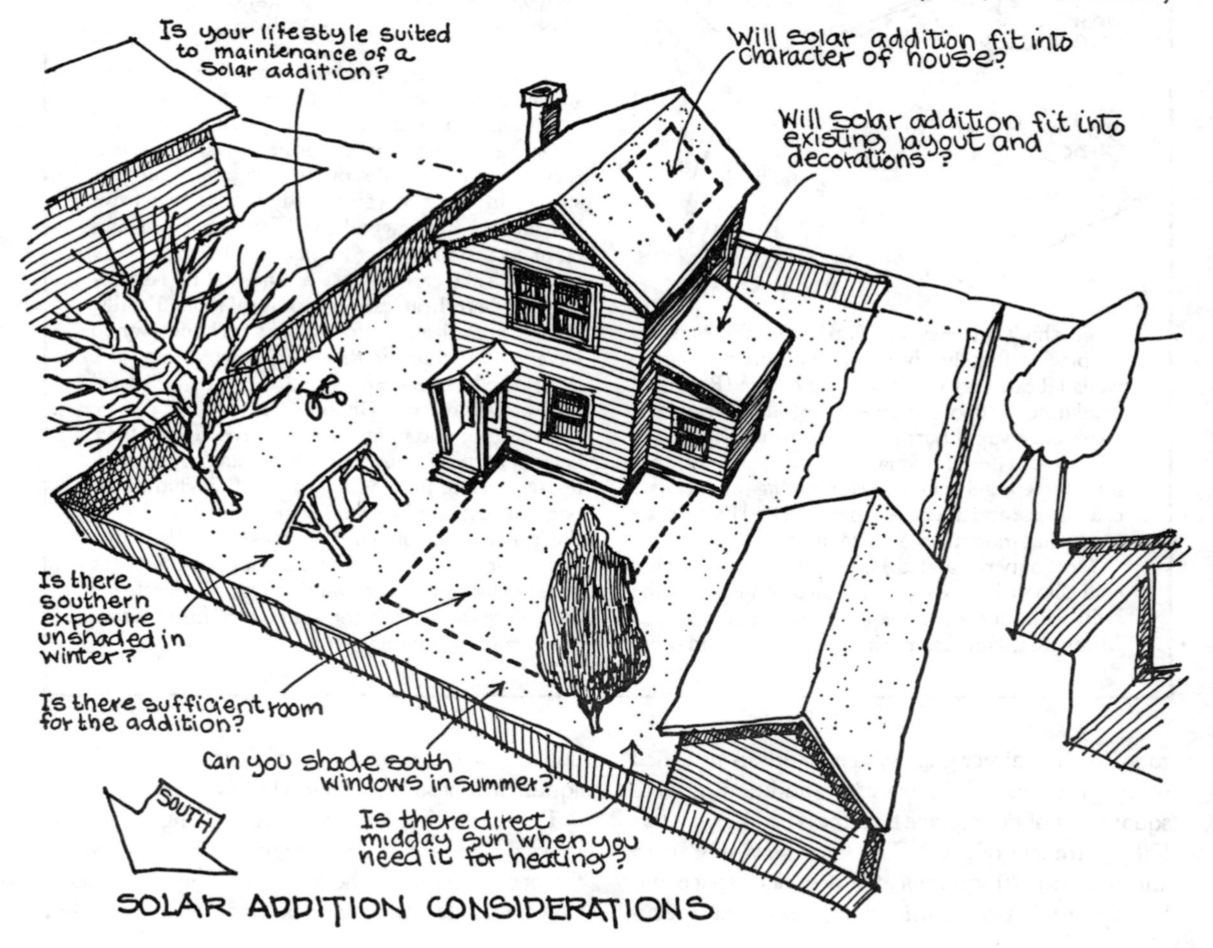

SOLAR ADDITION CONSIDERATIONS

BOX 8-1
SUPERINSULATION: A SOLUTION FOR VERY COLD CLIMATES

A superinsulated house is so well insulated and airtight that its winter heating needs are met almost entirely by heat normally given off within the house by cooking activities, electric appliances, human bodies, and solar energy absorbed through the windows. These houses usually have a wood stove or electric heater but need no central furnace. Fuel use is 85 percent less than in a similar conventional house.

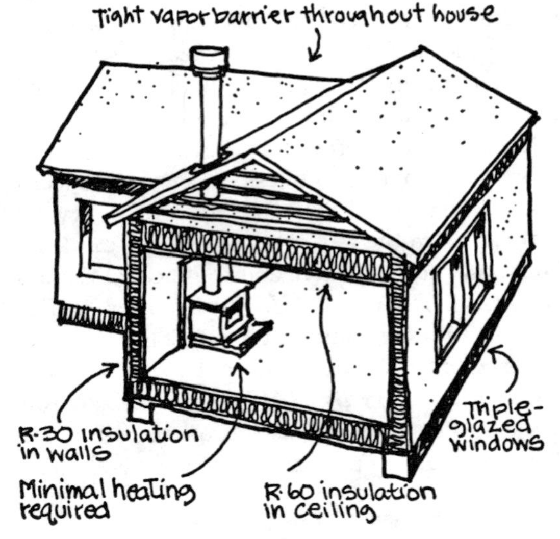

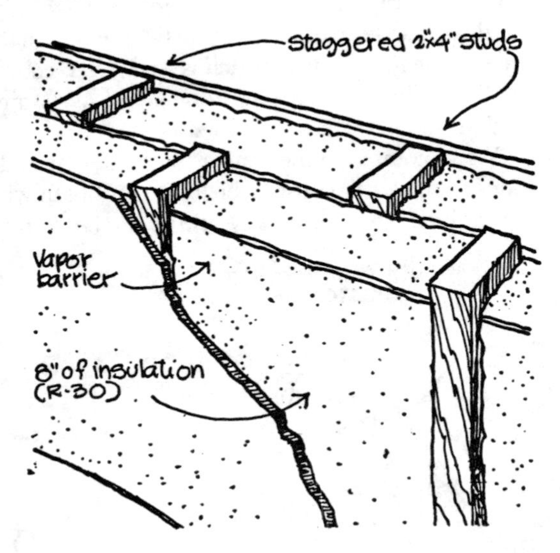

This high efficency level is achieved, for example, by placing 8 inches of fiberglass insulation in the walls (R-30) and 16 inches in the attic (R-60), by insulating the floors or edge of the slab, by installing a complete vapor barrier, and by using triple-pane windows. The additional cost for insulation and framing is largely offset by eliminating the expenses of a furnace and ducts. A superinsulated house costs somewhat more than a conventional home.

Most superinsulated homes are located in very cold climates. New superinsulated homes are being built with increasing frequency in Canada and in Minnesota, New Hampshire, Montana, and other cold states. There have been a number of retrofit superinsulation projects in these areas as well.

Consider superinsulation if you live in a cold climate and your house needs new plaster or sheetrock on interior walls or new exterior siding or stucco. In this case you already face an expensive job, and the incremental cost of the insulation and labor to install it may be justified by the energy savings. Take care to close all thermal bypasses—places where heat can get by insulation. Finally, plan to install an air-to-air heat exchanger or to have your indoor air thoroughly tested to assure that no pollutants are present. (See the discussion of indoor air quality in Chapter 4.)

Superinsulation can be expensive. There have been reports of superinsulation retrofits of small houses costing from $2000 to $5000, including labor, but costs are likely to fall near the upper end of this range. To avoid costly mistakes, find a homeowner or contractor who has superinsulated a house before embarking on this kind of project. See the reference section for sources of information about superinsulation.

room with a direct-gain system; and an attached solar greenhouse. The bedroom addition has 170 square feet of floor space and the Trombe wall has 100 square feet of glass. The kitchen/family room addition has 170 square feet of new floor space and 100 square feet of south-facing glass. The greenhouse has 100 square feet of floor space and 200 square feet of south-facing window area.

Each addition has external shading and insulated drapes (or exterior night insulation), which the occupants use. The kitchen/family room addition has a slab floor for mass with other exposed

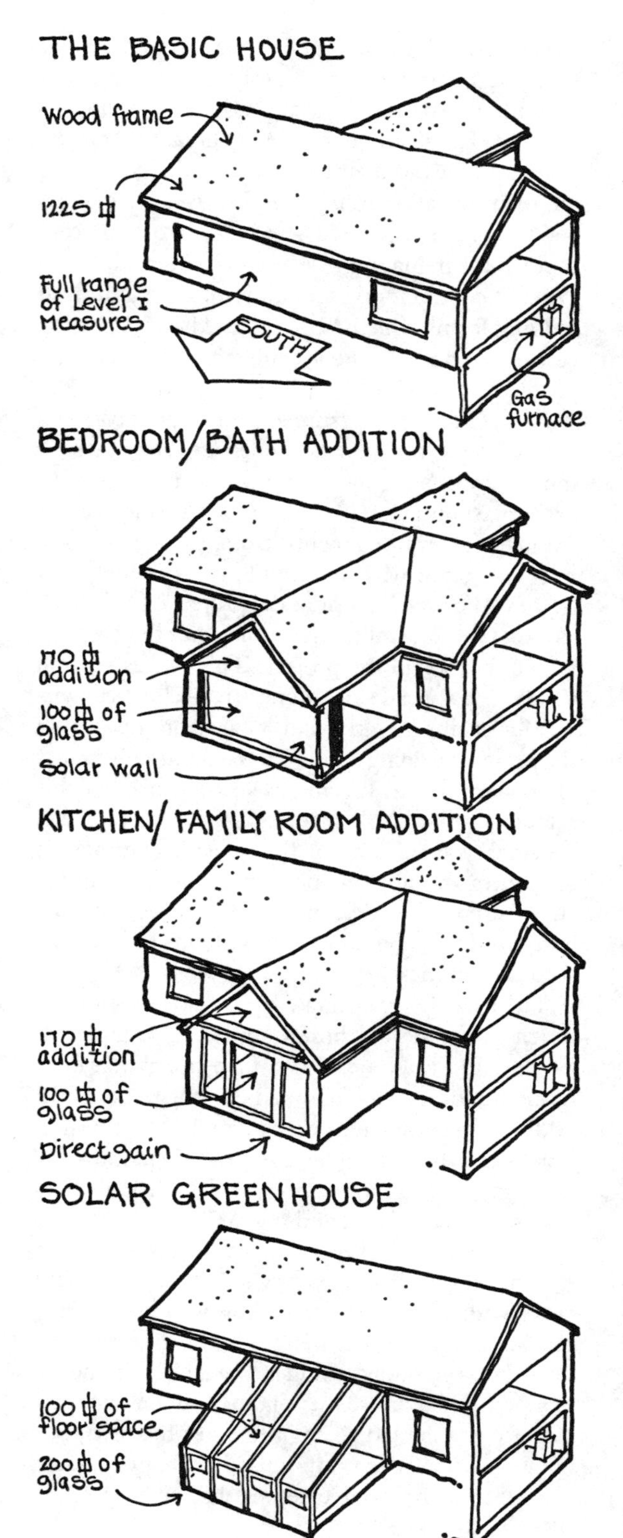

mass such as plaster walls or tile counters in warmer climates. The greenhouse shares a masonry wall with the house.

Solar performance varies with location and type of system. In Cheyenne, the Trombe wall bedroom/bath addition provides 15 percent of the entire house's heating needs. In Colorado Springs it provides 27 percent, in Albuquerque 34 percent, and in San Francisco 30 percent. These patterns of performance are similar to those in the case studies of Chapter 7. A Trombe wall in the bedroom/bath addition provides roughly half the energy savings of the indirect solar wall in Chapter 7, primarily because the wall in Chapter 7 has only half the area we assume for the room addition.

The direct-gain kitchen addition meets 19 percent of home heating needs in Cheyenne, 30 percent in Colorado Springs, 48 percent in Albuquerque, and 45 percent in San Francisco. In Tulsa it provides 21 percent of home heating needs; in Phoenix it provides 50 percent. These savings are also similar to those for the direct-gain south window addition in Chapter 7, but they have a greater dollar value because of the added heating requirements of the house with the new addition.

In colder climates, the kitchen addition in an average house contributes little more than do daytime heating strategies with little thermal mass. In warmer climates, the thermal mass provides improved performance in a nighttime heating strategy and helps lower summer cooling loads.

Greenhouses can be effective in providing heat—supplying 15 percent of the heating needs in a Minneapolis energy-conserving home and 95 percent of the heating needs in an energy-conserving San Diego home using an indirect-gain heating approach.

For an average, less efficient home, a simple greenhouse with 200 square feet of south-facing single-pane glass can supply 10 to 20 percent of heating needs in cold climates, 30 percent in moderate climates such as the Middle Atlantic states, and up to 60 percent in warm climates. In cold climates, double glazing is recommended; mass with night insulation increases a greenhouse's performance by more than 50 percent.

Because the roof and sides are glass, the performance of the greenhouse is relatively insensitive to orientation; heating contributions are 15 percent less at 60 degrees away from true south. Performance declines by only 3 percent at 25 degrees east or west of true south.

The case studies in Chapter 7 can give you an appreciation for the value of the solar energy available to your addition and climate zone. But remember that the costs for the measures in an addition are *less* than the costs for altering the existing wall assumed in the case studies. If you install a solar wall, for example, you don't have to pay the full costs (listed in the case study) but only the difference between the Trombe wall and a conventional south wall.

Whether you choose to invest in a solar addition or greater energy efficiency, keep in mind that the benefits go beyond energy savings. A solar room or a highly efficient addition increases the resale value of your home. Survey research has shown that energy features add to a house's value, and homebuyers are going to become increasingly sensitive to energy factors.

These same features also add to your personal security. A solar addition or highly efficient space leaves you less vulnerable if energy supplies are disrupted. In most climates, an energy-efficient addition, along with Level I measures throughout the house, creates a home that remains livable without external energy supplies.

Choosing a Contractor, Architect, or Designer

Level III energy improvements involve major construction. Except for the most skilled persons with abundant time on their hands, most people will want to work with a contractor, architect, or designer. Which route you choose depends on how involved you want to be and how confident you are in shaping your project.

The term contractor is often used to refer to a general contractor who will take responsibility for the whole project. General contractors look after the tasks of obtaining permits, purchasing materials, scheduling, hiring subcontractors, helping the client select fixtures and paint, and making sure the client is satisfied with the job—in short, all the many details of a successful project. They know what it takes to orchestrate a home addition but may not be involved themselves in the actual work.

General contractors prefer to bid from drawings that you, an architect, or a designer can supply, or they may work with you to produce the drawings for a fee. For all these services, general contractors build into the bid their costs and profit. Depending on their profit margin, working with a general contractor can cost anywhere from 10 to 25 percent more than managing the project yourself. Many general contractors use standard state-approved bidding forms which require that they specify the cost of the parts of the job and their fee including profit.

Most of the tasks assumed by a general contractor are ones you can do yourself. You can save money by managing your own addition, but in exchange you must commit time. This means that *you* get bids from subcontractors, *you* get the permits, *you* work with the building inspectors: You become the orchestrator of the project.

What if you want to use a contractor but contribute your labor to the project? This makes sense if you have a special skill in one area—electrical wiring, for example—and want to save on this part of the project by doing it yourself. General contractors often work out arrangements such as this. For this relationship to work successfully, it is best if you consider yourself one of the general contractor's subcontractors for this portion of the job and assume responsibility for meeting his or her schedule and standards of quality. If you don't the relationship can get messy.

The rules for choosing a general contractor are much the same as those outlined in Chapter 4. Because this is a much larger investment, it is even more important to follow these suggestions. In addition to getting and checking references, visit a job that has been completed for over six months. By this time, the homeowners will have had time to assess ther experience and find any flaws.

Further, ıf the general contractor claims to have expertise in designing energy systems, you should check with other clients to see how well the contractor has integrated the design and engineering aspects into the project and learn whether the house has performed as well as planned. Some contractors are as talented as engineers or architects, but others have next to no training in energy systems. You need to find out whether they're as good as they say they are.

Designers and architects are particularly helpful to a project if you have strong aesthetic concerns, if you're planning an energy system whose success depends on design features, or if you know you want an energy-efficient addition but have no idea how to approach it. Technically, the title "architect" can only be used by licensed members of the American Institute of Architects (AIA). This does not mean that all architects design good energy systems or that someone with good practical expertise but no license is not an excellent designer. Don't discriminate against designers because they are not licensed or assume that all architects know something about energy. The best way to escape this dilemma and avoid paying for anyone's "learning curve" is to visit a completed project and talk to the homeowners about the skills of the person whose work you are appraising.

Selecting an architect or designer can be intimidating, particularly if you have not worked with one before. They have extensive training in how to make a building work both functionally and aesthetically, and their pupose is to help the client conceptualize a project and give it form. Good architects and designers have an aesthetic point of view but know how to balance their client's tastes against their own to achieve a mutually satisfying design.

Architects and designers are usually willing to work out several types of arrangements with their clients. Total costs for design work can run between 3 and 7 percent of total construction costs, depending on the project's complexity and the extent of the designer or architect's involvement. Some charge an hourly fee that averages between $30 and $35 an hour but can range from $15 to $75 per hour depending on the professional's reputation and experience. Others work for a fixed fee; their involvement can range from simply doing the design and construction documents (the drawings required to get a building permit and used as a basis for bids, scheduling, and construction) to supervising the project from beginning to end. While these fees may seem high, the cost may be warranted if you are investing $15,000 and up. The extent of the designer or architect's involvement depends on what you need and can afford. If you are hiring an architect or designer simply to work out a design, you will probably be charged on an hourly basis or a fixed fee.

Because of their training and understanding of current equipment, good architects and designers can save you time and help you avoid expensive mistakes. Since they are in the business of design, however, they can easily give you more than you really want or can afford. To avoid nasty surprises, clearly define in your own mind what you want and need from your home addition *before* you see a professional. And be honest from the start about how much you can afford.

As in any relationship that involves personal tastes and habits, human chemistry is important to your project's success. If you find that you have trouble working with your designer or architect in the initial stages, pay him or her for the work done to date and call someone else.

Chapter Nine
Home Economics

Home Economics

Energy improvements are among the best financial investments you can make. Whether you are considering Level I measures or a combination from Level I, II, and III, you need to calculate costs and savings to determine whether it's a good investment. The first part of this chapter deals with project economics; it will help you estimate costs and savings. The second part presents different tools for analyzing the rate of return on energy projects and for comparing them with alternative financial investments. It also offers guidance on bank loans and other methods of financing your project.

Weighing Economic Factors

Chapter 3 helped you determine how much you are now spending for energy. The case studies in Chapters 5 and 7 gave you percentage savings estimates for conservation measures. Together these estimates give you an idea of your dollar savings potential. In this chapter we extend the analysis a step further and provide you with several methods for comparing your future savings with other investment opportunities.

ESTIMATING PROJECT COSTS

The case studies in Chapters 5 and 7 include assumptions about the cost of each measure. These estimates were based on average nationwide costs in 1983, using a contractor, for a typical house. Your costs could be more or less, but they will be much less if you do all or part of the work yourself.

Cost estimating is an art, not a science. If you are going to be using a contractor, he or she will develop a detailed cost estimate, and you can choose among contractors according to total cost and the quality of previous work. Get more than one bid, though, since contractor costs vary by as much as a factor of 2.

If you plan to do the work yourself or act as your own contractor, you have to develop your own estimate. First make a rough list of all project elements. Then develop an estimate based on a survey of building material suppliers and consultation with a carpenter or other skilled worker.

The insulation, weatherstripping, caulking, and window treatment measures of Level I present few difficulties or surprises when it comes to estimating costs. Most of these measures can be installed by the handy homeowner.

If you intend to install some or all of the measures of Level I yourself, you have two costs to be concerned with: the cost of the material and the cost of any equipment or tools you'll need to rent or purchase.

When you begin shopping for materials such as insulation, watch the newspapers for advertisements. Most retailers don't like to carry a large stock of insulation through the summer. With a little foresight, you may be able to take advantage of off-season sales.

In most areas, Level I measures are also offered by local licensed contractors. Always arrange for at least three separate bids. Since insulation contractors tend to be busiest just before and during the heating season, you may be able to negotiate a significant price break if you can schedule your work during the late winter or spring.

Cost estimating for Level II measures presents greater uncertainties. Estimating remodeling costs is difficult, and contractors who do mostly new construction tend to underestimate the time involved in work on an existing building. Even contractors who specialize in remodeling find accurate cost estimating a challenge. The increased care and cleanup entailed when working on a lived-in home tend to add time to otherwise straightforward tasks. A careful cost estimate by an experienced and realistic contractor can help you avoid overruns.

If you plan to do all the work yourself, draw up as complete a list of required purchases as possible. The large items—new windows, skylights, solar panels—are easy. But the smaller pieces add up quickly. For example, there are requirements for lumber, electrical materials, hardware, and perhaps new roofing.

If you plan to hire a carpenter by the hour, develop an estimated labor cost. There are useful books for making these estimates—the *National Repair and Remodeling Estimator*, for example, gives average labor and material costs for most construction tasks, including an adjustment factor for regional variations.

Don't forget the surprise factor. Whenever you begin probing beneath the skin of an existing structure you are likely to find surprises: damage or decay, substandard construction, a need for wiring or plumbing changes, unforeseen complexities. One cost may lead to another. Enlarging a south-facing window, for example, may require replacing an entire wall of sheetrock, installing new trim around the window, and repainting the entire room. And if you are considering an extensive remodel, local codes may require that you upgrade the entire structure to current codes—potentially a very large expense. Allow a contingency for cost overruns. How large a factor depends on the condition of your home and the scope of your project. Start with 30 percent of the total job cost at the outset; revise this margin downward as you learn more about your project and your house.

Level III projects are expensive and require a contractor's estimate for most homeowners. Home additions are much like new home construction; they don't entail as much uncertainty as Level II measures. Rules of thumb that apply to new buildings are likely to apply also to room additions. There are factors, however, that add to the costs. Joining the new roof to the old may pose a problem, for example. Or you may discover substandard construction in your house that needs to be upgraded.

Additions can cost anywhere from $25 to $75 per square foot, more for kitchens and bathrooms. To get an idea at an early stage of the costs of an addition for your area and your type of house, talk to people who have added on recently, or talk to a contractor. They may be able to give you a rough estimate for planning purposes. Most contractors, however, do not attempt a precise estimate until you provide detailed drawings of the addition and specifications of the material to be used. For more on working with contractors and architects, see Chapter 8.

ESTIMATING ENERGY SAVINGS

Developing an estimate of savings helps you determine how your project affects your cash flow. And if you are planning to finance it with a loan, the estimated savings may help you convince your lender that you can afford the payments on a home improvement loan or second mortgage, personal loan, or other financing mechanism. Earlier in the book we outlined two ways to estimate savings. One is to get a professional audit. One of the products of a good audit is a list of measures, their cost, and their estimated payback. If the written audit report does not provide a translation into monthly dollar savings for a specific set of measures, ask your auditor to help you make that computation.

The second way to develop an estimate of savings is with the case studies in Chapters 5 and 7. The case study that most closely approximates your situation tells you the reductions in your heating, cooling, and water heating fuel use you can expect from various measures or combinations of measures. Multiplying the appropriate percentage by your heating, cooling, or water heating costs gives you an estimate of your dollar savings potential.

How much confidence can you have in these estimates? How much financial risk are you taking? There is always an element of risk in an estimate of savings, but there is very little danger of losing money on the Level I measures and many of the Level II items. As your project gets higher in cost, more elaborate in design, and more dependent on *you* to operate it well, the risks get greater. The case studies are based on conservative assumptions about the cost and performance of Level I measures. Most utility audits also use an analysis that is on the conservative side. In contrast, you can expect a person trying to sell you insulation or some other conservation material to make much higher claims for energy savings.

No estimate of savings comes with a guarantee. There are too many variables—weather, patterns of use, housing type, and energy price changes, for example—to estimate savings with a fine degree of precision. But you can be reasonably confident of savings within a range of 20 percent more or less than the estimate.

One important factor to consider is the effect of future energy prices on your dollar savings. How will your savings change with time? Your percentage savings will remain constant as long as your patterns of use don't change. As energy costs rise, the dollar value of your savings rises proportionately even though your utility bill itself is higher. In the years immediately following your energy improvements your bill will actually be lower. (Tables 9-1 and 9-2, presented later in the chapter, provide a way to factor projected energy cost increases into an analysis of the economic benefits of a project.)

Later, as utility bills increase, more and more of your savings will be in the form of avoided costs—that is, costs you would have had to pay if you had not made your home more energy efficient. If your annual heating bill would have been $1000, for example, and you make investments that reduce it by 20 percent, you will pay $800. Suppose utility rates or heating oil prices increase by 20 percent this summer. Your heating costs next year will be $960—only $40 below your original, inefficient level. But your inefficient heating bill would have been $1200. You are therefore saving $240: $40 in actual savings and $200 in avoided costs. If heating fuel prices keep rising, your savings will soon be only in the form of avoided costs. Avoided costs aren't as tangible as real reductions in your energy bill, but they are just as important.

How fast are energy prices likely to rise? There are as many answers as experts, and the past is a poor guide. The U.S. Department of Energy (DOE)—which in the past has consistently guessed low on price increases—published an official price forecast in 1983. In that forecast, DOE projected that world oil prices would rise little if at all above the annual rate of inflation, that residential electricity price increases would be only about 1 percent greater than the rate of inflation, and that natural gas prices would rise at a rate of 6 to 8 percent above inflation. These projections rest on a number of assumptions, perhaps most important a stable international oil market. And they are national averages; in some areas prices will grow faster than indicated, and in others not at all.

Understanding Your Investment

Most people are not used to thinking about a home improvement in the same way they would an investment in a money market fund or a treasury bill. Yet there are similarities. Each involves an initial cost that is expended with the expectation of a monetary return. Each involves some planning and comparing of investment options. And each entails some risk. There are tax laws affecting each investment that are essential for the investor to understand, and there are financial penalties for doing nothing. Where the home energy investment differs from other financial investments is in the homeowner's ability to improve the quality and function of the "capital"—the home itself—and add to its resale value.

If your improvement project is simply one among several possible investments, think of it in the same way you would think of any other investment. Suppose you have $2500 to invest in a money market fund that yields a 10 percent return before taxes. If you invest that same amount in energy efficiency measures, you may realize a return of 15 to 20 percent, tax-free, each year.

If you're taking out a loan for your energy project, however, you need a way to compare the return on your investment to the costs of the loan. There are three commonly used methods for analyzing and comparing financial return: *rate of return*, *simple payback*, and *life cycle savings*. Table 9-1, presented later, is a worksheet for performing these calculations.

Rate of return measures the annual savings as a percentage of the original investment. Calculating a rate of return allows you to compare an energy project with the yields of money market funds, bonds, savings accounts, and other investments with an annual interest rate. But remember that

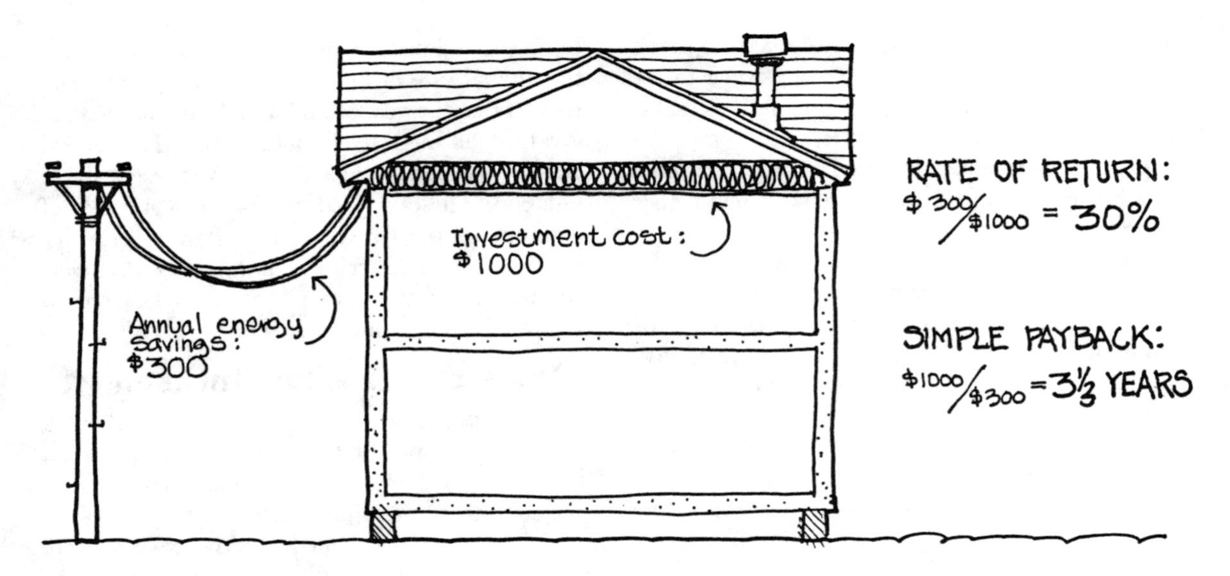

returns on home energy investments, unlike most others, are tax-free.

The formula for determining rate of return is

Rate of return = annual net savings ÷ investment

Suppose you spend $1000 to insulate your attic and reduce your heating and cooling bills by $300 a year as a result. In this case the rate of return (ROR) on your investment is 30 percent (ROR = $300 ÷ $1000). Because it isn't taxed, this yield has an even greater edge over most other investments. And if tax credits are available, your return would be even better.

Simple payback measures the time it takes for an investment to "pay for itself," generally expressed as original investment divided by annual savings, or 1/ROR. To continue with the previous example, if you spend $1000 on attic insulation with a $300 annual savings the payback of your investment is three and one-third years ($1000 ÷ $300 = 3.3 years).

Life cycle savings are the total savings over the life of an investment. (This figure is sometimes referred to as life cycle costs.) *Life cycle savings* are generally expressed in dollars and as the net savings that result after the cost of repairing and maintaining an investment has been subtracted.

Each of these three economic measures gives you an idea of the value of your investment. If you're primarily interested in short-term benefits or your yearly cash flow, use one of the first two measures—rate of return or payback—as your guide. The problem with using these two measures alone is that they can lead to shortsighted decision making. Buying low-quality weatherstripping may increase your rate of return from 20 to 35 percent, for example, but the materials may only last three or four years. High-quality material costs more initially, but it may last ten years, returning two to five times the total financial benefit of the cheaper materials that have to be replaced more frequently.

If you plan to be in your house for a long time and the investment requires annual maintenance or periodic repairs (for example, solar water heaters or insulating curtains), you should look at the life cycle savings of an investment before making a decision.

In contrast to short-term financial planning tools (rate of return and simple payback), long-term measures of benefits, such as life cycle savings, allow you to evaluate the project's value over the years in light of increases in energy costs. Tables 9-1 and 9-2, presented later, will help you make these calculations.

Tax issues are also important in analyzing the financial aspects of an energy investment. There are three principal tax aspects to consider when choosing an energy project: tax credits, tax deductions, and real estate taxes.

A tax credit is a direct offset against your tax liability. A 40 percent tax credit on a $2000 solar water heating system allows you to subtract $800 directly from your tax bill.

Many states as well as the federal government provide tax credits to encourage energy conservation and solar energy investments. Box 9-1 lists the states that offer solar energy credits or deductions. Contact your state energy or tax office for details on the benefits provided in your state.

The federal government allows a 15 percent tax credit for energy conservation measures and 40 percent for solar measures and wind energy systems. The conservation credit applies to measures installed in homes built prior to April 1977 and covers insulation, storm or thermal windows, clock thermostats, electronic ignition for gas furnaces, oil furnace burner replacement, and duct insulation for furnaces. Shading measures, window insulation, and furnace replacements are not eligible for the credit. The credit is available only for expenses up to $2000; in other words, the maximum amount of credit is $300. The credit can be claimed by renters or homeowners for their principal residence; landlords do not receive a conservation credit for investments in rental property.

The federal solar credit covers space and water heating systems, both active and passive. The credit is not available for costs or materials related to the structure of the house, however. This exclusion applies to the glazing for direct-gain systems and to the masonry portion of a Trombe wall system if it supports the weight of the roof. The maximum amount of credit allowed is $4000. Renters are entitled to the 40 percent solar credit, but landlords receive only a 15 percent credit for solar investments in rental property.

BOX 9-1
STATES WITH SOLAR TAX INCENTIVES

Alabama	Maine	Ohio
Arizona	Massachusetts	Oklahoma
Arkansas	Michigan	Oregon
California	Minnesota	Rhode Island
Colorado	Nebraska	South Carolina
Delaware	New Mexico	Utah
Hawaii	New York	Vermont
Idaho	North Carolina	Virginia
Indiana	North Dakota	Wisconsin
Kansas		

This list is accurate as of March 1983. Contact your state taxing authority for further information.

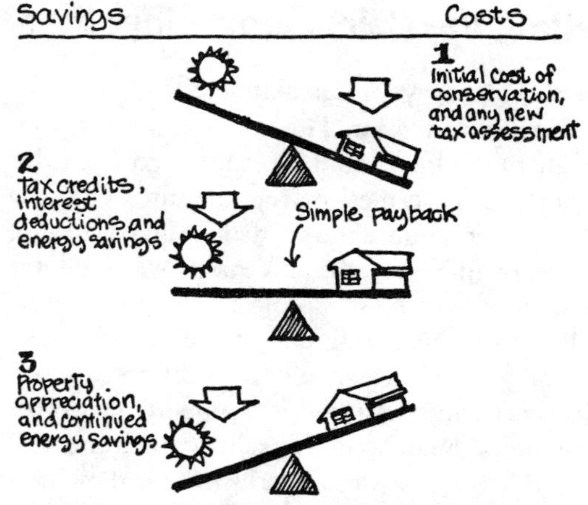

ENERGY CONSERVATION PAYBACK

Tax deductions are less attractive than tax credits because they do not lower your tax liability dollar for dollar like a tax credit. Nevertheless, they're an important incentive in states that provide them, particularly for upper-income taxpayers. A tax deduction is subtracted from gross income, and it reduces tax liability in proportion to your marginal tax bracket. If you are financing your project with a loan, the interest you pay is also tax deductible.

Finally don't forget property taxes. Major energy projects such as the addition of a sunroom or greenhouse can result in your property being reassessed, increasing your property tax bill. In some states solar water heating systems have been exempted from reassessment. Check with your state or county energy office or the state taxing authority for information. If your state doesn't offer this exemption, you may have to figure in the full costs of a property tax reassessment to get a complete financial picture.

Apart from these tax matters, keep in mind that the energy cost savings you realize are not taxable. Therefore, a rate of return of 10 percent for an energy investment is equal to a taxable 13.3 percent yield if you are in a 25 percent tax bracket or 20 percent if you are in a 50 percent tax bracket. If you're in a 30 percent tax bracket and paying $100 a year in interest, for example, your tax deduction of $100 reduces your tax bill by about $30. Because tax policies often change quickly, call your local IRS office and state taxing authority for up-to-date information.

Putting the Calculations Together

In completing your calculations, there are several items to watch for. The dollar value of tax or investment credits should be subtracted from the cost of the project in estimating the rate of return. Moreover, the value of the tax deduction you get for payment of interest on the home improvement loan should be added to the project savings column. Finally, your rough estimate of the added resale value of your home should be subtracted from project costs, and the additional property taxes you anticipate paying should be subtracted from savings. Table 9-1 provides a worksheet for these calculations. Use Table 9-2 to obtain a value of long-term energy savings in light of rising fuel costs.

Remember, all this work gives you a sense of what your financial benefits should be. Your actual savings may occur in the form of avoided costs—the difference between what you now pay for energy and what you would still be paying if you hadn't made the improvements. Loan payments are very real, however, which means you must guard your "savings" very carefully by making sure that high quality work goes into your house and you don't use your newly energy efficient house as an excuse to go back to an energy wasteful lifestyle.

If you're counting on both savings and avoided costs to help pay for the home improvement loan, allow yourself a margin of error in performing all cost and savings calculations. Unless you have included in your cost estimates a big contingency for cost overruns or you've been very conservative in your projections of energy savings, it may be appropriate to pick measures with a calculated rate of return 30 percent higher than the interest rate you must pay.

After you have completed the calculations, you need to decide whether the predicted rate of return for the measures you are considering is acceptable. Your answer depends in large part on your motives. Are financial motives your main concern? Or are you also inclined to weigh heavily the other benefits that come with energy conservation?

TABLE 9-1
PUTTING THE CALCULATIONS TOGETHER

	Example		Actual
Step 1: Estimate Net Costs			
1. Purchase and installation costs	$5,000	A:	$____
2. Tax credits	750	B:	$____
3. Increase in resale value (or salvage value)	1,000	C:	$____
Net Cost: (A − B − C)	3,250	D:	$____
Step 2: Estimate Net First-Year Savings			
1. Estimated energy savings	$700	E:	$____
2. Maintenance and repair costs	0	F:	$____
3. Property tax increase	120	G:	$____
4. Total first-year costs (F + G)	120	H:	$____
Net First-Year Savings: (E − H)	580	I:	$____
Step 3: Estimate Rate of Return			
1. Rate of return (savings divided by costs × 100; I ÷ D × 100)	18%	J:	____%
2. Tax bracket	33%	K:	____%
After-Tax Rate of Return (J ÷ K × 100)	54%	L:	____%
(Use the after-tax rate of return when comparing your energy investment opportunity with an alternative opportunity, say a money market fund.)			
Step 4: Compute Life Cycle Savings			
1. Expected energy cost inflation rate	5%	M:	____%
2. Expected lifetime of investment	20 yr	N:	____yr
3. Escalation rate multiplier (see Table 9-2)	54.4	O:	____
4. Lifetime value of energy savings (first-year energy savings × escalation rate multiplier; O × E)	$37,800	P:	$____
5. Lifetime maintenance and repair costs	1,200	Q:	$____
6. Lifetime increase in property taxes	3,000	R:	$____
7. Total costs (Q + R)	4,200	S:	$____
Net Life Cycle Savings (P − S)	33,600	T:	$____

TABLE 9-2
COMPUTING FUEL COST INCREASES

Year	2%		5%		10%		15%		20%	
	Projected Rate of Increase									
1	1.02	(1.02)	1.05	(1.05)	1.1	(1.1)	1.15	(1.15)	1.20	(1.20)
5	1.10	(5.31)	1.28	(5.80)	1.61	(6.7)	2.0	(7.75)	2.5	(8.9)
10	1.22	(11.07)	1.6	(13.2)	2.6	(17.5)	4.04	(23)	6.2	(31)
15	1.35	(17.54)	2.08	(20.7)	4.2	(35)	8.13	(55)	15.4	(72)
20	1.48	(24.69)	2.65	(54.4)	6.7	(63)	16.3	(108)	38.3	(210)

Use this table to project your future fuel costs (or your savings) at various rates of increase for fuel prices. The chart can be used to estimate fuel cost increases with or without inflation. To determine a rate of increase apart from inflation, select an estimated rate of fuel cost increase from which the projected rate of inflation has been subtracted. If you want to determine actual future dollar costs, select a rate of increase that includes an appropriate amount for inflation.

Find the pair of numbers on the chart that correspond to the rate of increase you are assuming and the year in question. The first number is a multiplier that enables you to project fuel costs for a single future year. The second number, in parentheses, enables you to project cumulative fuel costs from the present to the year selected.

For example, suppose you now spend $200 a year for natural gas and your utility estimates that natural gas prices will rise at a rate of 5 percent a year. Your costs next year (year 1) will be $210 ($200 × 1.05), and your costs in the tenth year will be $320 ($200 × 1.6). Your cumulative costs for the ten-year period will be $2640 ($200 × 13.2).

Now suppose you estimate savings of $150 from a heat pump this year, and you assume that electricity prices will rise by 10 percent a year. Your savings next year will be $165 ($150 × 1.1), and your savings for the tenth year will be $390 ($150 × 2.6). Your cumulative savings over the ten-year period will be $2650.00 ($150 × 17.5). Use the result of your calculation of cumulative savings with Table 9-1 to project the long-term benefits of investing in energy efficiency.

If financial concerns are foremost, be sure to compare this investment with the opportunity cost of not putting your money somewhere else. This means that your final rate of return (with all financial aspects taken into consideration) should be a figure larger than the after-tax return on an alternative taxable investment.

If you are inclined to weigh concerns about comfort, environment, and security along with financial objectives, you will be willing to invest in a package of measures with a rate of return less than that of an alternative investment.

Balancing Economic and Noneconomic Factors

The energy investment decision is a balancing act that ultimately turns more on subjective factors and personal values than on economics, some of which argue for the energy investment and some of which argue against it.

The "no" factors include a big economic hurdle —the dollar cost of a project—and several less tangible elements: mess, stress, and time. How much weight should be given to these intangibles depends partly on the scope of your project but mostly on you.

On the "yes" side there are two economic factors and several values that defy precise measurement. Economic factors are the dollar savings you realize from a more energy efficient home and the increased resale value of your home when you come to sell it. The unquantifiable factors are the comfort improvements, the increased space (or increase in usable space), and the increased self-reliance that result from an energy project. Moreover, it may be important to you that your lower energy use reduces environmental damage and contributes to national security by lessening your dependence on foreign energy sources. Weigh these factors in light of your personal values and goals.

Financing Your Project

There are several ways to pay for your energy improvement project: out of savings, out of monthly cash flow as you go along, or with a loan from a utility, bank, or other lending institution. Most people need a loan of some kind. Financing programs that specifically recognize energy-saving projects are becoming more common, but they are by no means readily available. If you plan to complete only Level I energy investments, your utility may have a program you can use. Some may even provide loans or incentive programs for solar water heaters or heat pumps. If you plan a larger construction project it is likely that you'll need to seek conventinal financing.

UTILITY FINANCING

Some utilities provide financial assistance to homeowners for basic conservation retrofit projects. The nature and scope of these programs vary as do the terms and the quality of assistance. If utilities are offering RCS audits, described in Chapter 3, they must also give you information about the measures recommended and assistance with financing them. Box 9-2 describes some typical financing programs offered by utilities.

Some large, privately owned utilities have determined that it is in their interest to help customers by

BOX 9-2
SOME UTILITY FINANCING PROGRAMS

Seattle City Light: Seattle City Light in Washington State is a public utility that sells electricity only. It does not participate in the Residential Conservation Service, but it has a far better auditing and financing program than many that do. The utility offers zero-interest loans of up to $5500 for approved conservation measures in houses using electricity for 70 percent or more of their heating. The customer does not make payments on the loan for five years; then the utility bills them for sixty equal monthly payments to retire the loan. Low-income households are eligible for grants of up to $3300 and loans for approved conservation measures. These loans have been augmented by the Bonneville Power Administration, which gives the customer dollar credits on the cost of insulation, depending on how much energy the insulation is expected to save.

For low-income customers, the city and a local bank offer low-interest loans payable over five years for insulation, caulking, and weatherstripping. For low-income customers using oil or gas as a heating source the city offers low-interest loans. The city pays 20 percent of the cost of the measures outright. This program covers attic, floor, and wall insulation, weatherstripping and caulking, smoke detectors, pipe and duct insulation, storm windows, flame retention burners, electronic ignition for gas furnaces, and flue vent dampers. Landlords also qualify for these programs.

Arkansas Power and Light: Arkansas Power and Light, a privately owned utility, offers zero-interest conservation loans to customers using electricity for heating or cooling. The loans are payable over ten years. The conservation investments are compared for cost effectiveness with building and operating a new power plant. The utility borrows money to finance the program from local banks. All customers benefit and the interest the utility pays is included in everyone's rates.

Pacific Gas and Electric Company: PG&E, which serves Northern California, offers what it calls ZIP loans —Zero-Interest Program loans. The utility loans up to $1000 for these basic conservation measures: ceiling insulation, weatherstripping, water heater blanket, low-flow showerheads, caulking, and duct insulation. After you complete these measures, you are eligible for an additional loan of $2500 at zero interest for such measures as wall and floor insulation, clock thermostats, lighting conversion, intermittent ignition devices, and storm or thermal windows and doors. Payments for the loan are evenly divided over fifty months.

Renters also qualify for ZIP loans. If the renter moves before the loan is paid, payments must be made by the following renter or by the landlord if the unit goes unoccupied.

Baltimore: The City of Baltimore and Baltimore Gas and Electric offer loans for energy conservation measures and renovation projects. The loans cover all types of insulation, storm windows, and new or upgraded heating systems. Moreover, the loans can be used to finance a new roof, new kitchen or bathroom, basic structural repairs, exterior painting or gutter repair, new wiring, and new plumbing. The minimum loan amount is $2000, the maximum is $15,000, and the customer can select a loan term of two to fifteen years. Lower-income households are eligible for a loan rate of 7.5 percent; others pay 12.5 percent. The program is financed by tax-exempt bonds issued by the City of Baltimore.

lending money for energy conservation projects. Some have zero-interest loans, and some have low-interest loans. The utility bases the amount of the loan available on the results of their audit and their estimate of costs and savings. Utilities with financing programs often offer loans at below-market interest rates so the customer has an incentive to finance the retrofits through the utility program. Some may not advertise the program widely, so even if you haven't heard about it, ask anyway. If you are served by two utilities, we recommend that you contact both and compare their loan terms.

Because the utility is securing the loan, it usually inspects the work to ensure proper installation. Some utilities may offer loans covering Level II measures such as solar water heaters, but this is rare.

Many public utilities buy their power from large federal power agencies such as the Bonneville Power Administration (BPA) in the northwest and the Tennessee Valley Authority (TVA) in the southeast. Utilities that purchase power from BPA and TVA are required to have a conservation financing program.

HELP FROM PRIVATE LENDERS

There are several ways to finance a home energy project through private lenders: a personal loan, a home improvement loan, and a second mortgage. If you plan to complete only a Level I basic conservation investment, your most likely options are a home improvement loan or a personal loan. The desirability of one over the other depends on the terms that lenders are offering. Be sure to ask the lender to itemize all the final costs of taking out a loan including all transaction, appraisal, and other fees.

Most home improvement loans are based on the owner's equity in the house. Frequently the maximum size of the loan is a percentage of the difference between the market value of the house and the existing debt.

Most lenders insist that large home improvement loans take the form of a second mortgage. If the home improvement loan becomes a second mortgage or you decide to take out a second mortgage to finance the project, the combined totals of your present mortgage and the second usually cannot exceed 90 percent of the appraised value of the house. If you have lived in the house a long time, the chances are excellent that your equity has increased and that loan size limitations will present few problems for you. If your equity has not increased greatly, only a modest loan will be available to you and you may have to take out another type of loan to finance your project.

Terms of personal loans are calculated differently than those of home improvement loans. Personal loan eligibility is based on income and cash flow. The drawback of the personal loan is that the term is usually shorter and the interest rates generally higher than for home improvement loans—particularly if the home improvement loan becomes a second mortgage on your house.

Your calculation of costs and savings may help convince the lender that you qualify for the loan. If you're planning a set of Level I or Level II measures, you may be able to show that the monthly costs you are avoiding by saving energy will help you meet the loan payments more easily.

To make this case effectively, you should have the estimates of an energy auditor to calculate costs and savings or your own cost and savings analysis based on the case studies or on your detailed research. In almost every case, the lender requires a cost estimate from a licensed contractor before processing a home improvement loan. If you approach a lending institution with well-thought-out figures on savings in relation to monthly payments, you can make a more convincing case for qualifying for the loan.

Table 9-3 gives the annual loan payment on a $10,000 loan with varying interest rates over different periods of time. If you borrow $10,000 at 10 percent with a five-year term, your annual payment will be $2600 a year, or $220 a month. Since the annual payments change in proportion to the loan amounts, Table 9-3 can be used for any size loan. The payments on a loan of $12,000 are 1.2 times the payments indicated for the $10,000 loan; for a $5000 loan, payments are half the amount shown.

Using the Washington, D.C., example again, if you were to hire a contractor to complete the first five priorities (seven measures) listed in the case study in Chapter 5, the cost would be nearly $1700. Your heating and cooling and hot water bills would be reduced by 42, 37, and 24 percent respectively—a total savings of about $510 each year at today's energy costs.

TABLE 9-3
BALANCING LOAN TERMS AND ENERGY SAVINGS

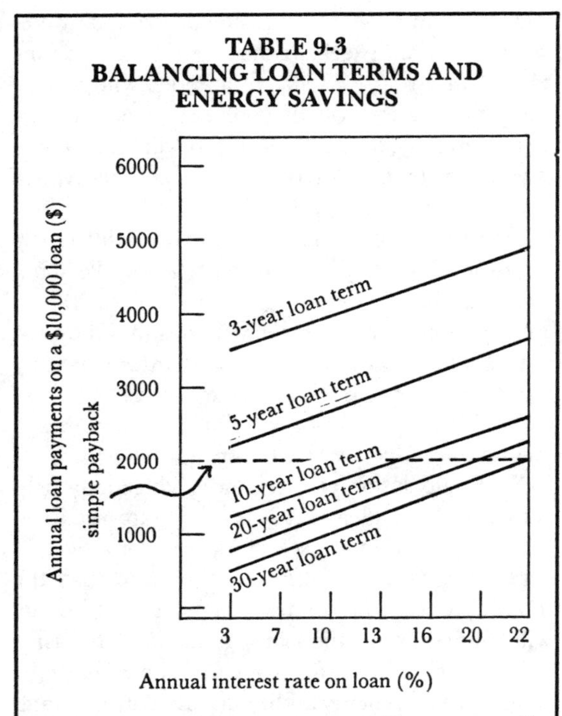

This table shows the combinations of loan terms and interest rates that produce the same annual loan payment. The annual loan payment can be compared to the value of first-year energy savings.

If you took out a five-year, $1700 loan at 10 percent interest, your annual loan payment would be $448, or 12 percent less than your savings without considering any tax benefits. If you obtained a low-interest utility loan, tax credits, or deductions, or if you did the work yourself, your savings would exceed your monthly costs by an even greater amount.

LOW-INCOME ASSISTANCE

Very few utilities provide loans or grants to people with low income, and usually these loans are subsidized by the federal government. The most extensive low-income energy assistance program is a weatherization program offered through local Community Action Agencies (CAA). In this program, a person receives up to $1000 in materials and a supplementary grant to pay for installation. The funds are available to people meeting certain income-level requirements through the CAA or a neighborhood organization. Particulars of this federal program change annually. The best way to get detailed information is to contact your Community Action Agency.

Although they're not specifically targeted at low-income groups, low-interest or no-interest utility loans, discussed above, offer a particular advantage to those who would have trouble qualifying for a conventional loan or meeting its higher monthly payments.

LANDLORDS AND RENTERS

One of the greatest opportunities for energy savings nationwide is in rental housing. Unfortunately this is where conservation assistance and financing programs are weakest. Some utility financing and audit programs for homeowners also include landlords, and both landlords and renters qualify for some energy tax credits, as discussed earlier in this chapter. Moreover, some landlords are finding that energy improvements—with or without tax benefits—give them a marketing advantage as potential renters become more conscious of energy costs.

Some new firms are making a business out of improving apartment efficiency. These firms, referred to generally as energy service companies, finance, construct, and sometimes maintain energy improvements in large apartment buildings in return for a share of the savings. Typically the company receives a large share of savings for the first two or three years after installation. At that point, either the building owner takes over maintenance and operation responsibilities or the energy service company retains that role in return for a smaller share of savings. These arrangements provide benefits for all parties: landlords, renters, and investors.

Some utility financing programs specifically target renters and landlords. Some utilities make the same low-interest, long-term loans available to landlords that they offer to homeowners.

References

AUDITS

All Through the House: A Guide to Home Weatherization, by Thomas Blandy and Denis Lamoreux. New York: McGraw-Hill, 1980. [Contains a detailed self-audit.]

Computerized Instrumented Residential Audit, by the Lawrence Berkeley Laboratory. Berkeley: Lawrence Berkeley Laboratory, 1982. [Computer software and reference manual.]

The Home Energy Audit, by Richard H. Montgomery. New York: Wiley, 1982.

The Residential Energy Audit Manual, by the U.S. Department of Energy with Oak Ridge National Laboratory and the University of Massachusetts Cooperative Extension Service. Atlanta: Fairmont Press, 1980. [A technical audit manual.]

For a list of trained house doctors nationwide write:
Princeton Energy Partners
P.O. Box 1221
Princeton, NJ 08540

For a list of trained private auditors nationwide write: Cornerstones
21 Stanwood Street
Brunswick, ME 04011

GENERAL CONSERVATION

Stop Burning Your Money: The Intelligent Homeowner's Guide to Household Energy Savings, by John Rothchild. New York: Penguin Books, 1981.

The Energy Saver's Handbook for Town and City People, by the Scientific Staff of the Massachusetts Audubon Society. Emmaus, Pa.: Rodale Press, 1982.

The Energy Wise Home Buyer: A Guide to Selecting an Energy Efficient Home, by Technology + Economics, Inc., for the U.S. Department of Housing and Urban Development. Washington: Government Printing Office, 1979.

HOME HOW-TO: ENERGY CONSERVATION, RENOVATION, AND COST ESTIMATING

Do-It-Yourself Energy Saving Projects, by the editors of Sunset Books. Menlo Park, Calif.: Lane, 1981.

Home Renovation, by Francis D. K. Ching and Dale E. Miller. New York: Van Nostrand Reinhold, 1983.

National Repair and Remodeling Estimator, by Albert S. Paxton. Carlsbad, Calif.: Craftsman Book Co., 1983. [Updated annually.]

Renovation, by Michael W. Litchfield. New York: Wiley, 1982.

ENERGY-EFFICIENT LANDSCAPING

Homeowner's Guide to Landscaping That Saves Energy Dollars, by Ruth S. Foster. New York: McKay, 1978.

Landscape Design That Saves Energy, by Anne Simon Moffat and Marc Schiller. New York: Morrow, 1981.

INDOOR AIR QUALITY

Air to Air Heat Exchangers for Houses, by William A. Shurcliff. Andover, Mass.: Brick House, 1982.

Household Pollutants Guide, by the Center for Science and the Public Interest, edited by Albert J. Fritsch. New York: Doubleday/Anchor, 1978.

SHADING AND WINDOW INSULATION

A Comparison of Products for Reducing Heat Gain Through Windows, by the U.S. Department of

Energy. Publication 8.15(dUS). Washington, D.C.: Government Printing Office, 1981. [Available from Lawrence Berkeley Laboratory, University of California, Berkeley, CA 94720.]

Movable Insulation, by William T. Langdon. Emmaus, Pa.: Rodale Press, 1980.

Thermal Shutters and Shades: Over 100 Schemes for Reducing Heat Loss Through Windows, by William A. Shurcliff. Andover, Mass.: Brick House, 1980.

Windows for Energy Efficiency, edited by Steve Selkowitz. Vol. 1, no. 1 (January 1979); vol. 1, no. 2 (January 1980). Berkeley: Lawrence Berkeley Laboratory. [These volumes are out of print but may be available in libraries.]

WOOD HEATING

Jay Shelton's Solid Fuels Encyclopedia, by Jay Shelton. Charlotte, Vt.: Garden Way, 1983.

Wood Heat, by John Vivian. Emmaus, Pa.: Rodale Press, 1976.

SOLAR HOW-TO

Build Your Own Solar Water Heater, by Stu Campbell and Douglas Taff. Charlotte, Vt.: Garden Way, 1978.

Solar Air Heater, by Ray Wolf. Emmaus, Pa.: Rodale Press, 1981.

Solar Retrofit: Adding Solar to Your Home, by Daniel K. Reif. Andover, Mass.: Brick House, 1981.

Solarizing Your Present Home: Practical Solar Heating Systems You Can Build, edited by Joe Carter. Emmaus, Pa.: Rodale Press, 1981. [Contains sun path charts.]

The Homeowner's Handbook of Solar Water Heating Systems, by Bill Keisling. Emmaus, Pa.: Rodale Press, 1983.

The Integral Passive Solar Water Heater Book, by David S. Bainbridge. Davis, Calif.: Passive Solar Institute, 1981.

HEATING, VENTILATION, AND AIR CONDITIONING

Heat Pumps: An Efficient Heating and Cooling Alternative, by Dermot McGuigan with Amanda McGuigan. Charlotte, Vt.: Garden Way, 1981.

Heating and Cooling, by the editors of Time-Life Books. Chicago: Time-Life Books, 1977.

TOOLS FOR SELF-RELIANCE

More Other Homes and Garbage, by Jim Leckie et al. San Francisco: Sierra Club Books, 1981.

The Integral Urban House Book, by the Farallones Institute. San Francisco: Sierra Club Books, 1979.

SUPERINSULATION

Superinsulated Houses, by William Shurcliff. Andover, Mass.: Brick House, 1981.

The Super-Insulated Retrofit Book: A Homeowner's Guide to Energy Efficient Renovation, by Robert Argue and Brian Marshall. Toronto, Ontario: Renewable Energy in Canada, 1981.

PASSIVE SOLAR DESIGN

Passive Solar Energy: The Homeowner's Guide to Natural Heating and Cooling, by Bruce Anderson and Malcolm Wells. Andover, Mass.: Brick House, 1981.

The Passive Solar Energy Book, by Edward Mazria. Emmaus, Pa.: Rodale Press, 1979. [Contains sun path charts and rules of thumb for passive solar design.]

The Passive Solar Handbook, by Douglas Balcomb and others. Newark, Del.: American Solar Energy Society, 1983. [Extensive and technical. Contains methods for balancing solar and conservation.]

GENERAL ENERGY TOPICS

A New Prosperity: Building a Sustainable Future, by the Solar Energy Research Institute. Andover, Mass.: Brick House, 1981.

Brittle Power, by Amory Lovins and L. Hunter Lovins. Andover, Mass.: Brick House, 1982.

Energy Future, by Robert Stobaugh and Daniel Yergin. Revised third edition. New York: Random House, 1983.

Energy, Vulnerability, and War, by Wilson Clark and Jack Page. New York: Norton, 1981.

Our Energy: Regaining Control, by Marc H. Ross and Robert H. Williams. New York: McGraw-Hill, 1981.

FINANCIAL CALCULATIONS

Depreciation, Investment, and Credit Manual, by Martin E. Holbrook and Lawrence H. MacKirdy. Englewood Cliffs, N.J.: Prentice-Hall, 1983.

Glossary

active solar heating: A system that uses mechanical devices (such as fans), requiring electricity, to collect, store, and, distribute heat.

air ducts: Sheet metal tubes that carry heated or cooled air to outlets or registers within the house.

annual fuel use efficiency (AFUE): A percentage indication of the average efficiency of boilers and furnaces over the course of a heating season. The AFUE takes into account efficiency losses due to equipment cycling on and off.

batch water heater: A solar water heater in which a black-painted water tank is located within a glazed, insulated, and weathertight collector box. The sun enters the collector box and heats the "batch" of water in the tank.

breadbox water heater: Another term for a batch water heater, so called because the glazed box resembles a breadbox.

Btu: Stands for British thermal unit, a measure of heat energy. Approximately the heat released by one lit match.

clerestory window: A vertical window placed in the roof that can be used for lighting, ventilation, and collecting heat.

coefficient of performance (COP): A measure of efficiency used for heat pumps and air conditioners. The COP measures the Btu's of cooling or heating that the appliance provides versus the Btu's it uses.

collector: A glass box, wall, or window that captures sunlight to heat water or air.

collector angle: The tilt of the collector surface in relation to a horizontal surface.

collector area: The amount of collector surface presented to the sun.

condensing furnace: A type of furnace that achieves high efficiencies by passing hot exhaust gases through several heat exchangers, reducing the temperature enough to condense the water vapor in the exhaust and capture additional heat. Also called recuperative furnace.

conduction: The transfer of heat through materials.

convection: The transfer of heat in a liquid or air that results from the movement of the colder and warmer portions.

convective loop: A continuous current of air or water that results from the rising of lighter, warm air or water and the sinking of heavier, cool air or water.

cooling degree-day: A measure of annual cooling requirements. Reflects the number of degrees per day that the average outdoor temperature exceeds 75°F. A day with an average temperature of 85°F has 10 cooling degree-days. These daily counts are added to achieve an annual total of cooling degree-days.

degree-day: A measure of climatic severity. See *heating degree-day* and *cooling degree-day*.

direct gain: A passive solar design in which the sun enters a living space for direct heating and storage.

energy efficiency ratio (EER): A measure of the cooling efficiency of air conditioners and heat pumps; the number reflects the Btu's per hour of heat extracted from the air for every watt of electricity used by the appliance.

envelope: The building surfaces that separate heated space from unheated space or the outdoors; normally the walls, windows, doors, floor, and ceiling.

fireblock: A 2 × 4 cut to fit at right angles between wall studs at mid-wall level in order to slow the progress of fire through a frame wall. Contractors will need to know the location of fireblocks before insulation can be blown into a frame wall.

furnace efficiency: That amount of heat a furnace puts out as a percentage of the total heat value of the fuel burned. See *annual fuel use efficiency* and *seasonal efficiency*.

glazing: A glass or plastic covering.

heat gain: An increase in the amount of heat contained in a space; results from direct solar radiation and the heat given off by people, lights, equipment, machinery, and other sources.

heat pump: A mechanical device that removes heat from one medium, concentrates it, and distributes it in another. This device can be used to heat or cool indoor space. The heat source can be air or water.

heat pump water heater: A heat pump designed to extract heat from air or water and concentrate it in water for domestic use.

heating degree-day: A measure of annual heating requirements. Reflects the number of degrees per day that the average outdoor temperature falls below 65°F. A day with an average temperature of 55°F has 10 heating degree-days. These daily counts are added to achieve an annual total of heating degree-days.

heating seasonal performance factor (HSPF): The total seasonal heating output of a heat pump relative to the total electricity use of the appliance, taking into account efficiency losses in normal operation.

hybrid solar system: A solar heating system that combines both passive and active features—for example a solar greenhouse used as a heat collector with fans to distribute heat throughout the house.

indirect gain: A passive solar design (such as a solar wall) in which the heat storage medium is placed between the collector and the living space.

infiltration: Passage of air through holes and cracks in the building envelope.

insolation: The amount of solar radiation striking a surface; usually measured in Btu's per square foot per hour or per day.

insulating glass: Multiple-pane windows.

insulation: Material used to slow heat loss or heat gain.

kilowatt-hour (kwh): The standard measure of electricity consumption. A kilowatt-hour (kwh) is consumed when a 1000-watt appliance operates for an hour or when a 100-watt light bulb burns for ten hours.

life cycle costs: The sum of purchase price, maintenance costs, and operating costs (including energy) over the life of a device, appliance, or system.

light well: A shaft leading from a skylight on the roof; used to bring daylight into living areas through the attic.

natural convection: Heat transfer through a medium such as air or water by currents that result from the rising of lighter, warm air and the sinking of heavier, cool air. See also *convective loop*.

natural ventilation: Ventilation that occurs as a result of design features without the assistance of fans, pumps, or other mechanical devices.

orientation: The compass direction that a solar collector faces.

passive solar system: A solar heating system that relies on convection, conduction, and radiation without the use of fans, pumps, or other mechanical devices.

pulse combustion: A furnace or boiler combustion system using a pressurized combustion chamber. Since fuel and air are fed intermittently into the chamber, complete burning of the fuel results in high efficency.

R-value: A measure of resistance to heat flow. The higher the R-value, the greater the insulating value.

radiation: Heat waves emitted from a material or body.

rate of return: The annual return from an investment, expressed as a percent of the original investment.

recuperative furnace: See *condensing furnace*.

retrofit: A term used to describe energy measures that are added to an existing structure.

rockbed heat storage: One form of thermal mass; a method of storing solar heat for later use. Fans blow solar-heated air through the rockbed, heating the rocks inside. When heat is needed fans draw air through the rockbed—where it gathers heat—and into the living space.

seasonal efficiency: The average efficiency of a heater or air conditioner over the heating season, adjusted for efficiency losses due to normal use and equipment cycling on and off.

seasonal energy efficiency ratio (SEER): The energy efficiency ratio (EER) of the cooling cycle of a heat pump or air conditioner adjusted downward to account for efficiency losses that occur in normal seasonal use.

simple payback: The original investment divided by annual savings. The time it takes for an investment to pay for itself without considering ongoing costs.

skylight: A glazed opening in the roof used for lighting, ventilation, or solar gain.

solar gain: An increase in the amount of heat in a space as a result of solar radiation.

solar greenhouse: a glazed structure attached to a house; used to grow plants and capture solar energy for home heating.

solar wall: A passive solar heating system in which the thermal mass is between the glazing and the living area. Trombe walls and water walls are examples of solar walls.

solar water heater: An active or passive system using solar energy to heat water for domestic use.

solarium: A glazed room or structure for capturing solar energy.

steady-state efficiency: The efficiency of a furnace or boiler without considering normal losses from cycling on and off. Steady-state efficiency is expressed as a percentage reflecting the amount of useful heat produced in relation to the amount of fuel consumed.

therm: 100,000 Btu's. Usually used to measure natural gas; 100 cubic feet of natural gas is equivalent to 1 therm.

thermal bypass (thermal bridge): A gap in insulation, or a segment of material offering little resistance to heat flow, which allows heat to conduct *around* insulation—either directly to the outside or an unheated area or indirectly by creating convection in a flue or a convective loop within a wall.

thermal mass: Material capable of storing heat such as water, concrete, rocks, or masonry.

thermosiphon: Movement of air or heated water upward as it is heated, drawing behind it cooler air or water.

thermosiphoning air panel (TAP): A low-cost solar collector design that heats air and discharges it directly to the living space; for daytime heating only.

Trombe wall: A passive solar heating system consisting of a concrete, stone, or masonry wall and a layer of exterior glazing. The sun warms the wall and the air between the wall and the glazing, which circulates by convection through the vents. Heat also conducts through the mass of the wall and radiates into the living area.

vapor barrier: An impervious material used to stop the passage of water vapor; usually polyethylene, aluminum foil, or coated paper. The vapor barrier is always placed between insulation and the heated living space.

water wall: A type of solar wall using water-filled containers as thermal mass.

whole-house fan: A large fan that cools by drawing warm air from a house when outdoor temperatures are lower than indoor temperatures.

wind chill factor: An index of the combined effects of wind and low temperature on perceived temperature.

windowbox heater: A low-cost solar collector designed for attachment to a window for daytime heating. Heated air circulates through the collector and into the room.

Index